# BICYCLE RACING IN THE MODERN ERA

*Twenty-five years
of cycling
journalism
from the editors
of* VELONEWS

**Library of Congress Cataloging-in-Publication Data**

Bicycle Racing in the Modern Era : twenty-five years of cycling journalism / from the editors of *VeloNews*. -- 1st ed.
    p.   cm.
    ISBN 1-884737-32-3
    1. Bicycle Racing.    I. Velo-news.
  GV1049.B46  1996
  796.6'2--dc21

97-9518
CIP

**PHOTO CREDITS**

**Front cover** Graham Watson; **Back cover** Robert Oliver
**Page 1** Cor Vos (1), photographer unknown (1), Tom Moran (1)
**Page 113** Sergio Penazzo (1), John Pierce/Photosport Intl. (1), Cor Vos (1)
**Page 145** H.A. Roth (3)
**Page 177** H.A. Roth (2), Tim Murphy (1)
**First photo spread:** M. Chritton (4), T. Loose (1), T. Moran (3), R. Oliver (1), S. Penazzo (3),
    J. Pierce (2), H.A. Roth (10), C. Vos (7), G. Watson (4), photographer unknown (1)
**Second photo spread:** M. Chritton (1), S. Clarke (1), R. M. Collins III (1), T. Moran (2), G. Peters (1),
    J. Pierce (3), H.A. Roth (17), C. Vos (5), G. Watson (5)

ISBN 1-884737-32-3

VeloPress
1830 N. 55th Street • Boulder, Colorado 80301-2700 • USA
303/440-0601    FAX 303/444-6788
E-Mail: velonews@aol.com   Web site: www.VeloNews.com

TO PURCHASE ADDITIONAL COPIES OF THIS BOOK OR OTHER VELO PRODUCTS,
PLEASE CALL 800/234-8356. FOR INTERNATIONAL ORDERS CALL 303/440-0601

# introduction

In the 25 years that *VeloNews* has been chronicling competitive cycling, the leading U.S. bicycle racing publication has published thousands of articles on every aspect of the sport. So choosing the 60-plus stories that make up this commemorative book was a gargantuan task. We haven't simply listed the names, results and statistics that have defined cycling's modern era; we tried to detail the emergence of competitive cycling in North America, while reflecting some of the sport's great moments worldwide.

The book opens with an extensive "Milestones" section, followed by three smaller sections that include significant feature stories, personality pieces, and technical and training articles. Each of the four sections is chronological, to enhance the reader's enjoyment of the book. Stories were chosen also to reflect the diversity of cycling — road, track, mountain biking and cyclo-cross.

To adapt the selected articles to book form, most have been shortened or re-edited. Many of the stories we wanted to include were left out because of space restrictions. For instance, the book includes significant milestones such as George Mount's breakthrough sixth place at the 1976 Olympic road race in Montréal, but not the fourth place of Frankie Andreu at Atlanta 20 years later. The first official world mountain-bike championships in Durango, Colorado, are covered here, but not the subsequent and just as successful world's at Bromont or Vail. We do include the benchmark world hour records of Francesco Moser and Chris Boardman, but not the ultimately less-significant rides by Tony Rominger and Miguel Indurain. Also, Greg LeMond's 1989 comeback Tour de France is included, but not his repeat victory in 1990. And for 18 of the 25 years, mountain-bike racing either did not exist or was not reported in the pages of *VeloNews*. Consequently, most of the off-road stories here come from the 1990s.

We would like to thank everyone who has contributed to this book, particularly the former editors and correspondents of *VeloNews* whose many fascinating pieces we were able to republish. Thanks are also due to the colleagues and interns who pored over bound issues of the magazine and typed in those articles that were printed before the age of desktop publishing. We certainly had a great time editing this book; we hope you have as much fun reading it.

*John Wilcockson*
*Boulder, Colorado*
*February 1997*

# table of contents

## III - FEATURE STORIES

## IV - PERSONALITIES

MILESTONES

One of the first stories to appear in VeloNews — when it was still called Northeast Bicycle News — was a report on the then biggest single-day race in America: the Tour of Somerville, New Jersey.

# Somerville climaxes Memorial weekend

BY BARBARA GEORGE

Roger Young, a 19-year-old sprinter from Detroit, Michigan, took the 28th annual Kugler-Anderson Memorial race Monday. The 50-mile Somerville race was the feature event in a 3 ½ day weekend that saw Olympic Development competitions for both road and track men and then a series of criteriums which brought the two specialties together.

Though track men won the sprints, road racers appeared in the breakaways and on the result sheets, achieving their objective of "getting in a little speed work" before their final Olympic Development race next Sunday.

Monday's course was a one-mile-plus circuit of Somerville's main streets — mostly black-topped but with a long concrete backstretch that had tar between sections. Most dangerous of the corners were numbers one and three, which are slightly more than 90 degrees and force riders from a wide street to a more narrow one.

Crowds clustered on these bends, making the Tour of Somerville, which is frequently called the Kentucky Derby of cycling, smack more of the Indy 500. White-jacketed stretcher bearers were much in evidence but no field-annihilating crashes occurred.

Occasional shrieks were heard when riders would miss turns and go into the crowd or over a curb. As this happened, one policeman who had been warning spectators to keep back exclaimed, "Now you people believe me!"

The first 25 miles were covered in 58 minutes and 16 seconds as a number of individuals opened gaps as wide as 20 seconds on the field. Somerville's own Joe Saling soloed for several laps until he had bike trouble and had to change machines at one of the corners. But even his experienced pit crew couldn't help him to regain the field, though he chased for several laps and was loudly cheered by the crowd.

Top-seeded Olympic hopeful and 1971 Pan Am Games competitor Jim Huetter rode three laps alone but he was pulled in and soon all were together again.

Just before the halfway mark, 1971 winner of the Tour, Ed Parrott, and 1951's François Mertens, got away for the longest break — five laps – but 1963 winner Olaf Moetus helped to catch them.

It seemed that Patrick Gellineau might take the race as he opened up a 20-second gap with eight laps to go, but a group of Metros, whose teamwork had gained them many of the top places last year, were some of those who reeled him in.

All this chasing served to thin the field, which had shrunk from its original over 150 to about 60 at the halfway mark.

With three laps to go, the winning order was established. Ten men were away — those who had caught Gellineau — with Slivinski, Lannigan, Fraser, and Swaim between them and the field, now numbering about 30.

Young took the sprint, with another sprinter, Chris Meerman, second. Included in the winning break were road men Parrott, Moetus, Allis and Guazzo and all-arounders Gellineau, Fischer and LeNavenec. The field arrived in 15th place.

The 19-year-old victor, who was on a successful prize-hunting trip east, has been racing since he was five and stands at the top of the Midwest Olympic Development track seedings. Young was second in the nationals as a junior and an alternate for the 1971 Pan Am team. He took the junior race at Somerville in 1970.

The Detroit native comes from an athletic family which includes sister Sheila — fourth in speedskating in the 1972 Olympics and a national bike champion — and father Clair, whose racing career included a fourth in the Tour of Somerville in the early-1940s.

Trophies were awarded behind the judges stand on the steps of the church. Lap prizes of $5 merchandise certificates went to John Allis (six laps), Jim Huetter (five), Guazzo, Mertens, Parrott and Gellineau (four), Saling and LeNavenec (three) and others.

As the four-hour affair drew to a close and traffic resumed on the streets of Somerville, one man exclaimed to another: "Forty-three dozen!"

What was it? Spectators? Competitors? Crashes?

He had sold 43 dozen hot-dogs at his luncheonette on the corner of Main Street.

*In 1975, VeloNews reported the Tour de France for the first time with its own correspondent. Eddy Merckx was attempting to win the Tour for a record sixth time....*

# Thévenet outclimbs Merckx for Tour victory

BY OWEN MULHOLLAND

From the beginning, the 1975 Tour de France did not go quite the way King Eddy planned. Since a mini-time trial has been used for some years now to open the race, Merckx has been able to don the yellow jersey right from the start (with the exception of 1969). He has long disclaimed any desire to hold the *maillot jaune* throughout the race, but his actions on numerous occasions have shown otherwise. There can be little doubt that he would have liked to have won this year's opening prologue in front of his home fans in Belgium and keep it for the next three weeks on his way to an unprecedented sixth win in this famous race.

But the acrobatic young Francesco Moser, youngest and most talented of a long-established family dynasty in Italy, had skipped the Giro d'Italia and concentrated on getting ready for the Tour. He showed that his preparation was perfect by blasting around the 38 bends (in only 6.5km) to pip Merckx by just two seconds.

For the first time since 1966, time bonuses for the first three on each stage were eliminated so Merckx really didn't have a chance to grab the jersey until the second time trial a week later at Merlin-Plage in the west of France. Two days later another time trial gave him the chance to add to his lead over the by now second-placed Bernard Thévenet. And at the time, it seemed that his 2:20 lead would be a sound basis for improvement in the mountains to come.

The other favorites, Joop Zoetemelk, Lucien Van Impe, Luis Ocaña, Raymond Poulidor, Vicente Lopez-Carril, Moser and Giovanni Battaglin, were all clustered in the top 15. For them, these first nine days from Charleroi down to Pau were just a time of shadow-boxing and waiting.

Serious hostilities began in the Pyrenees. The 1965 Tour winner, Felice Gimondi, showed surprising life by taking the first stage a few seconds in front of all the others one expected to be there. The next day, covering the notorious Tourmalet, Aspin and a third nasty climb, never used before, up to the new ski station at Pla d'Adet. Thévenet launched a vicious attack on the final climb, an attack that only Zoetemelk was able to follow. The Dutchman got up to Thévenet, hung on for 6km, and then sprinted by as Thévenet slowed with a puncture just before the finish line. Merckx finished with Van Impe and the Belgian's lead dropped to under two minutes.

The Puy-de-Dôme's terribly steep slopes were destined to be the scene for the next round in the Thévenet-Merckx battle. As he had done so effectively before in the Tour of Italy, when he hadn't been able to match José-Manuel Fuente in the mountains, Merckx attempted to gain time elsewhere, notably through the hilly Midi area.

But Thévenet is no Fuente. Not only is he considerably stronger than the diminutive Spaniard on the flat, he is also a well-seasoned professional by now. Actually, he has ridden as many Tours as Merckx and he knows all about marking an opponent closely. Of course, Merckx wouldn't be Merckx if he didn't try at least 20 attacks a day, but in the end it was all for naught, and they arrived at the foot of the Puy-de-Dôme, an extinct volcano just outside Clermont-Ferrand, *en peloton*.

Thévenet didn't waste much time in banging away in his rather rough, but quite effective style. The surprise came when Van Impe got up to him, waited until the last kilometer, and then had reserves enough to dance away from the thumping Thévenet. The real loser was Merckx, who now saw his lead on overall classification shrink to 58 seconds.

**Course stresses Merckx's weakness**

In recent years, Merckx has used his strong team and considerable sprinting powers to build up a lead on general classification with time bonuses acquired at the stage finishes. Conversely, his climbing powers have steadily declined since 1969, when he was in a class by himself. Knowing all this, the fathers of the latest Tour de France designed a Tour devoid of time bonuses and including no less than five uphill stage finishes, thereby accentuating the very abilities which Merckx has been slowly losing.

Thévenet had long ago announced — since about one week after the issuance of the details of the 1975 Tour — that this would be his year to win.

From the Pyrenees on, the pendulum began to swing in the Frenchman's favor, and as the momentum built up so did the fervor of the French public at the prospect of having one of their countrymen finally take the maillot jaune to Paris for the first time in eight years.

Alas, although a more sporting public would be impossible to imagine, there are always the exceptions, one of whom managed to get near Merckx just before he finished on the Puy-de-Dôme and socked him in the stomach.

That injury must have affected him on the four days from Nice up through the Alps, which obviously held the answer as to whom would arrive in Paris for the victory promenade up and down the Champs-Elysées.

The decisive day was the tremendous 217.5km stage from Nice to yet another ski station searching for instant notoriety: Pra Loup. This stage was so difficult that the winner averaged only 28 kph (17.4 mph), a speed which nevertheless represents superhuman efforts in view of the distance and 5400 meters (17,700 feet) of climbing.

The Alps are quite different from major mountain chains in America. Although the Alps are generally inferior to the Rockies and the Sierra Nevada in terms of sheer altitude, in some ways they present more dramatic terrain because of the enormous contrasts between the summits and deep valleys, which run through them everywhere. If one desires to go directly from one point to another, the trip usually entails traversing a series of peaks and near-chasms. The roads that buck up and down through these stupendous giants are rarely more than one Cadillac wide and often, much, much less. For most of the route, they are hacked straight out of the rock walls — indeed, there are even roads hung from the walls — and what paving was done when the roads were first constructed rarely has been improved on since.

Such obstacles make the Tour de France a true ultimate test of the capabilities of a human being on two wheels. It staggers the imagination to see men battling away for four hours and realize that only half the stage has been ridden and the hardest is yet to come! Yet the likes of Merckx and Thévenet and Gimondi accept such terms as suitable grounds on which to establish a hierarchy of the *grands*.

**Merckx gains on downhills**

As usual, Merckx opened the account by accelerating on the descent of the second col. Fifteen men became detached, but in the subsequent valley a group from behind arrived, the most notable beneficiary of this regroupment being the venerable Poulidor. It was the last time he was to show himself at the front; in the days to come, the 1974 runner-up slipped down through the placings, plagued by a breathing difficulty.

Serious hostilities began on the Col des Champs as Thévenet attacked several times only to have Merckx reply immediately and have a go himself just to show he was in good health. He survived a puncture at the expense of considerable energy, for at the same time Raymond Delisle was insuring that Thévenet had a fast wheel to follow. At the summit, Merckx led over the top, unknowingly taking advantage of flats to both Thévenet and Moser, the latter showing much better in these mountains than in the Pyrenees. Thévenet got back up to Merckx on the succeeding *faux-plat*.

At the village of Allos, situated at the foot of the col of the same name, the bell sounded for yet another round, only in this case the seconds, Delisle for Thévenet, and Ward Janssens and Jos De Schoenmaecker for Merckx, stayed in the ring to run interference for their captains. The Allos is a real monster, which several times flatters that the summit is near only to reveal the deception around the next turn of yet more interminable *lacets* winding up some new and higher face of the mountain.

By now, Merckx knew that there was no getting rid of Thévenet uphill, but there is the other side of the col which has to be negotiated, and he intended to use it to full advantage. He shot away in the last kilometer to the top to take eight seconds on Thévenet, 15 seconds on Gimondi, and much more on everyone else.

The descent was as wicked as a descent could be and still be called paved. Snow banks here and there fed steady streams across the road, and so torn up was the surface in many places that gendarmes with yellow flags stood by the worst parts to warn those coming of the dangers ahead. The road never grew to more than one car wide, and I don't have American standards in mind when I say that. Covering it all was a fine layer of gravel and dust sufficient to make the slightest slip a permanent one.

This was Merckx's big chance and he knew it. He looked to be on skis rather than wheels, being airborne as often as not, as one after another he passed the cars and motorcycles in front of him, truly a stupendous achievement on such a surface where motorcycles and cars can slide with less danger. He thundered on, white eyes staring with absolute concentration through a cloud of dust and fumes, screaming all the while at those in front to move over. The cars and motorcycles were only too willing — finding a place to pull off was the problem.

Behind, Gimondi utilized his considerable talents in the same department to pass Thévenet and keep the gap on Merckx close to the original 15 seconds. His team car was desperately trying to stay near, a little too desperate as it turned out when the car shot off a cliff and fell down the absolutely sheer precipice at least 300 feet. One occupant was ejected (he wasn't using a seat belt, of course) and all received injuries, but rather mild ones in view of the apparently mortal plunge.

This was one of a succession of such crashes. Two days before, a Dutch press car had tumbled down a hillside and later the Kas team lost two cars in two days, one of them being in a grave accident with a gendarme coming the opposite way on the course.

In front, Merckx continued his offensive in great style, calling to mind the great Grand Prix drivers such as Juan Fangio, Sterling Moss and Jim Clark, who went faster than their competition and did it more safely.

### Thévenet passes

The transition to the final climb was immediate and here, as everyone knew, the Tour was to be played out. Merckx had 33 seconds on Gimondi and 1:10 on Thévenet and

Zoetemelk. Seven and a half kilometers at eight percent: quite a test after more than seven hours of battling.

Suffering as he rarely has, Merckx attempted to maintain his rhythm but bit by bit he weakened. Later, he recalled, "At four kilometers, I felt my strength declining. I tried with all my energy to regain myself but 1500 meters later I just couldn't maintain it. At one moment, I thought of getting off the bike."

It was terrible to see, his whole body heaving with every turn of the pedals, eyes glazed, head lolling, his face a river of sweat, as first Gimondi and then Thévenet went by. Thévenet was absolutely unbelievable. He set such a searing pace that neither Zoetemelk nor Van Impe could hold him — he simply flew. In his almost awkward yet speedy and punchy style, he pounded an enormous gear up through the thousands of ecstatic fans.

Past Merckx, with hardly more than a second side by side, he gave the same treatment to the elegant Italian ahead, taking 23 seconds out of him the last 500 meters. Merckx continued to slow and had no resistance whatsoever when Zoetemelk and Van Impe clawed their way past. In the end, he lost 1:56 on Thévenet, thereby acquiring the same deficit that Thévenet had that morning, 58 seconds.

Merckx wouldn't be Merckx though if he accepted one verdict like this. Next day on the relatively short stage of 107km, made notable by the inclusion of the Cols of Vars and Izoard, Merckx was soon on the attack again, down Vars this time, but in the succeeding Gorges of the Guil, Thévenet and Moser got back to him.

The Izoard is one of the most famous cols in the Tour itinerary. There's a monument to Fausto Coppi near the summit, and several men since him, including Merckx himself, have found fame and the key to a Tour win on its wicked slopes. This time, Thévenet wanted to show himself in yellow before his own public, as well as put a bigger cushion between himself and Merckx; and when he attacked, there was no stopping him. Merckx, as usual, led the chase all the way, and his efforts were rewarded with second place, sadly for him, 2:22 after Thévenet had arrived at the finish.

Yet another marathon mountain stage faced the Tour on the next day, and once again Merckx did his very best to attack his antagonist at every bend in the road. But Thévenet wisely remained prudent on the descents, preferring to lose some time downhill, before gathering his men around him to reel Merckx back in.

**Merckx battles on**

One can hardly praise Merckx too much, though, for his combativeness, refusing always to accept the apparently inevitable. After making the pace all day long, he still had enough left on the final climb to attack Thévenet several times and finally beat him by two seconds. Van Impe and Gimondi were actually dropped, so ferocious was the pace.

Only one opportunity now remained for Merckx to get himself back in yellow, and that was in the succeeding time trial. At 40km it was quite long and if it had been anything like normal, the five-time Tour winner might well have had some chance of taking a big hunk of time out of Thévenet, but several factors worked against him.

First, was his stupid crash before the start the day before. At five kilometers per hour, he touched Ole Ritter's rear wheel and fell sharply on his face, fracturing his left cheekbone. Naturally, his breathing was impaired, though one would never have known it by the stupendous ride he put up that day.

Further complications arose that night when he discovered great difficulty in eating. A specialist at a nearby university advised him to abandon, but Merckx wouldn't hear of it.

A nasty six-kilometer col was stuck right in the middle of the time trial course, weighing the odds in Thévenet's favor. Merckx, trying to gain time where he could, picked up 34 seconds on Thévenet in the opening 12km to the base of the col. But from that point, he steadily lost ground, not only to Thévenet, but also to nearly all his rivals. At the summit he was in fifth place, 1:11 down on Van Impe; 26 seconds on an amazing Ritter; 21 seconds on Zoetemelk, who was destined to puncture a little later and lose enough time to slide down the ranking; and 17 seconds on Thévenet.

The descent was an utter corkscrew allowing acrobatic Eddy to pull back to second place. From here though, it was all gradually uphill and Merckx finally slipped behind Ritter by one second to finish third to little Van Impe who is *petite* in size only. Thévenet had underestimated the severity of the course and found himself overgeared for much of the way. He collapsed at the end, but the 15 seconds he had lost to Merckx still left him with a comfortable margin of over three minutes.

**French triumph in Paris**

All that remained now was the long run up to Paris, days filled with *"peloton groupé"* announcements over the radio. The final stage, finishing on the Champs-Elysées for the first time, was run off in the style one expects from the French: bands, a procession, the President of the Republic, and no less than 700,000 spectators.

There was still the possibility that Merckx might pull something off. Thévenet followed him like a shadow, so closely in fact that on the first lap the crowds were treated to the dazzling sight of their jerseys racing at great speed down the course well ahead of the others. It couldn't last, of course, but Merckx was at the front with his usual frequency throughout the rest of the race, and right behind him was his shadow, Thévenet.

**62nd TOUR DE FRANCE. June 26-July 20, 1975.**
1. Bernard Thévenet (F), Peugeot-BP-Michelin, 3999.1km in 114:35:31 (34. 899 kph); 2. Eddy Merckx (B), Molteni, at 2:47; 3. Lucien Van Impe (B), Gitane, at 5:01; 4. Joop Zoetemelk (Nl), GAN-Mercier, at 6:42; 5. Felice Gimondi (I), Bianchi, at 13:05; 6. Vicente Lopez-Carril (Sp), Kas, at 19:29; 7. Francesco Moser (I), Filotex, at 24:13; 8. Joseph Fuchs (Swit), Filotex, at 25:51; 9. Ward Janssens (B), Molteni, at 32:01; 10. Pedro Torres (Sp), Super Ser, at 35:38.

*An extraordinary night of track sprinting — and more — took place at the 1975 Pan American Games in Mexico City. VeloNews editor Barbara George was there to report it.*

# Tire-slashing and sabotage at the Pan Am Games

### BY BARBARA GEORGE

'One of the most emotional nights in cycling," was how U.S. coach Jack Simes described the protest-filled and dramatic Thursday evening, October 20, the last night of track events at the 1975 Pan American Games. Politics, sabotage, and tire-slashing were some of the ingredients of this "first-ever" in both international and American cycling.

Steve Woznick and Carl Leusenkamp of the U.S. easily won their first rides, and Leusenkamp posted the fastest 200-meter time of the round: 11 seconds flat. Both advanced to the quarter-finals.

Top-seeded from the start was Argentina's Octavio Dazzan, the world junior sprint champion and winner of both sprints and kilometer at the 1974 Pan Am Championships, when he was a mere 16 years old. Both he and Commonwealth Games silver medalist Xavier Mirander of Jamaica rode sub-11-second times to also reach the quarter-finals.

Favored with two-up rides thus far, Dazzan continued to cruise through when Leslie Rawlins of Trinidad-Tobago fell just after the 200-meter mark while trying to look behind.

The other Trinidad-Tobago rider, Ian Atherly, and the Cuban Lezcay matched jumps on the back stretch and each won one. Possessed of an astonishing turn of speed on the pedals while out of the saddle, the Cuban took the run-off from the front. Meanwhile, Leusenkamp put out the second-seeded Alvarez.

Early seeding would have dictated that Woznick meet Lezcay, and Mirander meet Atherly but the Belgian commissaire, without explaining why to U.S. commissaire Bill Lambart, changed this for the quarter-finals, saying such was his privilege.

With an early wind-up in their first ride, Woznick led out a long one from before the bell. On the second, he got a gap of 10 meters on the back stretch of the second lap, while Mirander was up near the fence, and did a 500-meter time trial.

"I was waiting for him to die," said Mirander later, "but he didn't." Although Mirander seemed to gain fractionally at the 200-meter mark, Woznick maintained his flat-out pace and posted an 11.2, an amazing time for such an effort, said his opponent.

With two Americans, an Argentinian and a Cuban in the semi-finals, the U.S. was assured of one medal at least and looked forward to the last night of racing. Confusion and even pandemonium were to reign throughout the evening, and at one point the entire team almost pulled out.

First up were Leusenkamp and Dazzan. The American took the inside and the lead going into the 200-meter mark, but both left their sprints very late. On the back stretch, they were still not at speed. When Leusenkamp came down into the pole and shut off his opponent just before the third turn, Dazzan rode into the infield and raised his hand. Leusenkamp continued around and even did a fourth lap — the officials had forgotten to ring the bell a lap earlier. Infield judges (a Belgian, an American, a Uruguayan and Colombian) gave Leusenkamp the verdict.

In the second ride, Leusenkamp again took the lead on the last lap, staying high and using the banking to come down directly but cleanly in front of Dazzan as they went into the third turn. This time, there was no overlapping and Leusenkamp won by a wheel.

Meanwhile, Woznick had lost his first ride with the Cuban when Lezcay kept him up against the fence on the back stretch and then came out of the pole in the final turn to win in a photo-finish. Against such a quick jump, Woznick then rode two long ones. Winding up after lap one, he gained a five-meter gap, which the Cuban almost closed, only to give up on the back stretch.

In the deciding ride, Woznick again led it out and was moving well by the bell, keeping the Cuban back and staying out of the pole. Finally, on the very last turn, the Cuban managed to come inside and they elbowed briefly but Woznick won.

According to the results, Woznick and Leusenkamp would sprint for the gold and silver medal, just as they had in the U.S. nationals, and it was a great moment for the U.S. Warming up, Woznick gave Leusenkamp a friendly push as if to say: "I can't talk to you now; you're my opponent." Both chatted with the Cuban as they rolled slowly around the track.

The final for third and fourth was due to start, but no contestants had been announced. The Argentine and Cuban managers were presumably still protesting Leusenkamp's first and Woznick's last ride. Judges, officials, and translators were clustered around the videotape machine or standing in little knots arguing. In spite of a band which played intermittently, the crowd was getting restless.

Abruptly, after half an hour of deliberation, the judgment on the first ride, in which Dazzan had gone into the infield, was reversed and Leusenkamp was disqualified. They would have to go to a third ride to determine the winner of their semi-final.

Coach Simes looked angry and manager Mike Fraysse was kept busy explaining to both the coach and the rider about the judges' decision. Larry Swantner massaged Leusenkamp's legs, and the turmoil continued among the officials.

By riding up the banking into the turn, Leusenkamp forced Dazzan to take the lead, but left a gap of several bike lengths. This he barely closed on the third turn and was still trailing at the last corner, pulling even with a mighty kick on the long finishing straight.

The infield judges and eventually the announcer awarded it to Leusenkamp, but Dazzan continued to point to his protégé as the winner. Minutes later, the Omega photo revealed that it was indeed Dazzan who had won. A very disappointed Leusenkamp let off steam by charging around the darkened infield on his road bike and later showed his teeth to the crowd as he warmed up for the final for third and fourth place.

But who would ride for first and second? There was still no announcement. Americans who had been filled with elation at the prospect of a U.S. sweep of the gold and silver now had to face the possibility that the U.S. might share the bronze.

For spectators in the stands, the hour-long scene in the infield was like a pantomime, a silent war film, in which there were no uniforms to guess who was on which side.

"There's a lot of tension when a sprinter rides a big meet," explained Simes later, and the waiting, reversed decisions, confused announcing and heated arguments were having their effects on Woznick. Clearly tormented, he walked out into the middle of the giant infield, away from the crowded pit area, and sat with his head in his hands. His coach patted him on the back and talked to him, torn between his duties to the pursuiters and his friend the sprinter. Leusenkamp came over and replaced Simes, sitting on the grass with his arm around the distraught rider.

Suddenly, Woznick took his bike and strode over to the track. Holding up the front wheel, he struck downward with his hand and there was a loud explosion; he had cut the tire with a knife. Wrenching the bike around, he did the same to the rear tire, then threw the whole machine on the sloping track, directly in front of the crowd. Deliberately, he began stripping off his uniform — shoes, jacket, warm-ups — while the crowd watched aghast, wondering how far he meant to go.

From the stands, the secretary-general of the Federation International Amateur de Cyclisme, the amateur branch of the Union Cycliste Internationale, jumped the fence and rushed down to push Woznick off the track, hustling him back toward the pits. Woznick collapsed on the shoulders of Leusenkamp and his other supporters.

Photographers went wild, crowding around the sobbing rider and then returning to shoot the still life — "Bicycle with Uniform" — as it lay on the track. No one seemed to want to touch it. "It was like a monument," said Simes later. "Those South American judges really deserved that." The Cuban Lezcay soon strutted out jauntily, bowing to the crowd, sure that he was about to profit from Woznick's display of temper by a ride for a gold medal.

What did it all mean? Was Woznick's display just poor sportsmanship? Had he been disqualified? Would he be thrown out of the competition. Suspended for life?

No word came over the public address system, and U.S. commissaire Lambart later revealed that the announcer sometimes refused to read items the judges gave him if he didn't like them or didn't agree with them.

As it turned out, Woznick had been told before he made his demonstration that he would go into the final for first and second. But the resentment and protest he had built up by that time had to find its outlet and he risked his career to make this statement, retiring to the cabin afterward completely upset and determined not to ride for the final.

It was the Italian Pacchiarelli of FIAC who came down to the cabin and talked to Woznick for half an hour, urging him to come back, sympathizing with him for his protest, telling him he was a real champion, and encouraging him to go out there and win.

"When you see Pacchiarelli come down out of the stand and take charge, then you know…." said Jamaican coach Ted Gray. "It's unusual for the head of the appeals jury to come into the pits to ask a rider if he's ready." Pacchiarelli was so incensed at the proceedings that he threatened to throw out one of the protesting managers.

Team pursuit rides intervened, and later Woznick reappeared, rolling around the track by himself while the pursuiters prepared for their medal ceremony.

Riding for the bronze as he had done in the 1967 Pan Am Games in Winnipeg, Leusenkamp's matches against the Cuban Lezcay were eventful, but the Oregon rider was able to keep his cool, in spite of all that had happened.

In the first one, Leusenkamp gloved his wheel and stopped abruptly in front of the Cuban just before the banking. The surprised Cuban almost ran into him and dropped down to the flat, raising his hand. Officials raced to check out the problem. Apparently Lezcay had pulled some tread off his tire while trying to stop.

In the reride, Leusenkamp used the tactic that had served him so well thus far, leading out but staying high and coming down in front of his opponent in the third turn to effectively shut off his sprint.

In their second match, they were both very high and moving fast along the back stretch. Leusenkamp had just made what looked like a winning jump from behind when the lights went out and the entire stadium was plunged into darkness. Two flames paralleled the report of the gun as Lambart canceled the match for another reride.

After a few minutes, the lights came on as suddenly as they had gone off, indicating not electrical failure but probable sabotage. By whom and for what purpose other than sheer mischief was never revealed.

When the lights went out, Woznick sitting on the warm-up bench, dived down behind it, certain that someone was going to try and shoot him.

"How many times do you have to ride to win," wondered the U.S. Olympic Committee bulletin the next day. Leusenkamp began his fourth attempt against the Cuban, and his 13th start of the series. It was a clear-cut victory; Lezcay never even came close. Leusenkamp took the inside in the first turn and got a gap which the Cuban couldn't close; Lezcay gave up in the straight. Both the final rides for Leusenkamp were 10.9s.

Winding up after the bell, Woznick won his first match against Dazzan from the front, coming out of the pole in the last turn onto the straight.

The second ride was a thriller, Woznick again led it out, trying to keep Dazzan on his back wheel, but the Argentinian snuck inside on the back stretch and opened the gap. It seemed as if all was lost but Woznick closed and sat in until the straightway, where he put on a tremendous burst to win the photo-finish by millimeters. The time was the fastest of the entire sprint series: a 10.78.

A gentleman from the very start, who always shook his opponent's hand and whose riding displayed great strength and heart, Woznick earned the cheers and admiration of the crowd. Later, he was congratulated by fellow competitors who sympathized with his protest, saying it was the only way a rider can express himself to officials against whom he is helpless.

The next day Woznick was given a 30-day suspension ("for conduct unbecoming to the spectators....") by the UCI commissaires. Most felt this was so lenient that it amounted to agreement by the officials that his protest was justified.

For Woznick, it was a case of all's well that end's well, but Leusenkamp was not so lucky. Better trained and going faster than ever before in his career, master of the banking and the track, the 28-year-old had to accept the bronze and flew home the next day in complete depression.

Although Leusenkamp was given the chance of a third ride, many thought his first semi-final ride should not have been disqualified. He never touched Dazzan, who was suspected of purposely riding into the grass when he knew he had lost.

The appeals jury (an Italian, a Mexican and a Colombian) pointed to the film and said that Leusenkamp had been overlapping Dazzan's wheel slightly, had gone below the pole himself briefly, and thus was at fault. Others suspected this reasoning to be solely aimed at preventing a U.S. gold and silver medal or at least to be a political compromise.

*Since 1912, no American cyclist had been remotely close to medaling in the Olympic road race. Then, on the very hilly circuit at Montreal in 1976, Californian George Mount was in the winning break....*

# George Mount: 'I died a hundred deaths'

BY **BARBARA GEORGE**

After placing sixth in the Olympic road race in Montreal, George Mount is now known all over America to people who have never even been to a bike race, or who didn't know there was such a sport. Twenty-one this month, Mount comes from Lafayette, California, where he is the third child of five. He left home after high school and moved to Berkeley where he has a winter job in the Velo Sport bike shop and is coached by Velo Sport's owner Peter Rich, also the sponsor of the Velo Club Berkeley.

**VeloNews** How did your season progress? What was your build-up for the Olympics?

**George Mount** The Olympic trials were a good build-up because they were at a proper time after the Tour of Baja, where I was finally beginning to come on. Then we rode the five-day race in Quebec, which was important for two things — one for just general high-speed racing. In one of the stages, for 10 miles, we were in what I would consider a full-out sprint, and I was just hanging on from the back of the group. We were in, like, 54x13s in the flat into the wind and we were going as fast as we could go and some sonofabitch would come from the back. And I'd go, "Oh no, I can't go again," and I'd go again and again and again, hanging on.

And then it was important also because, for me, to get the competition with the Europeans. It was so important to ride that race. What that did was it told me that these guys aren't supermen....

And so that gave me the confidence and more strength and we just rested up a little bit, a little racing here and fine tune yourself, and by the time the Games rolled around, I peaked. I physically peaked, very, very high. I did a super carbo-load for the race and ... I wasn't nervous at all until five minutes before the race.

**VeloNews** Did you have a plan for the race?

**George Mount** No. I was just doing like everybody else. We were going to watch the Poles, but because of the nature of racing you have to know that the guy who won it two years ago is more than likely not going to be the guy who wins it this year. So I didn't keep my eyes exactly on one person but watching the overall thing. I will admit that tactically I'm not the smartest rider. But I have the power....

**VeloNews** It seems like you did have good tactics in a way — I mean, you stayed in the front. It must be very hard to stay in the front in a race like the Olympics.

**George Mount** No, it's easier to stay in the front, because with all those corners you get the yo-yo effect and if you're in the back then you have to make up that time each time.

It's kind of like a miss and out. A guy starts coming by you and you just go a little bit harder and push him over a little bit. That's the way Mike Neel was riding, too. The other guys were kind of playing in the back, being careful and watching people....

**VeloNews** How did you get in the big break?

**George Mount** There were about five or six major breaks in the race, and I was in every one of them. I'd see a break go and I was in it. It's just the only way to ride that race. You can't sit in and wait for the last minute and then go 'cause you ain't going to do it. I know.

You kind of have to have a sixth sense. It's a certain point, and you've got to go with it. Certain riders, and you've got to go with it. Certain combinations of riders, and you've got to go with it. Those are the things that you've got to know and that's where experience comes in, which is something I'm lacking in. So I go with more breaks than I should. But at this point, this is the way I have to ride. That's why I need to race in Europe now.

**VeloNews** Were you worried or nervous when you were out there in the break?

**George Mount** I wasn't nervous. I was just really ruined. I was trying to hang in there. About a third of the time going up that mountain I felt just fantastic, but I was being cool, saving my strength. Usually when I'm feeling fantastic, I attack like a son of a bitch, and then I'm really dead. But this race, I knew was really big and I had to conserve all my strength. And then about a third of the time I felt sort of okay. And the other third of the time, forget it. I was just ruined. I never hurt so bad.

I learned so much in that hard kind of racing with those guys, because I would be hurting so bad, worse than I'd ever hurt, and some son of a bitch would attack. And I'd go with him. I surprised myself. They surprised me and I surprised myself. I just kept saying what I'd read in some cycling thing somewhere, Coppi or someone, "Remember, the other guy is hurting as much as you are." Of course, that's providing you're both just as fit. They're just as much as I am, it's just that they know how to hurt. That's a big difference.

**VeloNews** How did the Swede, Bernt Johansson get away?

**George Mount** We got to the top of that hill (on the last lap), and everybody was just whacked. There was nothing left of any of us. Except Johansson, and he looked around with disbelief in his eyes, and a kind of rode on a little bit. I yelled something at the Italians who were sitting up for the sprint already and they kind of shrugged.... Johansson just kind of rides off the front. And we're going, "There's no way." The guy was just stronger than everybody else, and he just rode right off the front. He rode down the hill and nobody could do anything. Fourteen times up that mountain and there was just nothing left. The last time up that mountain I never hurt so bad in my life. I mean, I died a hundred deaths. It was so bad.

**VeloNews** People will think that your sixth place has some meaning for American cycling. Was it just you, was it just luck, or does it have some relationship to the sport in this country?

**George Mount** I think that it shows that the sport in this country is advancing to the point now where we are competitive with the Europeans. I think that the sixth place was kind of like a trophy, but we've been proving it all along. Like in that five-day stage race, when I got fourth place and Neel won a stage, I think that was proof right there. But the sixth place in the Olympics was, like, you know, everybody could see it. It's right there, I proved it.

**VeloNews** Since you got the sixth place, has your life been any different?

**George Mount** I think that a lot of good things have happened to the sport in general. If getting sixth place in the Olympics hadn't been good for the sport, I wouldn't have done it. I'm just so glad because we got eight minutes of prime-time television coverage. A lot of people watch the Olympics.

**VeloNews** Do you think you can stand the life over there in Europe?

**George Mount** That's why I don't want to turn pro now, because if I turn pro and go to Europe, it's even harder. But rather I want to test myself out as an amateur, see if I can hack it. If I can't handle the situation, I'll quit racing. I won't race in this country any more. I won't race for the federation any more, forget it, I'm done. The Olympics are over with. I'm tired of losing money … and we never have any support. We go to a 12-day stage race and all we have is a mechanic and a coach. Theoretically, you can't ride a stage race without a soigneur, and we've done it many times, and that's why we don't do very well in a lot of the events.

The Olympics, I've got to say, you've got to give so much credit to mechanic Steve Aldridge and soigneur Frank Westell, because they are so important. Westell was just incredible. He was the guy who convinced me to shoot for a medal. A month before, I was going to go for the top 10. He says, "Why shoot for the top 10? Why not shoot for a medal?" So I was, I was trying. If I was just shooting for the top 10, I would have sat up for the sprint and got ninth or something, but instead I kept going and I was sprinting as hard as I could go. I beat a couple guys in the sprint.

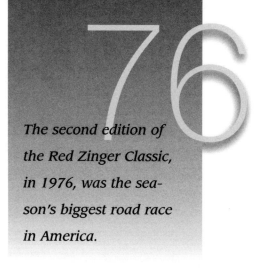

*The second edition of the Red Zinger Classic, in 1976, was the season's biggest road race in America.*

# Red Zinger goes international

**BY ALICE KOVLER**

Spectacular is the term that comes closest to suggesting the scale of the U.S. season's only recognized international road event, which brought an array of cycling talent into action in the soaring mountains along the splendid and awesome Continental Divide.

Celestial Seasoning's second annual Red Zinger Bicycle Classic on August 6, 7 and 8 in Boulder, Colorado, was in some ways almost the road counterpart to Rodale's North American Championships on the track the week before in Pennsylvania.

In Boulder, as in Trexlertown, a major company with a conscious interest in natural, healthful lifestyles has lavished heart and money to promote bicycling. The results to some are heartening.

Celestial Seasonings, thus far, has been putting its enormous wallop — $50,000 this year — into the three-stage Red Zinger Classic and is projecting the growth of this event, over a period of years, into something of an American Tour de France.

Large crowds, drawn from the young, easy-going, fitness-conscious populace of Boulder, were attracted through one of the most extensive promotional campaigns American cycling has ever seen. Advertising for this August weekend started in May and culminated with a blitz of ads and public service announcements in all media.

"This year we're international," as the ads put it. The participation of a Commonwealth team, comprised of Olympic riders from Australia, Great Britain and New Zealand, and a squad from Mexico, with a mix of Olympic and non-Olympic riders, fulfilled the terms. With the presence of the U.S. Olympic "A" and "B" road teams, and about 100 of the top American cyclists, it was, indeed, a classy brew.

Making up the Commonwealth team were Englishmen Bill Nickson, this year's Milk Race winner, and Dudley Hayton; Australians Clyde Sefton, the 1972 Munich silver medalist, and Ian Chandler; and Gary Bell of New Zealand.

With the international threat and a prize list in excess of $20,000, the ante was dramatically higher than last year, but John Howard again captured victory in the affair by his supremacy in the time trial.

"This was his key to winning," explained race coordinator Dave DiPane. With a fifth place in the road race and 28th in the criterium, Howard's victory must be traced to this event.

A few hundred people showed up at the site of the opening time trial east of Boulder on Friday morning. It was a typical hot dry Colorado day with benign wisps of clouds floating by. (Ironically, this had not been typical lately. It had, in fact, rained almost every day the first week of August, causing some embarrassment over an early promotional claim that, "Rain in Boulder during August is about as likely as snow in Hawaii.")

But the time trial started in perfect weather, with defending champion Howard going first and other riders following at spaced intervals. Some wind came up as the event went on and gave resistance to later starters.

Howard came through with a 22:42 on the 10.8-mile course, a full 20 seconds up on second-place finisher Tom Doughty of the U.S. B team — and not far from his 25-second edge in last year's slightly shorter time trial.

Commonwealth men Hayton, Chandler and Nickson were third, fourth and fifth, respectively. Sixth through 10th place, in order, went to Americans Dicky Dunn, Jim Flanders, David Mayer-Oakes, Mike Neel and Jack Janelle.

The 93-mile road race course was close to perfect, too. The promoters added over 15 miles of rolling hills and an additional canyon hurdle to last year's route in response to rider criticism that it was too short.

And, incredibly, people were omnipresent along this entire extended and variegated way. Even in remote mountain passes, spectators were in evidence.

"I've never seen this many people come out for a road race in this country," exclaimed Bill Woodul, whose appearance at most of the important races in the U.S. as the technical support man in the Campagnolo van gives credence to his pronouncement.

Someone even likened craning viewers along the most steep and searing descent to vultures. Well, no one could deny that audience involvement was high, but the prevailing mood was quite positive.

Sefton of Australia was the dominant figure in the race from first to last. He took all the primes; three for the King of the Mountain title, and one given by Caribou Ranch in front of its entrance on the Peak to Peak highway at about the halfway point.

Sefton and an American rider broke away in the first three miles of the race and gained a half-mile edge, but were rounded up just before the climb to Coal Creek Canyon where the road begins its sharp upward ascent from the 5000-foot level.

In a pre-race interview with Gary Burns of the *Boulder Daily Camera*, Howard said, "I expect a break somewhere near that place with the strange name — Wondervu, that's it." And, wondrously, that was it!

A chase-proof seven-man group worked itself away from the field on the climb to 8500 feet at Wondervu (the 30-mile point). From there, a "grudge match" ensued between the Americans — Howard, Dale Stetina, Mark Pringle, Doughty, Dunn — and the Commonwealth riders, Sefton and Hayton.

Sefton finally flew off on his own along the steep and twisting descent of South St. Vrain Canyon (the 60-mile mark). He accelerated to over 50 miles an hour on the wildly winding road and was picked up by the others 10 miles out of Lyons (the 80-mile mark). From there, said Sefton, it was a matter of waiting for the sprint.

For Howard, Lyons was probably the place he lost his chance to win the stage. There he killed his front wheel while crossing the railroad tracks and, though the Campy support crew supplied an almost immediate wheel change, he never felt quite right with it.

Howard was returned to the front by his teammates for the weekend, Stetina and Pringle, who dropped back to pick him up — a show of teamwork and spirit that brought pleased comments from many observers. But he never managed to get in position for the sprint. It was obvious, though, that he rode a very good race.

At the finish line in downtown Boulder, about 7000 people were present to see Sefton take the sprint, with Pringle in his wake. Sefton's teammate Hayton was third.

Sefton was overwhelmed by the expressiveness of the crowd, which cheered wildly as he came across the line. "I received the Olympic silver medal at Munich in 1972," he commented, "but this reception was twice as good as the one I got there."

The 50-mile criterium was routed around the perimeter of North Boulder Park where 15,000 people watched the race while enjoying a *be-in*–like "Sunday in the Park." A 19-piece jazz band made music and the concessions offered iced Red Zingers, fresh and imaginative salads, and whole-grain sandwiches. Down to the last detail, a natural, healthful consciousness prevailed. The imported master of ceremonies, Vern Grimsley, has an awareness-type radio show in San Francisco and his presentation was spiced with healthful information.

An atypical, 30-minute downpour during the 69-lap race did nothing to douse the high spirits of the enthusiastic audience. The rains came with 25 laps to go, but the pace-setting nine-man break was so far ahead of the 120-man field, it didn't seem to make any difference. These reeling mavericks went on to lap the entire field, causing no little havoc among the pickers.

Entering the last lap, Nickson was led out by his teammate Chandler. Rounding the final curve, Nickson snapped out like a slingshot to win the race. Second was Dave Boll, third Chandler, and Mayer-Oakes was fourth.

Howard, having carefully calculated his margin in the overall standings, went easy in the criterium (he finished 28th), satisfied that none of the lapping riders was in contention for the overall victory. His calculations proved to be quite clear-headed, as none of Saturday's first seven overall places were changed by the criterium results.

Throughout the international gathering, Americans rode with class and in the overall team standings, they came away with the first two places. The Olympic A team was first, the B team second, and the Commonwealth team third.

The awards ceremony later in the day provided a touching finale. Huerta made a moving speech in appreciation of the warmth and conviviality the Mexicans had been met with in Boulder. The constant attention of two interpreters during their entire stay made their visit inconceivably homelike and comfortable, and he invited American riders to test Latin hospitality at the Tour of Mexico in October.

Criterium winner Nickson will probably be remembered for his kindness even more than for his speed. During the criterium, over $1000 had been collected from spectators, with half to go to the race winners and half for victims of the recent devastating flash flood in nearby Big Thompson Canyon. On behalf of teammate Chandler and himself, Nickson rechanneled their share of the money to the flood victims. Everyone was elated by this gesture of goodwill.

When it was all over, Celestial Seasonings was clearly pleased. Media coverage of the event was extensive locally, with front page headlines springing out of all the papers and a 15-minute news special on TV. *Sports Illustrated* and *East-West Journal*, a counter-culture magazine, had reporters on the scene. The foreign teams went home bursting with goodwill, and a sizable chunk of the population of Boulder came to be seen and have a good time.

Coordinator DiPane is already thinking of next year's Classic, which may have an Aspen to Denver stage and possibly a night criterium in downtown Denver. But the No. 1 goal, he says, is to try to connect with other promoters around the country to establish greater uniformity of events in cycling.

With the Zinger's great success, others may well want to hear from these master promoters. "They have a gold star as far as I'm concerned," said Woodul, who's seen it all.

*In 1978, long before mountain biking became an official branch of competitive cycling, a small group of riders began racing "clunkers" in Northern California...*

# California bikies are 'mountainside surfing'

**BY OWEN MULHOLLAND**

Remember when California was celebrated as the land of surf and sun, some sort of mystical isle known best to most Americans through pop classics like "Surfer Girl" and "Santa Catalina"? Yeah, just laying about all day in the sun with some beautiful member of the opposite sex, beer in hand and surf on the horizon. Mmmmmmmmmm, California dreamin'.

And those who got a little closer to the fantasy found that surf and sun weren't the only ways to enjoyment. A regular hedonistic paradise of endless mountains, deserts, forests and beautiful cities — all inhabited by like-minded folks working hard at not working hard — either took the puritanical starch out of one's dedication to dutiful labor or sent the curious back home where right and wrong were still not matters of debate.

In the subculture of bikedom, the vision of California, with just some twists here and there, remained pretty well the same. The *real* roadies came only from California. Everyone knew that. Who else could get up those mountains like goats? The results of such up-and-down races as the Aspen Alpine Cup and Clarksville, or the composition of the U.S. road teams (and almost as frequently the track teams) for the Pan Am and Olympic Games seemed to confirm that "Out West" was the only place one could reach the top level.

Then John Howard from Texas came along in 1968. Howie went on to play foster father to a whole new era in which the star of California definitely dimmed to some degree.

The Beach Boys had to come back as some hip artists, and the likes of Mike Neel and George Mount were only two of numerous top-rate bikies across the land. Even the Haight-Ashbury is a regular respectable middle-class neighborhood these days. Very boring.

Well, fear not! The California quest for ever new highs is still alive and well, just a little underground that's all. The secret can now be revealed that a growing cluster of California bikies has discovered yet another stairway to nirvana. Depending on whom you talk to, it's called either bombering or clunking....

The origins of this subliminal quest for self-annihilation are lost in the misty, time-obscured depths of the past decade, but a few men are still around who claim to have been around at the inception of the effort to conquer California mountains on two wheels. One of these hoary old men is Charly Kelly; another is Gary "Wild Man" Fisher. Actually, it's only in conventional cycling circles that Gary is known as "Wild Man." Compared to Charly he is a very tame man. Regardless, it seems that Charly grew accustomed to navigating the tiny tracks of Mount Tamalpais, his back door volcano in Marin County just north of San Francisco, on an old Schwinn newsboy's bike.

Trouble was, that single hub brake was meant, as Charly recalled the other day, for a "75-pound newsboy, not some 200-pound fool." Eventually, Charly met Gary, the latter mounted on his "cruiser," or heavy-duty get-around-town bike. They got to talking about their steeds' limitations, Gary mentioned the bike parts warehouse he occasionally referred to as "home," and pretty soon the two were hard at work on some heavy modifications.

First came the front drum brake, then five speeds, then 10 speeds, with the usual alloy crank setup, then 25-year-old Schwinn cantilever brakes , a Brooks B-72 saddle and, finally, the logical outcome of such a line of development, their own frames, these being made by the local master craftsmen, Joe Breeze. The frames are real jewels and run for something like $275, bare. At the moment, Joe can't keep up with the orders.

All of this was hardly in the service of idle touring up the countryside. The competitive spirit never lies far below the skin, and hardly were the bikes on the trail than the races were on. In time, two types developed: infrequently held mass start "enduros" that involve as much up as down, and the weekly time trial runs down "Repack," a three-mile-long fire trail that drops a thousand feet. In other words, *steep*.

A peculiar mixture of U.S. Cycling Federation riders and locals has swollen the ranks to nearly 100. Other contingents from around the Bay Area frequently attend bomber blasts, and rumors of an annual Colorado bomber race from Vail to Aspen have already prompted much talk of an "invasion" back there.

What this all portends is anyone's guess, but those who remember surfing back in the early '50s could perhaps hazard a theory or two. And those California bikies who have been suffering from an inferiority complex of late can take heart that theirs is still the land of two-wheeled kamikaze crazies.

*In 1981, his first season as a pro cyclist, Greg LeMond faced off against the all-conquering Soviet national team in Colorado's Coors Classic.*

# Red Guard fails to shake LeMond

## BY BJARNE ROSTAING

Dave Chauner spoke for many when he said he could be very happy if he never read another course description. But Morgul-Bismarck, once again the decisive Coors Classic stage, deserves a bit of scrutiny. At 93 miles (seven 13-mile laps), it's a little distance-shy by world standards but it has, like the Coors Classic itself, emerged as a premier test with its own unique character. Europeans who laugh off many of race promoter Michael Aisner's criteriums as "entertainment," talk about this sun-baked monster as a world championship course.

Morgul-Bismarck tests completeness: Riders who lack strength, reasonably good climbing, speed and good recuperation are simply eaten up, because the constantly shifting terrain allows for constant attacking. Nothing holds steady long enough for things to get dull and, because the climbs are not long (900 feet of climbing per lap), Morgul-Bismarck can be very fast. Power-climbers hit the hills hard, zooming over the top in the big ring most of the time. It's a Soviet course, you might say — made to order for a 100km team time trial specialist.

The opening move is almost traditional now — a few riders go off the front early, gambling that they will hook onto something more powerful which is sure to come by a bit later. This year's gamblers were Alan McCormack, Greg Demgen and Mark Frise. They were given plenty of rope — about two and a half minutes' worth in a relatively short time. Behind them, the pack was not under real pressure until the break gained another minute and people began to remember that McCormack has gotten away with this sort of thing before and that Demgen was due for another good day.

As the chase began heating up behind them, McCormack and Demgen dropped Frise and moved smoothly on, waiting for the inevitable — and the inevitable looked like it would be mostly red jerseys. By the time the first of the chase groups reached them, Demgen was looking poorly, soon to be dropped, but McCormack is used to pro distances and tempos, able to hang on. When the final joining-up was accomplished, the survivors included the entire Soviet squad except for Sergei Zagretdinov, plus Alessandro Pozzi, McCormack and race leader Greg LeMond. Not a single U.S. amateur.

The Soviets went to the front, as they like to do, and began to roll up time on the pack. Behind them, the three outsiders conversed, perhaps about the fairly cool, overcast weather with its threat of rain. Perhaps about working for their mutual advantage. Without a single Renault man in sight, LeMond was looking at 50 miles of fun and games. Rumor had it that Renault-Celestial negotiations had fallen flat — but with Pozzi getting stronger and stronger, his services could be decisive for LeMond, whose four-minute-plus overall lead no longer looked very solid.

With a break established, Soviet team director Viktor Kapitanov came alongside to lecture his troops, steering his motorcycle driver with an iron grip on the shoulder. The red jerseys hunkered down into their echelon, with LeMond choosing to stick right behind them, trailed by Pozzi and McCormack. The Soviets wasted no time going after LeMond's lead. They began with a combination of psychological warfare and a little rough riding. If LeMond were going to insist on a Russian wheel at all times, they were going to make that wheel tricky. Especially 1980 Rider of the Year Sergei Soukhoroutchenkov, whose hooks, bumps and general bad behavior indicated that trouble lay ahead.

LeMond's almost casual handling of this steady harassment was amazing. But when the very composed and efficient Pozzi flatted on the next lap, the noose appeared to be tightening. Kapitanov was there again on the motor with instructions and the locomotive *really* began to move. Pozzi made a game effort to close but there was no way, and the Soviets were whipping back off the front of their echelon *very* close to LeMond's front wheel, unmistakable in their intent. By now, however, commissaire Ian Anderson was watching from his car with an experienced eye and the tactic had to stay within reason.

The speed just seemed to keep climbing for miles and miles of TTT, and still there was LeMond and there was Mighty Mac. The Red Guard never seemed to realize that this lonely pair might survive the tempo. With total victory within their grasp, the Soviets confined themselves to muscle-flexing until the last lap, when the schedule apparently called for a *coup de grace.* Suddenly they were doing what they should have been doing earlier — sending riders up the road and blocking LeMond.

Somehow the blocking did not mesh and, with a bit of help from McCormack, each attack was covered. The imperious TTT effort had taken more out of the Soviets than those sitting behind — when LeMond tried a solo he got twice as big a gap as any of them had managed.

With only a few miles to go the Soviets were extremely glum, not to say defensive, which tempted McCormack to shoot away up the Hump as they closed in on the finish. But just as the outrageous move looked possible, he was hauled in. Then *everything* exploded — Yuri Barinov in particular, driven by Kapitanov's guttural expletives.

LeMond had the Soviet's wheel and might have had the stage until screams from the Renault team director ordered his final attack. The American pro was around Barinov like a shot and passed him, only to die on the line. He would have done better to go with his instinct, but no one cared that much. Against all odds, Morgul-Bismarck had seen a miracle and the eternal question of amateur versus pro had been cast in a new perspective.

81

*In 1981, three years before Greg LeMond debuted in the race, Jonathan Boyer became the first U.S. rider to finish the Tour de France.*

# Jonathan Boyer: first U.S. Tour rider

**BY THE EDITORS**

Twenty-five days and 3766km after his historic start in the 1981 Tour de France, Jonathan Boyer crossed the finish line in Paris July 19 and joined the third Tour victory celebration of his teammate Bernard Hinault. Boyer was the first American to complete the Tour de France.

Fifth highest finisher on the 10-man Renault-Gitane squad, Boyer placed 32nd of the 121 riders who completed the event. Though he certainly deserved to join the festivities, Boyer didn't stick around for much of them. He flew back to the U.S. just hours after the race was over and spent two days being interviewed in New York City.

The non-stop schedule was nothing new for the 25-year-old professional. Boyer said that during the Tour he had absolutely no free time beyond his racing, eating, sleeping and interview responsibilities. "I got an incredible amount of attention, but it didn't distract from my concentration on the race at all," he said.

While in New York Boyer appeared on "The Today Show," and was featured in *The New York Times*.

For those already familiar with cycling and Boyer's career, the important questions were "What was it like?" "How do you feel now?" and "Were you satisfied with your performance?" His voice muffled by a stuffy nose, Boyer answered these questions and others in a telephone interview with *VeloNews* July 21.

"How can I be disappointed — Bernard won," Boyer said in response to a suggestion that his 32nd overall was a letdown after being among the top 15 after the first third of the race. "My job was to work for Hinault. He was the only rider on our team with a shot at the win and we had to make sure that he had minimum effort throughout the race.

"That meant bringing back any breakaways and making sure that at the end of a race we kept up a good pace," he continued. "If Hinault didn't want any breakaways to get away, then all nine of us would get up front and take pace at 25 or 26 miles per hour. We worked very effectively as a team."

With an average speed of more than 23 mph, this year's Tour was the fastest ever — perhaps because lucrative hot spots were strategically placed to speed up the pace. This meant that the early miles of the long stages were not always an easy warm-up, Boyer explained. "Sometimes the warm-ups would last 50 or even 60 miles, but not always. Everybody wanted to go for the hot spots, and after the hot spots there would be attacks. It was kind of hard to relax."

Boyer talked of burning pain in his legs and being very tired toward the end of the Tour. But, charged with the responsibility of getting Hinault to Paris in the yellow jersey, he seemed to downplay his own stage performances — almost as if they weren't real.

It was the dramatic 12th stage from Compiègne to Roubaix which shattered Boyer's chances of a higher general classification finish. He flatted five times and crashed into a team support vehicle that stopped abruptly in his path. For the rest of the Tour, he admitted, he didn't feel quite right and he lost more than 50 minutes in the last seven stages.

Boyer seemed to recover quickly, however. In New York he said, "I don't feel run down at all, and I'm feeling no long-term physical effects either."

Boyer's strength is built on a diet (no red meat, lots of whole grains and nuts) that has been the subject of considerable attention in the European cycling press. It's been rumored that Renault team director Cyrille Guimard is highly critical of this regimen, but Boyer said that's not true.

"Guimard has supported me in my diet," Boyer asserted, "because he realizes that even though I don't eat meat, everything I do eat is of good quality." Boyer did say he had a hard time buying dried fruits and nuts overseas and he added that the diet maintained by most European pros is partially a factor of convenience. During the Tour, his 125-pound supply of California dried fruit shrunk to less than 50 pounds.

*In 1982, two years after placing fifth at the world's, Jonathan Boyer was in a solo attack 800 meters from the finish of the pro road race at Goodwood, England...*

# Boyer-LeMond rivalry clouds world's

**BY TIM BLUMENTHAL**

In a year marked by two U.S. world championships and other important victories, the most memorable race was one that ended both in controversy and without an American winner.

The 1982 World Professional Road Championship, 275km long, was completed Sunday afternoon, September 5, in Goodwood, England. But it still goes on. The extraordinary final kilometer remains a hot topic in the U.S. and in Europe.

For a few seconds in the final minute, U.S. cycling was on top of the world. Jacques Boyer was clear of the bunch with the finish line in sight. Greg LeMond was at the front of the powerful first group.

But less than 30 seconds later, Italy's Giuseppe Saronni was the world champion. A jubilant LeMond took the silver medal. An anguished Boyer finished 10th.

Second and 10th — it was the best performance by the U.S. in pro road championship history. Normally such results would prompt an unrestrained celebration. Instead, the post-race moods of LeMond and Boyer bordered on bitter.

From the press came immediate accusations that LeMond chased down Boyer, that he intentionally prevented him from winning the world championship. LeMond did not deny it, and only a few people in the U.S. delegation congratulated him for his ride. Boyer reportedly spent much of the night in tears.

The finish raised many questions that can never be answered. But this only serves to make discussions of the race more lively and opinionated, especially among U.S. cycling fans who've never before had much to talk about following a pro road championship. Among the questions being asked:

• Could Boyer have taken the rainbow jersey if LeMond had ridden the final kilometer differently?

• Could LeMond, a strong sprinter, have won the world championship with Boyer's support?

• If LeMond hadn't jumped, would Saronni and Ireland's Sean Kelly, each a powerful sprinter, have neutralized each other and handed Boyer the world title?

• What effect have LeMond's tactics and post-race statements had on his reputation in Europe?

To gather some expert views on these matters, *VeloNews* talked at length with Boyer, LeMond, bronze-medalist Kelly, U.S. pro George Mount, former pro Mike Neel, U.S. pro team director Jack Simes, and others who watched the event in person and/or on videotape. Our intention is not to draw conclusions, but to share with you what these people are saying.

The bad blood between Boyer and LeMond so apparent in the race aftermath did not begin in England. Nor did they always dislike each other.

Boyer and LeMond first met in the winter of 1977-78 when Boyer returned to his Northern California home from France. Then 22, Boyer already had five years of European experience. He had turned pro on May 2, 1977, after a strong early season on the prestigious French amateur team, U.S. Creteil.

"If there is anybody I'd like to be like, it'd be him," 16-year-old LeMond said of Boyer (*VeloNews,* March 10, 1978). "(He is) ... the ultimate in cycling."

Their first stage race confrontation came in the 1979 Coors Classic. LeMond, still a junior, ended fourth on final G.C. Boyer finished second and would have won easily if not for a controversial five-minute penalty.

Two years later, both LeMond and Boyer signed to ride for France's powerful Renault-Gitane pro team. Just a month before beginning his European career, LeMond told *VeloNews*: "(Boyer) is a good friend. I don't think there will be any problem. He's an older guy ... he's more mature ... Jacques has raced for two years as a professional in Europe and he knows what the races are like and what to expect. It will be good for me."

While LeMond was quickly successful with Renault-Gitane, he didn't get along with his American teammate almost from the start. LeMond says that Boyer needled him all the time, comparing their results.

Boyer says he thinks their current problems stem "mostly from envy and jealousy when (LeMond) turned professional." Further, he states that the bad feelings were all on LeMond's part. He says he helped LeMond as a translator and worked for him during the mountain stages of the 1981 Dauphiné Libéré, where LeMond was fourth.

LeMond on the other hand, says that Boyer was upset by the frequent press attention he received as a 19-year-old neo-pro. "At first, I got more publicity than I really deserved," LeMond admits.

Strained relations between the riders' wives appears to be another reason for the falling out. It's not easy to adapt to the restrictions imposed on the wife of a pro cyclist. Women are not permitted to follow most races in the caravan and so must spend a lot of time away from their husbands. For an American woman in Europe, it can sometimes be boring, sometimes tense, and it's not easy to make friends. Somehow this climate produced friction between Elizabeth Boyer and Kathy LeMond that carried over to their husbands.

Until the world's, Boyer and LeMond did not cross paths often during the 1982 season. LeMond broke his collarbone April 11 in Liège-Bastogne-Liège and rode just a few stage races, criteriums and Belgian kermesses before the world's. Boyer, who had switched from Renault-Gitane to Sem-France Loire, competed in the Coors Classic, his second Tour de France, and spent much of August racing in Belgium.

Did the U.S. have a team in the pro road race? The riders' perception of teamwork was an important part of the event, as well as Europe's reaction to LeMond's tactics in the final kilometer.

"I felt we had — apart from Greg — a team that wanted to do something in the race," says Boyer. "Jackie Simes (team director and president of the U.S. Professional Racing Organization) talked with us before the race. Greg didn't come to any of the meetings because he just didn't want to be associated, I guess, with the team.

"I felt very good with the riders that we had," Boyer continues. "George (Mount) was willing to help anyone as much as he could. Eric (Heiden) certainly helped me out during the race. David (Mayer-Oakes) and John (Eustice) weren't as capable as any of the others in doing something, but they certainly would have helped me if I had asked them, though it never came to that point. I think we had a lot stronger team this year than any other year. We had a lot more team spirit also."

"Even the European press, they don't understand that a U.S. pro team really does not exist," he says. "I know that PRO is really trying to improve on things, but there are only 10 professionals right now. It's pretty hard to support a team and everything when you're such a new federation.

"I think the U.S. public has got to realize that I'm no longer an amateur. I'm racing for Renault and I'm racing for myself. It's a business and it's my living. To me, that second place was almost as good as winning, especially at my age."

In Mount's view, "everybody makes their own deals. Whether they make the deal to ride for themselves or whether they make the deal to ride for their national team captain, which some big teams do, or side deals. I'd have to say that I was riding primarily for myself, in as much as Greg and I are really good friends and I know what a good rider Greg is. The other riders, I don't know where they were at.

"If you're on the Italian national team, you get an additional monthly stipend all year long and you get enormous bonuses if the rider wins (the world's). Of course, they were paid — they're professionals. I wouldn't ride for somebody unless I'm paid."

LeMond says the fact that he had to pay his own way to the world's was one reason he discounted the notion of a U.S. team. He says other national team leaders (the Netherlands' Jan Raas, France's Bernard Hinault, Italy's Saronni) were able to select riders to help them in the race. Who should have been the U.S. team leader? Did the U.S. even have the depth to mount a team effort? LeMond says that Boyer was on form and not about to give up his own chances.

Perhaps this is U.S. pro cycling's new dilemma: to have two riders capable of winning the world road championship yet incapable of working together. LeMond says it's similar to the relationship between Moser and Saronni, Italy's two superstars. Moser reportedly was paid several thousand dollars to work for his long-time rival at Goodwood. His efforts brought results.

"No, there wasn't any money involved (in U.S. plans)," says Boyer. "But we have national pride. I was certainly proud to be there representing the United States."

Simes says he talked with LeMond before the race and told him that "nobody expects you to actively work for someone." Simes says he asked LeMond to consider not hindering and even helping a U.S. rider in contention to win.

Looking at the results, Simes says, "It's professional cycling and the killer instinct comes out after 170 miles." He adds that the idea of national loyalty *without a large financial incentive* may be too vague to dictate the tactics of a pro rider in a world championship.

There is little disagreement about the flow of the race up to the point where Boyer attacked and built a lead. Spain's Lejarreta escaped from the pack with less than a mile to go and Boyer rode onto his wheel. When the Spaniard slowed, Boyer went ahead on his own. He built a lead of 30-40 meters with about 800 uphill meters left to the finish. Behind in the bunch, Italy, the Netherlands, Belgium and Spain were all well represented with at least three riders each. LeMond also was in there.

After Boyer made his move, Dutchmen Hennie Kuiper and Johan Van der Velde were prominent at the head of the pack. And that's where the consensus ends.

At what point did LeMond shoot out of the pack? What did he do when he pulled even with Boyer? Was Boyer losing ground to the peloton as he approached the final turn? These key questions are addressed in the following analyses of the final kilometer.

"I knew who had the best sprint out of the whole pack and that was Saronni," LeMond told *VeloNews*. "Kelly is really fast, too, but on an uphill sprint nobody can beat Saronni. I raced with him in Tirreno-Adriatico in March and I was always sprinting against him for time bonuses and I kept getting second.

"But with a lap to go, I really didn't think of anybody. I was only concerned about myself, trying to be in good position for the sprint.

"Boyer got quite a good lead at the bottom of the hill — you know, 15 seconds, maybe 10 seconds in front of the group. When Boyer went, the pack really slowed down like they were setting up for the sprint. Kuiper started leading out and Van der Velde was behind him, and they were leading out one of the Dutch riders. I'm not sure who it was. At that time you are just going on instinct.

"Then Kuiper kind of died. It was a long hill and it was hard to maintain a maximum effort for any amount of time. Van der Velde was up at the front and at that time the whole field started really moving. I moved up and I was on Van der Velde's wheel. With about 300 meters to go, Boyer was, I'm not sure, 20 meters in front of us, and we were really coming up on him quick.

"Van der Velde died and I was left there right in front of the group. So there was nothing I could do at that point. And there was nothing Boyer could do. I think that if he was that much stronger he would have held on. I just ended up sprinting for the finish. With 300 or 400 meters to go it's pretty hard to do any kind of blocking for anybody.

"Boyer really did a good ride. He made a good move, but a move like that has about a five-percent chance of making it. It's not often that a guy can hold off a pack. It happens when there's a group of maybe four of five riders. But in professional racing when it comes to a sprint, the group moves at such a fast speed that for anybody dangling off the front it's like suicide.

"Everybody who has these knowledgeable theories about racing, they have no idea what it really takes. There's no way in the world that I could have helped Boyer in the last 400 meters. The only thing I could have done was throw on my brakes, crash in front of the pack, and hopefully hold off Saronni. I mean, what kind of tactics is that? At 400 meters to go you just don't put on your brakes, especially in the world championships."

"I know (LeMond) chased me down," Boyer says. "I saw him — his only intent was to chase me down. On the film, he shut off once he got to my wheel. Once he caught me, he shut off and that's when Saronni attacked. He shut off because he accomplished what he wanted to do.

"It wasn't up to LeMond to make the move. I am fully aware of Saronni's capabilities in the final 1000 meters or whatever it is, but Saronni was too much afraid of Kelly, who could beat him in the sprint. He wasn't about to chase me down with Kelly on his wheel. Or Kelly and Raas on his wheel, which was the case."

Boyer insists that he wasn't slowing down when LeMond and the bunch pulled even on the home stretch. In fact, he says he had just changed into a larger gear.

"I don't think that Boyer was fading," Sean Kelly told *VeloNews* from his home in Carrick-on-Suir, Ireland. "Anybody who got away at the moment he did had to be very, very strong. When he did get away I was quite close to the front of the group and nobody moved. He got quite a good gap. Nobody wanted to go after him.

"Saronni really wasn't intent on going *after* Boyer because I was on his wheel at that moment. I'd say he was afraid of me in the sprint. Then LeMond went after Boyer and Saronni followed him and I followed Saronni.

"I was quite surprised to see LeMond jump. Yes, LeMond chased down Boyer — Boyer was the only man up the road. If it was the same position with the Irish team where I was up the road and Stephen Roche chased me, I think I would be very, very vexed up for him to do that.

"When Boyer went away I definitely wasn't going to go after him. I wasn't going to make the pace to catch him because he's been on the same team with me all the year."

According to Kelly, if LeMond hadn't jumped, neither he (Kelly) nor Saronni would have moved. Who else was there to chase Boyer? Joop Zoetemelk, who ended fourth? Lejarreta, who took fifth after trying on his own earlier?

"Van der Velde was pulling the pack pretty good, but Boyer was still gaining on it a little bit," says former U.S. pro Mike Neel, who scored America's first big breakthrough when he finished 10th in the 1976 world road championship. Neel says he has seen several tapes of the Goodwood finish.

"Saronni and Kelly weren't going to jump, probably. Van der Velde jumped, then Greg jumped — real hard — and then Saronni was right on his wheel. Perfect, just like laughing. And then Greg pulled for it looked like 150 meters and got up even with Boyer and kind of looked back. He looked to the side at Boyer and then Saronni jumped right then. Greg looked over and saw Saronni and then went for his wheel.

"Greg might have done better to look behind him at Saronni. He didn't anticipate Saronni and that strong of a jump. I don't really think that Greg was really trying to chase down Boyer. He was trying to go for the finish, but he's inexperienced. He probably just jumped a little early. It was uphill, there were lots of corners. He could have waited a little longer.

"You have to be aggressive to win and (LeMond) got a lot of respect for it. The problem was that he was in second place, and when Van der Velde pulled over he probably should have waited. But he was in the lead so he just jumped. You just don't know what's going to happen. You could be devoured at any second. It's scary.

"They (LeMond and Boyer) should have talked about it. If they would have talked about it maybe they could have worked a better deal. If Boyer could have pulled that hard all the way up the finish with Greg on his wheel, nobody would have come around him.

"Who's to blame? Boyer because he attacked Greg? Or Greg because he wanted to win the race? I don't know. I just think that both of them were a little more aggressive than normal because both of them were there. It's all said and done, and they didn't cooperate. You can't blame Greg and you can't blame Jacques."

"LeMond didn't attack until a couple of hundred meters to go," says Mount, who ended 52nd, six minutes down. He says he's watched the race at least 20 times on video tape.

"In a pro bike race, especially the world's, the sprint starts winding up with about a mile to go, and with about 500 meters to go the sprint starts. Boyer made his attack with about 800 meters to go — he made a good move. At that point the sprint started. Van der Velde was the one who picked the pace up and started leading the sprint out with about 400 or 500 meters to go. Greg was in a good position — he was on Van der Velde's wheel. What's Greg going to do? The sprint starts and there's 400 meters to go.

"Boyer is going really slow. He's going at least 15 or 20 percent slower than the field at this point. He just died and the field is starting to sprint now. Just before the corner, Van der Velde dies and pulls off. It's less than 200 meters to go. What's LeMond going to do? Throw his bike down in front of everybody because Boyer is such a good buddy of everyone? Or because Boyer is paying enormous sums of money to everybody — which is not going on. Hell, no — he's going to start sprinting because it's less than 200 meters to go and the sprint's already been going for a couple hundred meters. Greg continues to sprint. He pulls away from Sean Kelly.

"Amateur riders, especially in the U.S., don't understand how pro sprints work. They are longer sprints, they are faster sprints, they are harder sprints. Of course, nobody was going to beat Saronni that day. He was just unbeatable. In that kind of sprint there is no one who can hold his wheel.

"LeMond made a good move and a good sprint. Boyer made a good move, he got good publicity, and he finished well. He should have been happy with it. Boyer was not going to win that race. The best he could have got was fifth or sixth place."

"I think the thing was really blown out of proportion mainly because of the journalists right after the race," LeMond says. "Every journalist came up (to Boyer) and started screaming, 'You would have won, you would have won, your teammate chased you down.'

"I don't blame Boyer racing for himself and I don't see how he can blame me doing what I did," LeMond continues. "I think if I was so worried about him being in front, I would have chased him, got on his wheel, and just sat there.

"I got second. I was so thrilled and all of a sudden I have all these journalists coming up and criticizing me for chasing down Jacques. I mean how can you chase somebody down in 400 to 500 meters before the finish? It's impossible. I didn't know what to say at the time. People don't realize that our country is such a new country (in cycling). There are so few professionals and our team is not structured like their teams."

*In August 1983, Greg LeMond, 22, was in his third season of pro racing. After a silver medal the year before, the American was favored to win gold in the world pro road championship at Altenrhein, Switzerland.*

# Reflections on the inevitable

BY TIM BLUMENTHAL

For a man who in 12 hours will race for the most important prize of his life, Greg LeMond is surprisingly relaxed.

He sits waiting for dinner in the palatial Hotel Bad Schachen, near Lindau, West Germany. Just across Lake Constance, maybe a mile or two by boat, is Altenrhein, Switzerland, site of tomorrow's world professional road championship.

LeMond is surrounded by family: his mom and dad, his wife Kathy and her parents, and other relatives. There are two outsiders at the table: Fred Mengoni, the New York City realtor who is one of U.S. cycling's best supporters, and this journalist from *VeloNews* who hasn't seen LeMond in nearly three years.

Wine is poured. LeMond sips slowly from a full glass. Now 22, he's been through three hard seasons as a professional bicycle racer, but his face is still fresh. The only thing that seems to have changed since our last meeting is his hair — it's shorter now. Maybe he's a bit smoother socially, too. He shows no anxiety at having his dinner interrupted by the visitors, and he is quick to call for more chairs.

The conversation ranges from how LeMond found this hotel (a guide book) to the baby Kathy expects in February. A crew from NBC television is setting up for an interview in one of the hotel's meeting rooms, and LeMond says he'll answer questions between courses. No problem.

After his second place in the 1982 world championship, people are expecting to see LeMond at the front of the field at Altenrhein. He has been named as one of the favorites by Eddy Merckx, who should know, and by a poll of French cycling writers.

LeMond surely is expecting a lot of himself, too. He has had what journalists call a season *à la carte,* which in his case means no Tour de France and no other serious challenges since the Dauphiné Libéré in early June. Whether riding the Tour is good or bad for a rider's world's chances is often debated, but Freddy Maertens (1976) was the last rider to finish in the Tour's top 10 and win the world's the same year.

There are great expectations this evening, but no apparent tension and almost no discussion of the race.

We walk down the 30-foot-wide hotel corridors toward a small TV crew that could produce the first significant U.S. exposure for LeMond. It's hard to believe that he has come so far in his sport without any national recognition. "Greg, I'd like you to meet Gary Gerould of NBC." The interview begins.

LeMond's face is whitened by the lights. He speaks confidently, but not cockily. He says his preparation, especially in the last 10 days or so, has been just what he wanted. He says he's healthy this time — he battled a bad cold just before last year's world's — and he feels well-suited to the course.

He speaks bluntly about the negative side of his 1982 silver medal, about the accusations that he led the bunch up to his soloing countryman, Jacques Boyer, on the final climb. That experience, LeMond says, has given him extra incentive to do well this year. "I ride for myself, for Renault and for money," he says for the millionth time.

LeMond still doesn't state it directly, but one gets the feeling he not only hopes to win tomorrow, he intends to win.

The interview complete, we walk back toward the dining room so he can continue dinner. I wish him luck, and good night.

Later I hear that at dessert he made his boldest prerace statement, though it came off lightly. A good-luck cake was brought to the table but then taken back because LeMond said, "We'll eat it tomorrow as a victory cake." Surely, everyone at the table laughed.

There must have been other journalists walking down other hallways with other big stars this evening, thinking that their companion would be the next world champion.

But the feeling that LeMond would win wasn't just some optimistic fantasy born of patriotism and pushed into my mind by a glass of wine. There's been an aura of inevitability surrounding his career since 1977, when he got up from two crashes to win the national junior road championship.

He said then that he wanted to win the junior world's — and he did it two years later. Next, he said, he wanted to be a pro with a top European team — and he was after two more years. Even as a junior, the stem on his bike sported a dollar sign. He had no doubts about his goals in the sport.

LeMond has always delivered. He is fortunate to have the physical and mental capabilities to be a champion cyclist, but like all champions he has worked hard to make good talent great.

There have been almost no disappointing performances, and the few setbacks in his career have been beyond his control.

One was the U.S. boycott in 1980 that snuffed out his chance to be the first American cyclist to win an Olympic medal. Another was the April 1982 crash that resulted in a broken collarbone and three months out of competition. But that accident spared him from the most arduous period of the season and allowed him to concentrate on the world's. He responded with the silver medal.

That feeling of inevitability continued the morning of the race. No one — not LeMond, not his father, not U.S. pro team director Jack Simes, not manager Jim Ochowicz — said Greg was going to win. But neither were they surprised when he did. Elated, yes. Surprised, no.

LeMond looked loose as the peloton rolled by the start-finish the first few times. There was a smile on his face and he appeared to be talking with riders around him. But he said later he was feeling lousy early on. Kathy commented that he had slept less than six hours and had gotten out of bed a few times.

Halfway through the 270km, LeMond joined a break with his good friend Phil Anderson. All the Americans in the stands stayed in their seats. Spoiled by last year's world's, they most probably expected to see both LeMond and Boyer in contention for the title on the last lap. The dream bubble we've been in since last September wouldn't get popped this day.

Twenty-five-inch color TV monitors hung from metal support pipes in the grandstands. There were four screens in the press tent, one with German commentary, one with Italian and another Dutch. Several cameras were mounted at roadside on the second rise, which made for great viewing.

One camera, located near the castle of Wartensee before the major summit, gave us a perfect close-up of the riders climbing. The pitch at that point was steep, and the slow-moving riders were in view for nearly 10 seconds each lap.

On the 16th circuit, American eyes were focused on the middle of the bunch, where LeMond was riding right at the front. Suddenly he attacked, prompting memories of Boyer's move at Goodwood. Swiss rider Serge Demierre was up the road, and LeMond was intent on catching him — or better.

From the side, U.S. stars-and-stripes jerseys are not easy to pick out. But from the front it's easy. When LeMond left the bunch, I looked for Boyer with the hope of seeing his reaction. However, by the time the camera returned from LeMond and the two who had caught his wheel, Spain's Faustino Ruperez and Italy's Moreno Argentin, Boyer and the others were rolling over the top at Vogelherd, their expressions showing only the fatigue of the 16th climb.

LeMond looked much fresher than the three riders out front with him. Demierre had ridden hard alone for a lap. Ruperez was in a fog of fatigue. Argentin, though I didn't know it at the time, is one of Italy's best road sprinters. But there was no need to ask the writer from Rome sitting next to me about him, because he was dropped on the penultimate lap.

There was just one moment when I feared LeMond was going to be caught. He was on the final rise to Vogelherd and the last split I'd heard was 25 seconds. Suddenly his body seemed to sag, his front wheel started swaying, and I thought I detected a different look in his eyes. It must have been my imagination. At the summit his lead had grown to 37 seconds.

And the rest, as they say, is history.

The stampede of the crowd toward the new champion was something I still don't understand. LeMond lives in Belgium, races mainly in France, and hasn't been in Switzerland that many times. Maybe the Swiss spectators simply had an emotional release after being so disappointed the day before when their Niki Rüttimann lost the sprint for the amateur title.

On the podium and in the press tent during the hour-long onslaught of questions, LeMond seemed totally in control. He appeared pleased but not overwhelmed. There never was a moment where he looked to the sky as if to wonder, "Can this really be happening to me?" He never said, "I don't believe it."

On this day, Greg LeMond was something of a knight in shining armor. As an American you'd have been proud of him. He performed valiantly, carrying himself in a manner befitting a world champion. But he kept his deep feelings of accomplishment to himself.

The emotional expressions of victory came from others — his wife, his father-in-law, and his father, who has coached Greg and trained with him since his intermediate days.

Finally free from the commotion, LeMond entered the copy machine room of the press tent. The door was shut behind him. There were about eight people — all Americans — in the room.

The conversation between LeMond and his father was 100-percent practical. Where should the party be held and what time? The plans were made quickly, then LeMond walked forward confidently, just as he had the night before. Somewhere a cake was waiting.

84

*January 1984 marked a turning point in the history of world cycling when 32-year-old Francesco Moser traveled to Mexico City to attack the legendary world hour record of Eddy Merckx.*

# Moser's finest hour

## BY TIM BLUMENTHAL

Francesco Moser has achieved cycling's most prestigious feat. He broke the world hour record. Not only that, he did it twice in one week.

Many thought the record would never be wrested from Belgian Eddy Merckx, who covered 49.431km on the wood track here in 1972 near the peak of his career. No subsequent attempt had come within a kilometer of Merckx's distance.

Then along came Moser, the 1977 world road champion and three-time winner of Paris-Roubaix. On January 16 on a new concrete track the 32-year-old Italian surpassed Merckx's mark by 1.4km, covering 50.809km.

Seven days later, Moser tried again and improved his own record by riding 51.151km. In the course of his two attempts he also set new world marks for 5km, 10km and 20km.

Few experts had seemed to think Moser had much of a chance at beating Merckx. They said he's too old and they cited his comparative lack of racing success during the past few seasons. Among those reported to be skeptical of Moser's chance were Italian great Felice Gimondi and Merckx himself. Merckx questioned Moser's gear selection and the timing of the attempt (Merckx set his hour record in October). Even Moser's team sponsor, the Gis ice cream company, refused to support him.

Moser was able to raise 100-million lire (about $60,000) from Enervit, a firm that makes a powdered energy food supplement. Enervit reportedly promised another 100-

million lire should Moser succeed. Among his other supporters were the bicycle manu-facturer Benotto and the Italian Cycling Federation.

Enervit's backing allowed Moser to hire four scientists and a physiotherapist to help him prepare. He flew to Mexico City in November to inspect the facilities.

Dr. Francesco Conconi, an Italian sports specialist, set up Moser's lap splits for the hour. Conconi even claimed that Merckx did not ride the optimum schedule.

The remainder of November and part of December was spent training at the Milan Sport Palace. In mid-December, Moser fine-tuned his equipment and aerodynamic riding position in wind-tunnel tests at Turin.

He returned to Mexico City just after Christmas, giving him three weeks to adjust to the 7400-foot altitude, before making his first try.

Moser's bike reputedly cost $35,000 to build. It is no lighter than Merckx's machine, but uses technical innovations that were unknown in 1972. It features dropped handle-bars, a smaller front wheel and a shorter wheel base (by 10 centimeters) than Merckx's bike. The rims are held together by solid carbon-fiber discs. Tires are narrow section, 17 millimeters wide.

The concrete track was varnished to make it smoother. Both Merckx and Ole Ritter (who held the hour record before Merckx) rode on a wood track.

Before going to Mexico, Moser acknowledged his technical advantages. "With all the help I will have," he said, "probably Merckx could have reached 51km."

In his first attempt, Moser covered five kilometers in 5:48 to beat Ritter's world best by more than three seconds. His 10km split was 11:39 — 14 seconds faster than Merckx's world record. The clock read 23:30.34 at 20km, which was 36 seconds under Merckx. Moser's second attempt established new world records for 5km (5:41.1) and the hour.

*Los Angeles 1984. The Olympic Games. This was the setting for the most successful week ever for American cyclists in international competition.*

# 'Hearts beat fast' for unforgettable week

**BY ED PAVELKA**

Eddie Borysewicz had about 50 pounds on his shoulders but he felt lighter than air. The weight of his son was nothing compared to the tons of pressure he had borne during the week of Olympic cycling, July 29 - August 5.

But now it was over. Little Eddy was being given a clear view of the final medal ceremony, in which the U.S. 100km team time trialists were receiving the bronze. His dad, an old 100km rider himself, was understandably proud. His team had finished in the top three to complete American cycling domination of the 1984 Games.

Yes, *domination.* U.S. riders could have won 15 medals and they did win nine, or 60 percent. The total was one shy of doubling the number won by the next best nation, West Germany. The U.S. took four golds while no other country took more than one. Not since 1912 had an American rider won an Olympic medal, and not since 1904 had a U.S. cycling team won more.

Is the U.S. now really so superior on a world scale? Of course not. The current world champions in four Olympic events were not at the Games because of the Soviet-led boycott. U.S. riders won three of those events — the men's road race, individual pursuit and match sprint. The Americans might have won regardless, but the cyclists of the USSR, East Germany and the other Eastern bloc nations would have certainly been in the thick of the medals fight in almost every event.

The boycotters aside, why this sudden U.S. success against the best of the rest? That was the question increasingly asked by the world's press as the week unfolded. The U.S. cyclists, sitting there in interview rooms after each medal-winning ride, unfailingly offered two reasons: (1) corporate sponsorship of the sport; (2) U.S. Cycling Federation head coach Eddie B. Not necessarily in that order, and not at the exclusion of their own athletic talent.

Without the money for advanced equipment and training and racing opportunities, U.S. riders could not reach their potential. Without the right person to design and carry out the program, the money would make little difference.

So the program is key, and that's a fact not lost on the rest of the world. According to U.S. team manager Mike Fraysse, one foreign cycling federation approached Borysewicz during the Games and made him this offer to take over its program: $100,000 a year base salary, a new house, and six expense-paid trips each year back to the U.S.

USCF executive director Dave Prouty said he too had heard about the offer. "Eddie's hot," Prouty acknowledged, but he emphasized that the federation doesn't intend to lose him. He said an attempt will be made to let Borysewicz do more of what he likes and less of what has caused him to say he would leave the USCF after this year.

"We're going to find somebody to manage the coaching operation and help Eddie get slotted to do pure coaching, which is what he wants," Prouty said. "A lot of discussion will take place by the end of the year."

Borysewicz was noncommittal about the subject other than to say, "I am pleased the federation has let me do it my way." He also declined to say much about the ultimate meaning of America's Olympic results.

"I am here to coach. You are here to make opinions," he told reporters. "Of course I am very happy. Who would not be happy with nine medals? But it is possible to win nine medals and possible to win zero medals. You can train athletes but you can't train luck."

Later, as he watched the final medal ceremony with his son, the coach seemed to feel that the glorious week really could make a difference for the sport.

"America has a different spirit that you can feel about cycling," he said. "More than 200,000 people came to watch at Mission Viejo and we gave them our best. How many hearts beat so fast? How many people smile? Many people will never forget."

For those who weren't roadside in Mission Viejo or trackside at the 7-Eleven Olympic Velodrome, ABC-TV was the next best thing. U.S. cycling's success paid off in unprecedented U.S. television coverage for the sport, followed by big splashes in *Sports Illustrated, Time, Newsweek* — and who knows what else will develop?

The weather was sunny and hot, the sky only light brown, and a breeze usually blew. Not perfect conditions for championship racing, but at least consistent. Some riders complained of tough breathing, but the killer smog failed to materialize. Same for the massive traffic jams. Maybe there was a connection.

The Olympic cycling week got off to an euphoric start for the U.S. with road race victories by Connie Carpenter and Alexi Grewal on July 29. Carpenter's win in the first-ever Olympic cycling event for women was embellished by Rebecca Twigg's silver medal and Janelle Park's 10th place.

Grewal's gold medal (the first in history by a U.S. roadman) was the crowning touch to a team effort that put all four Americans in the top 10. Davis Phinney finished fifth, Thurlow Rogers sixth, and Ron Kiefel ninth in a race that 80 riders couldn't complete.

The track events began the following day, with U.S. commissaire Bill Lambart serving as starter and chief referee. The velodrome was nothing like the bumpy, cracked and slow track some feared it would be. The surface did have a few ripples, but it was in excellent shape, having been refinished and coated with a special epoxy that measurably decreased rolling resistance.

The first final was the 1000-meter time trial, won by West Germany's Freddy Schmidtke. The U.S. team was brought back to earth somewhat when Rory O'Reilly finished out of the medals in eighth place. Still, it equaled the best-ever performance by an American in the event. Some 8000 fans packed the stands, as they would for each of the five days of racing.

The next gold medal was awarded in the 4000-meter individual pursuit. Steve Hegg set a new Olympic outdoor record on the way to giving U.S. cycling its third victory of the Games. He beat West Germany's Rolf Gölz in the finals, shortly after America's Leonard Nitz edged Dean Woods of Australia for the bronze medal.

The match sprint was another high point for the U.S. as Mark Gorski and Nelson Vails went undefeated to make it an all-American final. Gorski got the gold, 2-0, and both riders were champions with the press.

The 4000-meter team pursuit produced the moments of greatest drama for U.S. fans. First a loose rear wheel and then a crash forced the team to make three attempts at qualifying. Then it had to ride for the championship with just three men when Dave Grylls's foot pulled out at the start. Australia was given the golden opportunity, while the U.S. team of Hegg, Nitz, Pat McDonough and Brent Emery took home the silver.

The points race was the only abject failure for the U.S. as neither of the two entrants qualified for the final. Belgium's Roger Ilegems won the gold in an upset of Denmark's Michael Marcussen, the 1983 world champion.

A medal in the final event, the team time trial, was just what the U.S. camp needed to feel that the week really couldn't have been better. In fact, the successes had been so numerous that team assistant Ed Burke, for one, was reduced to using his fingers to recall and count up all the medals won.

He didn't need his toes, too, but there's always 1988....

*Five months after the 1984 Olympic Games in Los Angeles — where American riders won nine medals — it was revealed that a number of the U.S. cyclists had blood doped....*

# Blood-boosting news rocks cycling

## BY BARBARA GEORGE

The news first became public on January 9 when the Associated Press released a wire story with an Allentown, Pennsylvania, dateline, saying that "some U.S. cyclists received controversial 'blood doping' transfusions ... hours before competing in the Los Angeles Olympic Games."

The weeks following brought a storm of media attention — certainly more publicity than U.S. cycling has received in recent memory. How often do you see cyclists on "Good Morning America"? How often does *Sports Illustrated* devote six pages to bicycle racing topics? And who would have imagined a cycling-related story in *Rolling Stone*?

Some of the news and headlines were not nice. Cheating, illicit doping, tainted medals — these were among the words and phrases used in reports and editorials.

What happened? What effect will it have on the future of U.S. cycling? Neither question can be answered completely.

Blood doping or packing or boosting, as it is usually practiced, involves removing blood from an individual, spinning it down to condense it, and freezing it for storage. Weeks later, when the body has had time to bring its blood volume and red-cell count back to normal, the stored blood is re-infused. The result is a short-term increase in red blood cells, which raises the oxygen-carrying capacity of the blood. Some research studies have shown a 20- to 30-percent improvement in endurance in subjects using this technique.

Is blood boosting legal as a way of improving athletic performance? It's debatable. Apparently the International Olympic Committee does not include a definition of doping in its medical control rules or related brochure. Those materials merely state that doping is forbidden and include a list of prohibited drugs. Neither blood nor the practice of blood boosting appears on the prohibited list.

However, the IOC medical commission has been quoted elsewhere as saying that "doping is the administration of or the use by a competing athlete of any substance foreign to the body or of any physiological substance taken in abnormal quantity or taken by an abnormal route of entry into the body, with the sole intention of increasing in an artificial and unfair manner his performance in competition."

Some time ago riders asked the U.S. coaching staff — including national coaching director Eddie Borysewicz and technical director Ed Burke — about the procedure and Burke prepared an information package with photocopies of reports of various studies. Last spring at least one rider, Danny Van Haute, decided to try it. He did it privately, with his own blood, several months before the Olympic trials, with the hope of improving his chances of making the team.

Van Haute stressed that when the information was made available, there was no pressure from the coaching staff on the riders to do it. "It was your own choice," he said, adding that he knew there was a chance it might not work.

Van Haute rode very well at the Olympic track trials in Colorado Springs in July and he did make the team. Though many attributed this to the blood boosting, he said he's not so sure. "I can't say if it helped me or not," he told *VeloNews*. He explained that he had been riding quite well in the months before and that almost all the riders at the trials — because of the high altitude — significantly improved their personal best times.

Apparently, it was Van Haute's example which caused other riders to want to try blood boosting at the Olympics. There was no longer enough time to use the athletes' own blood, so they were given transfusions from others, a more dangerous method. The coaching staff arranged for a doctor, Herman Falsetti, to carry out the procedure.

In early November, another doctor who was there, Tom Dickson, contacted the U.S. Cycling Federation and the U.S. Olympic Committee and told them what had happened. An investigation was begun by the USCF.

At the suggestion of USCF executive director Dave Prouty, the attorneys who were helping with the investigation prepared a preliminary confidential report for the regularly scheduled meeting of the USCF executive committee (officers) in Chicago December 7-8. The attorneys recommended, and the executive committee agreed, that because of the potential impact on the federation, the matter should be brought to the full board of directors at its January meeting and kept confidential until then.

One who reportedly favored more immediate action at the time of the Chicago meeting was president Rob Lea and he subsequently resigned. Later, he sent a statement of his views to the board (*see statement below*).

The full board met as scheduled January 18-19 and, in closed session, considered the report of the investigation and what to do about it. It suspended Burke and Borysewicz for one month with no pay, postponed their salary reviews for six months, and reprimanded them. Olympic team manager Mike Fraysse, a board member, was removed as head of the competition committee, demoted from first to third vice president, and reprimanded.

Because there had been some confusion about who was responsible for supervising the individuals involved, the board clarified the chain of command by making executive director Prouty the person to whom the coaching staff must report.

Legislation was also drafted forbidding blood boosting and providing for disqualification and suspension for a rider who does it.

Asked about the errors in judgment which were the basis of the punishments and reprimands of the three individuals, both Prouty and newly elected USCF president Phil Voxland concurred. As Prouty explained it, the men erred in not considering the liability of the federation or the public relations aspects of the blood boosting. They were faulted, too, for not evaluating the risks and benefits sufficiently. Voxland said there were also possible grounds for complaint about the medical procedures used but that the board did not feel competent to judge that.

Some members of the board were in favor of stronger punishments and one of them, Lea's wife Tracy, resigned. In contrast, riders at the U.S. Olympic Training Center protested the suspensions as unfair.

In the meantime, what effect has the affair had on U.S. cycling? Public opinion seems to vary widely.

In contrast, former national road champion Wayne Stetina said in early January when the news first came out: "I think this is a total non-issue. Everyone else has just been smart enough not to get caught.... This thing is just like taking vitamins.... There's no way to prove it other than a confession. How can there be a ruling on something you can't prove? I just hope it doesn't hurt anyone's careers or reputations."

Sponsors of clubs and races interviewed at the bicycle trade show, BDS Expo, in Long Beach, California, seemed to be continuing business as usual. Though the news came out when the sponsorship contract for the 1986 world championships had yet to be signed, Southland Corporation subsequently signed the contract for $1.5 million.

Dave Karneboge of Schwinn, which is continuing its team sponsorships, said he felt the press had been good about presenting both sides of the controversy and that the people who are interested in the sport will read the information and make up their own minds. "There are enough people involved who have had good experiences with cycling," he said. "They understand what's going on and they're less quick to make snap judgments."

Karneboge said he thought part of the reason for the extensive publicity was that blood doping was a new topic for the public, one it hadn't heard of. Though he didn't feel necessarily that any publicity is automatically good publicity, he said the affair showed that cycling is sophisticated. The public has more understanding of athletes and to a great extent has forgiven its pro football and baseball heroes for using hard illegal drugs. Because blood boosting is such a gray area, he noted, the public will not get upset.

### Rob Lea's statement: 'It's cheating'

*After resigning from the board of directors in mid-December, former USCF president Rob Lea sent a report to the members of the board before their meeting January 18-19. It is dated January 2 and titled "President's Report on USCF Staff Participation on Blood Doping at the 1984 Olympics." Extracts:*

On November 10, Dr. Tom Dickson informed me that our coaching staff "blood doped" some of our Olympic team riders in order to enhance their performance at the Olympic Games, and that the United States Olympic Committee had the matter under investigation. I realized that if these allegations were true the federation would have serious ethical, legal and public relations problems. I therefore ordered a full and prompt investigation of the matter.

The investigation established that blood doping did occur; that it was done in most of the instances by the medically dangerous method of transfusing blood from a donor rather than by re-infusing the rider's own blood; that these transfusions were authorized and arranged by the coaching staff with full prior knowledge and support of our Olympic team manager; that the transfusions were performed in a motel room at the Ramada Inn in Carson; that the doctor performing the transfusions was paid through the federation office and that at least one donor's blood typing was also paid for through the federation office.

It was established that permission to blood dope had been requested by Ed Burke, and that request had been denied by Colonel Miller, Kenneth Clarke, Ph.D., director of USOC Sports Medicine and Dave Prouty; and further that blood doping is forbidden by the International Olympic Committee policy on doping, even though specific tests for blood doping have not yet been developed. It was also discovered in the process of the investigation that the coaching staff had experimented with the effects of massive doses of caffeine on riders with the specific purpose of enhancing race performance without being detected by post-race drug testing....

During the course of the investigation, Mike Fraysse, Eddie B, and Ed Burke were called to Colorado Springs to answer questions pertaining to the blood doping. They appeared with counsel, and also with Carl Leusenkamp and Tim Kelly. who vocally supported their position. At no time during that meeting or in any subsequent conversations that I know of have any of them admitted to having done anything ethically wrong or medically dangerous. On the contrary, they have consistently maintained that blood doping is legal, ethical, and necessary for successful international competition.

The Executive Committee did not see the need for immediate action at the recent Chicago meeting. The result of this lack of action … is that the federation is now *knowingly* continuing with the blood doping cover-up maintained since the Olympics, and also continuing to employ staff who were either directly or indirectly involved with the blood doping and who in some cases still support blood doping.

After the Chicago meeting, I decided that I could not serve either as president or as a member of the board of directors under these circumstances. I therefore resigned December 19. My resignation brings the blood doping cover-up to an end.

The wishful thinking that has led the principals and their supporters to believe that this affair might remain secret is now entirely without foundation, because it must be obvious to all that my resignation, and therefore the reasons for it, will not long go unexplained. I have decided to wait until the January meeting of the board of directors before making my reasons for resigning public, but after that meeting I will feel free to explain my position in any forum and to anyone interested. In the meantime, I am cooperating with the USOC investigation into the matter.

I have come to this stand after considering every weaker, easier position possible. However, all of the easier positions I have entertained ignore the fundamental moral issue in this and all instances of doping — that is, doping of all types is cheating and in most cases involves major health risks. As directors of a national governing body of sport, we cannot afford to tolerate either; and when cheating and health risks with riders are orchestrated by staff, we have no choice but to act with the most severe measures at our disposal. We owe this to our sponsors, to the United States Olympic Committee, to our national team riders and, especially, to the youth of this nation whom we hope to inspire to follow in the footsteps of our gold medalists. For what are they to learn from this? That the way to win is to cheat? And that going for the gold means taking dangerous health risks at the hands of medically incompetent staff? And what sponsor would want to identify its product with these values?

There is no weaker, easier position to take in this matter. I stand totally opposed to it, and I urge each of you to take this stand with me.

At the January meeting, you, the board of directors, will have your chance to redeem the reputation of the federation and its partners in sport — the USOC, USCF sponsors and the vast majority of our riders who do not dope up for races — from this disgrace. I wish you vision and moral courage. I know well the burden you are shouldering as you become aware of the full extent of this sad affair.

*85*

*The first edition of the CoreStates USPRO Championship in Philadelphia in June 1985 was won by the former Olympic speedskating champion Eric Heiden.*

# Heiden's best race

BY **CHERYL LINDSTROM**

For five years, Eric Heiden has been sacrificed to the media, often without the satisfaction of standing on the victory blocks. Patiently, he has answered the scribes' questions, politely explaining the fundamentals of cycling while his teammates have answered the call to glory. He has been a part-time cyclist whose successes have come in between semesters at Stanford University or stints as a television commentator. But he has always been a full-time celebrity — the drawing card the Southland Corporation wanted him to be when it formed the 7-Eleven team around him in 1980.

Yet quietly through all this Heiden has honed his cycling, trimming his 29-inch speed-skating thighs down to a more manageable size for the rigors of road racing. His teammates talk of Heiden's superior athletic ability, which allows him to gain more with less training.

Still, from a 7-Eleven point of view, the CoreStates USPRO Championship, June 23, was to be set up for Davis Phinney or Ron Kiefel. But when the cards didn't fall in the two Coloradans' favor, Heiden had a chance to show off what he had learned over the past few years — particularly at the recently completed Giro d'Italia. And he culminated it by blowing four others out the back door in a sprint to don his first stars-and-stripes jersey ever in front of a crowd of 25,000.

"I rode the best race I've ever ridden," beamed Heiden, 27, after he covered the 156 miles in 6:26:39 to earn $20,000 out of the $100,000 purse.

Heiden acknowledges that had he been able to devote all his time to cycling in recent years, his shift from a power sport to an endurance sport might not have taken close to four years. "It would have come sooner. Even now I have a big body for a bike racer, especially for climbing," said Heiden, who packs 180 pounds on his 6-foot 1-inch frame. ("I've dropped to 175 a couple times, but I've felt weak.")

Though Heiden manipulates those 180 pounds with considerable ease — climbing with conviction, sprinting with determination — it was his teammates who were to get the call June 23. "When we started, we were going to work for Kiefel and Phinney," he said of the 7-Eleven strategy. "We weren't sure how the race was going to turn out."

The field for the first-ever national pro road championship in this country had a lot of question marks. Few had the experience of racing the distance that was scheduled. Many were neo pros like Phinney, but without the benefit of a Giro in their legs. Those that were accustomed to a European-style event were listed but no-shows: Greg LeMond, Doug Shapiro, Steve Bauer, Dag-Otto Lauritzen, Noel Dejonckheere.

Though LeMond had shown a serious interest in the race, the date fell too close to the Tour de France, which was to start five days later. That and the fact that most European national championships were on the same day kept many riders on the Continent.

The heat, the humidity, the distance and the Manayunk Wall were the factors most felt would eventually shatter the field into small groups. Attrition would let the stronger riders move to the front without the need for serious attacking. 7-Eleven was the only team with experience and depth and, as so often happens in this country, it was assumed the moves would be keyed off those riders. "The repetition, the distance and the heat will start hurting people," predicted Phinney, after riding the course Saturday. "Whoever is riding best at the end will win." As for his team's strategy, "We'd like to have somebody go with any suicidal moves (early). The best situation would be if a group of six or eight go away with 40 miles left and work together until the last lap." As it turned out, Phinney's assessment of the race was close on target.

**Early break**

At the gun, a few of the 65 who started decided to make that early, suicidal break. Race directors Dave Chauner and Jack Simes had chosen a course that made three loops on a circuit approximately three-quarters of a mile long that passed through the start-finish line twice on each lap for the spectators' benefit. It then traveled away from the downtown area and into the blue-collar neighborhood of Manayunk, then back toward the center of the city through the area's historical district. That 14.4-mile circuit was to be lapped 10 times.

By the time the three laps of the initial circuit were completed, a five-man break had formed: Irishman Alan McCormack, American Matt Eaton; Rainier Valkenberg of the Dutch team, Fangio; Nigel Dean of Great Britain, who was riding for Texas-based Spenco; and a Swiss, Hans Ledermann, one of the many labeled free agents, but listed with the team from Sweden.

McCormack has been a colorful animator in U.S. racing, making bold moves and surprising recoveries. His fitness is at a higher level than ever before in his career and he was out to prove he is taking his riding considerably more seriously. But would he be able to pull it off for 156 miles? "If Matt hadn't gone when I did, I would have sat up," said McCormack. "We've been up front a lot this year."

Though Valkenberg was dropped on the first climb up the Manayunk Wall, the four were able to pull away from the main field without a chase attempt and they quickly opened up a six-minute-plus gap. "I wanted to get 10 minutes," explained McCormack, who spent several months rehabilitating from a painful and damaging encounter with a fire hydrant in Toronto one year ago. "I figured if we got that much we might be able to hold it."

McCormack was the aggressor up the Manayunk Wall, a half-mile-long climb that was the first and most significant of the three on the course. For the first five laps, McCormack easily outstroked the others in the break and eventually earned the $1000 prime for the climb.

And it was there that the thickest throng of spectators collected aside from the start-finish area. With each successive lap the crowd grew from two to three to five to eight deep. Most had never seen a bicycle race before, but a door-to-door campaign had obviously convinced the residents of these row houses that the event was worth watching, even if they had no idea how this climb factored into the race as a whole. "I was thinking this is what the Olympics must have been like," Heiden said later of Manayunk. "It gave you the chills."

By the fifth lap, though, a chase group had formed and was closing the gap on McCormack et al. Dean and Ledermann were struggling on the Manayunk climb and Eaton was showing signs of cramping.

With four laps to go, it was just McCormack and Eaton with only 2:15 over a chase group that contained Heiden, Tom Schuler, Tom Broznowski, Australia's Shane Sutton, Paul Sherwen of Great Britain (La Redoute), Greg Gilmore of GS Mengoni and two Danes: Jens Veggerby and Jesper Worre, who ride for Fanini-Wuhrer and Sammontana-Bianchi respectively. Phinney and Kiefel were at the front of the main field that was only 20 seconds behind the chase group.

McCormack and Eaton were caught on the approach to Manayunk and were blown out the back by the group of eight. "Now we've got a race," one spectator was overheard to say when the group of eight climbed up Manayunk. He was right.

**Where were they?**

Still, the question was: Where were Phinney and Kiefel? They didn't bridge when the chase group caught the leaders and the distance to them was increasing. As it turned out they were mired in a pack of wheel suckers, to hear their description later. "We were so marked, it was incredible," Kiefel would say at the race's conclusion. "They would let the little groups just walk away, but when Davis and I tried to go, they were right on us."

Throughout the time Heiden and Schuler were in the lead, 7-Eleven manager Jim Ochowicz had been passing the message "Don't work" to the two, who indeed were keeping a pace, but not forcing one. And they were continually looking over their shoulders to see the progress of their teammates behind them.

"We were waiting for Ron and Davis to come up," said Heiden. "They were the guys who had the best chance (of winning)." For one brief moment on the next to last push up Manayunk, it looked as though Phinney and Kiefel would bridge. But those two had already decided against it, figuring the odds were better with two out of five (only Heiden, Schuler, Broznowski and the two Danes were now left in the break), than five out of 20.

Once it became obvious that Phinney and Kiefel were not going to bridge, Heiden and Schuler started plotting the last lap and a half to the finish. Heiden was climbing well, and there seemed little chance he would fade in the final stretches. Schuler was protecting him on the flats. His sprint? Well, he had just won a series of hot-spot sprints at the Giro, edging Switzerland's Urs Freuler for one of them.

"The last time up the Wall, I came off the back and Broznowski attacked. Schuler and a Dane stayed with him and the other Dane stayed with me. Right about that time Och' didn't say anymore to wait for those guys," Heiden explained.

Though the two Danes tried to shake off both the 7-Eleven riders, the strategy didn't work, and the five stayed together with Schuler and Broznowski setting the pace. "Tom (Schuler) did a lot of work for me," said Heiden later. "He let me sit in. I didn't do any work those last 20 miles."

And in the chase group, Phinney and Kiefel were blocking to re-open the gap they had previously closed, so there was no chance for a late bridge to the leaders.

Five laps on the finishing loop were all that remained and by this time the race organizers had pulled all but the last two groups. (Riders who were pulled were given whatever placing they had as they came onto the finishing loop.) For those five mini-laps, Heiden's group stayed together; it seemed unwise for anyone to try and solo in.

The set-up for the sprint had Schuler in the second position and Heiden at the back of the group. The two aligned themselves for Schuler to give Heiden a leadout, but just as the sprint started to wind up, Schuler pulled his foot completely out of his shoe and was left to straggle in for fifth. Heiden picked his line along the left curb and blew by the two Danes and Broznowski by more than a bike length. The Danes were second and third and Broz fourth. all were given the same time while Schuler finished in 6:26:53.

"Man, when I came across that line I couldn't believe it," said Heiden.

Heiden's teammates were both surprised and yet not so. They had seen his strong riding, but had never seen him orchestrate a finish so well. "I'm really happy for Eric. This proves that Eric is a good pro, that his sprinting in Italy was no fluke," said Kiefel, who won the bunch sprint for sixth while Phinney followed in seventh. Collectively, the team took $40,000 home and probably would have had another $10,000 were it not for Schuler's shoe. All five riders were in the top 11.

*By becoming the first American to win the Tour de France, in 1986, Greg LeMond received unprecedented coverage in the U.S. media — including the big hitters of press and television.*

# 'Vive le Greg'

### BY MARILEE ATTLEY

"I want to be the first American to do really well in the Tour de France." That's what Greg LeMond told *VeloNews* in an interview in 1979. Just 18 years old, LeMond had made cycling history by winning three medals at the world junior championships. In the seven years since, LeMond has more than fulfilled all the promise of his youth with consistently high placings in the world's most important races.

But his victory in the 1986 Tour de France is something else again.

That an American won the Tour is astounding enough. That he did it over the most difficult, mountainous course in years compounds the achievement. That he did it despite a continued, calculated challenge from his own teammate and former mentor Bernard Hinault puts it in the ranks of sports' greatest triumphs.

Yet there was never a question that if any American could do it, it would be LeMond. The Nevada native had shown great promise from his first year of competition in 1977 when, as a 16-year-old, he won two of the three selection races for the world junior championship team. He was too young to compete in the world's, but later that summer he took his first national junior road title (the second came in 1979). The following year in Washington, D.C., he finished ninth in the world junior road race and, along with Ron Kiefel, Greg Demgen and Jeff Bradley, took a bronze medal in the 70km team time trial.

At the junior world's in Argentina one year later, he became the first rider in cycling history to win three world championship medals in one year: gold in the 120km road race, silver in the individual pursuit, and bronze in the team time trial (with Bradley, Mark Frise and Andy Hampsten).

Here are some other highlights of LeMond's career:

1980: He made the U.S. Olympic team but the boycott kept him from competing. Just 19 years old, he signed a professional contract with the French Renault-Gitane team, joining then-world champion Hinault on the roster.

1981: In his first year as a pro he won a stage at the Tour de l'Oise and finished fourth overall in the Dauphiné Libéré, a showing that prompted Hinault to predict that the American would succeed him at the top of cycling. That summer, LeMond won the Coors Classic for the first time.

1982: A broken collarbone kept him out of early-season racing, but he came back to win the 11-stage Tour de l'Avenir, finish second in the Tour of the Mediterranean and take third overall in Tirreno-Adriatico.

That fall in England he took the silver medal in the world road championship — the first senior men's world road medal in U.S. history. Along with the medal came controversy, including charges that he chased down U.S. teammate Jonathan Boyer in the final 400 meters. LeMond countered that the U.S. contingent was a group of riders who each paid their own way and that they were not a unified team. "I ride for myself, for Renault, and for the money," he said.

1983: He won three stages and was first overall in the Dauphiné Libéré (after "winner" Pascal Simon was disqualified), and he finished fourth in the Tour of Switzerland. Then in the fall he achieved a long-time goal: winning the world road championship. He left the field behind with 11km to go and crossed the line alone, 1:11 ahead of runner-up Adri Van der Poel. With his gold medal and second places in the Grand Prix des Nations and the Tour of Lombardy, LeMond earned yet another coveted prize — the Super Prestige Pernod trophy for top pro, a season-long points competition. He was only 22 years old.

1984: He was knocked unconscious in a crash in Belgium in late May but came back to finish third in the Dauphiné just a fortnight later. On June 29, he started his first Tour de France. Three weeks later, despite bronchitis and sore feet, he finished third overall, 11:46 down on winner and teammate Laurent Fignon. Hinault was second at 10:32.

That fall, LeMond signed a three-year contract with the French team, La Vie Claire, worth a reported $1 million.

1985: He finished second in the Giro d'Italia, second in the Tour de France and second in the world road championship, and won the Coors Classic.

1986: He started the season with third overall in Paris-Nice in March and logged a second in the one-day classic, Milan-San Remo. Other top placings included fourth in the Critérium International, fourth in the Championship of Zürich and fourth in the Giro d'Italia, despite a crash in an early stage. Just prior to the Tour de France, he finished third in the Tour of Switzerland while helping teammate Hampsten to the overall title.

LeMond's Tour de France performance received unprecedented coverage in the U.S. The *New York Times, Boston Globe* and *USA Today* all carried daily stories and results. CBS Sports televised five segments during the race, including same-day coverage of the final stage and LeMond's ascent to the podium.

CBS Radio also broadcast occasional reports, including the electrifying news on Sunday. July 20: "American Greg LeMond has taken over the yellow leader's jersey in the Tour de France bicycle race." (What did it matter that the announcer pronounced his teammate's name Bernard Hee-new?)

Coverage also appeared in several national magazines, including *Sports Illustrated, Time* and *People.*

The August 11 issue of *Time* called it, "the greatest cycling duel in the 83-year history of the Tour de France.... Greg LeMond, 25, became the first non-European to win the premier race in this most passionately parochial of Old World sports. And the easygoing American did it by triumphing in a fratricidal war with his teammate — and friend — Bernard Hinault, 31, who has become a two-wheeled French national monument."

Not only was the amount of Tour coverage unprecedented, but LeMond himself was the subject of several editorials, including one in the *New York Times.* The editorial appeared in the "Topics" section in the July 29 issue under the headline, "Champion du Monde." It read, in part: "The Tour de France is the world's premier bike race, one of the most grueling of all athletic contests and long a passion of Europeans. Now, thanks to a young man named Greg LeMond, it also belongs to America.... To wear the *maillot jaune,* the winner's yellow jersey, [LeMond] had to beat [Hinault], who pressed him to the limit, psychologically and physically. Congratulate Mr. LeMond for his historic achievement, and thank him for raising America's consciousness of this superb contest."

Syndicated columnist and *Washington Post* writer Coleman McCarthy praised LeMond as an athlete who "embodies self-discipline, not self-destruction.... In LeMond the country has a chance to look at an athlete who is conditioned, balanced and rightly hallowed. His glow is the intensity of his performance in the Tour, an event he has likened to doing a daily marathon for 26 days. Gaullish snobbery being one of the earth's pestilence's, there is the bonus of LeMond beating the French at their own sport on their own roads.

"LeMond's Tour de France success may prove to be as inspiring as Frank Shorter's winning the 1972 Olympic marathon."

To those of us who have followed it, LeMond's entire career has been inspiring. As McCarthy said, "Vive le Greg."

# Two medals delight Italian fans

BY PAT ENNIS

**86** *The world road championships were held in the United States for the first time in 1986. Colorado Springs was the venue. The highlight was the pro road race at the Air Force Academy.*

About a dozen Italian cycling dignitaries and journalists hovered around a TV monitor in the Air Force Academy's press area. Among them were Agostino Omini, president of the Federazione Ciclistica Italiana, Dr. Francesco Conconi, developer of the famous heart-rate test, former world champion Felice Gimondi, and well-known frame manufacturer Giovanni Pinarello. Amid a clutter of Styrofoam cups, half-eaten bagels, and stacks of results sheets, journalists from *La Gazzetta dello Sport* and other Italian sports dailies were jotting down lap times and discussing who was doing what to whom in the 17-lap world professional road championship.

A reporter from *La Gazzetta* asked me for a prediction. I refused to venture a guess. "I like Argentin or Van der Poel," he offered.

The usual early breakaways caused little concern among these seasoned observers, but when a breakaway of 11 riders formed in lap 13, the Italians searched eagerly for their blue national jersey. They found only one, that of pre-race favorite Moreno Argentin. The journalists quickly identified the other riders and noted that 10 countries were represented — only France had two riders in the lead group.

Suddenly there flashed on the screen an image of two riders in blue jerseys trying to pick themselves up from a tangle of bicycles. Giuseppe Saronni was the first to arise. As he moved aside, the pain-stricken face of Roberto Visentini, winner of the 1986 Giro d'Italia, was revealed. The Italians gasped: Saronni and Visentini down — what misfortune! Visentini was holding his right shoulder grimacing.

The TV coverage returned to the race leaders. Within minutes someone came by to announce that Visentini had broken his clavicle and abandoned. The press area chatter ceased briefly. Then a concerned voice asked, "What about Saronni? Why isn't there a camera on the field?"

Meanwhile, France's Laurent Fignon attacked and was caught. Then Jörg Müller of Switzerland and Charly Mottet of France escaped together, and Argentin reeled them in. When Mottet and Rolf Gölz of West Germany attacked and gained a few seconds, Stefan Brykt of Sweden bridged the gap.

The Italian *tifosi* watched intently as Argentin, apparently waiting for the right moment, launched a solo chase and passed the leaders. Gölz and Mottet caught his wheel, while Brykt dropped back to join Fignon and Acacio Da Silva of Portugal, who had escaped from the original breakaway.

Going into the final lap, Argentin, Mottet, and Gölz had 18 seconds on the pursuing trio, and they quickly increased their lead to 24 seconds. Anticipating a three-up sprint, the journalists recalled the recent successes of Argentin's adversaries. Gölz, they agreed, was the one to fear because he was faster than Mottet and the Frenchman had already done a lot of work in this race.

Fears diminished and excitement intensified as Argentin forced the pace on the long, gradual upgrade and dropped Gölz. Another shorter, steeper hill and Mottet fell back several meters. The excitement was nearly uncontrollable — would Argentin finish alone for the gold?

No. Mottet closed the gap on the descent. Argentin continued to pull insistently, as he had throughout this final lap. He looked strong, but was he overconfident?

The finish line was approaching fast. With 100 meters remaining, Mottet made his move, trying to come around on Argentin's left. The Italian increased his tempo and refused to yield. Mottet had played his last card. He could hold Argentin's wheel no longer. As the Italian pulled gradually but steadily ahead, the Frenchman threw his head back in a sign of exhausted surrender. Argentin glanced back quickly, sat up and raised his arms high, then blew a kiss to the screaming crowds as he coasted confidently across the line.

Meanwhile, in the press area, the small band of Italian journalists and dignitaries leapt to their feet, arms raised high as if to share in their countryman's victory. Seconds later, to their surprise and delight, Saronni crossed the line to take the bronze medal.

Two world championship medals — the Italians watched with deep satisfaction while the final moments were replayed. One woman cried with joy. A reporter from a local paper approached and asked if the victory had come as a surprise to the Italians. The reporter from *La Gazzetta* replied, "Not really. Cycling has a long tradition in Italy. Let us not forget that Italy has won more world championship medals than any other country."

Then, turning to me, he winked and said with a smile, "What did I tell you about Argentin?"

*Clockwise from above:*
**SLIPPIN'** The rain made the cobblestones on the Kemmelberg climb too slick for Phil Anderson at the 1989 Ghent-Wevelgem. **HITCHIN'** In 1988, bike sponsor Francesco Moser gave a youthful Maurizio Fondriest a nice ride the year Fondriest won the world's. **LEAPIN'** A member of the Czech national junior team had an unexpected Pole to jump at the 1991 cyclo-cross world's.

*Clockwise from top left:*
**HOT SPOT** Swiss rider John Baldi cooled off at the 1989 CoreStates Championship. **COLD SPOT** A change of shorts was needed by Jelle Nijdam in the 300km motorpaced Zuider Zee Tour in 1984. **EXTINCT** A world championship event since 1895, motorpacing had its final title race in 1994. **INDUREIGN** The '90s were ruled by Miguel Indurain. **OVER THE EDGE** Campagnolo support went above and beyond at the last Coors Classic in '88. **EGGS-TREME** In 1993, Graeme Obree broke the world hour record and won a world title using his infamous position. **CHAMPIONS** The inaugural Tour de France Féminin in 1984 went to Marianne Martin, while Laurent Fignon took his second "big" Tour.

W. Nelissen

E. Vanderaerden

R. Virenque

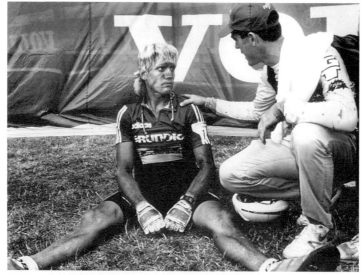

G. Duclos-Lasalle

*Clockwise from top left:*
**BUMMED!** Grundig leader
Dave Wiens crashed in the
final at Berlin and lost the
1991 World Cup to John
Tomac. **HELP!** There were
no airbags in the '70s.
**YES!** Bob Roll celebrated
7-Eleven teammate Dag-
Otto Lauritzen's victory at
the '87 Rund um den
Henninger Turm. **WATCH
OUT!** Fans made a hurried
escape at a Tour of Texas
criterium in '84. **YIKES!**
Rory O'Reilly strained to a
ninth-place kilo' finish at
the '85 world's. **WHEW!**
Greg LeMond never came
closer to a classic than in
this second-place finish to
Sean Kelly at the '83 Tour
of Lombardy.

S. Rooks

S. DeMattei

M. Martinez

J. Boyer

*Clockwise from top left:*
**SOLO** U.S. junior William Dolan plowed a lone furrow into 46th place at the 1988 cyclo-cross world's. **BIG CHEESE** Francesco Moser used a split-tubed bike to ride a 50.359km indoor hour record at Stuttgart in '88. **CELEBRATION** Alexi Grewal danced to the Morgul-Bismarck stage win in the '83 Coors Classic. **BELLISSIMO!** Who was happier? The Italian coach or motorpace racer Mario Gentili after winning a gold at the '86 track world's in Zürich. **BEST FOOT FORWARD** In the early days of mountain biking, everyone had crashes.

E. Berzin

*Clockwise from top:*
**WHO FELL ASLEEP?** In the 1985 Giro d'Italia, the slow early pace of the flat stages sometimes caused massive, but harmless pileups. **GUZZLER GREG** They say that winning the Tour de France can put 10 years on you. **THE EYES HAVE IT** Show and tell at the '84 Tour of Holland. **SHOWTIME** The camera was up, close and personal while shooting "American Flyers" during the Coors Classic.

*Tragedy overtook the reigning Tour de France champion Greg LeMond on an early-morning turkey shoot near Sacramento, California, in April 1987.*

# LeMond shot

**BY GEOFF DRAKE**

Greg LeMond, America's (and perhaps the world's) greatest cyclist, was shot in a hunting accident on April 20, 1987. He was hit by 20 to 30 shotgun pellets when one of his companions fired at a turkey. LeMond, 25, was initially listed in critical condition. He underwent two hours of surgery to remove the shot from his back and right side. He is expected to recover fully from the accident and left the hospital April 26.

During a time when most pro cyclists are competing in Europe, LeMond was at home in California recuperating from a broken hand he suffered in a crash March 14 in Italy. He was planning to return to Europe on April 23 to continue racing.

The accident occurred near Lincoln, California, on land belonging to LeMond's uncle, Rodney Barber. LeMond reportedly had his bike with him and was planning to ride home afterward, a distance of about 40 miles.

Barber and LeMond's brother-in-law, Patrick Blades, were hunting in some underbrush at about 8 a.m. when Blades fired the shot that hit LeMond. LeMond was transported 100 miles by a California Highway Patrol helicopter to the University of California Davis Medical Center in Sacramento. Within an hour of his arrival LeMond was undergoing surgery. Doctors removed a number of pellets, including one in his diaphragm and two that punctured his right lung. There were two punctures in his small intestine and a "nick" in his liver, according to a hospital spokesman. One kidney was also bruised. Most of the surgery involved repairs to the small intestine, the spokesman said.

The operation was performed by a team of doctors headed by Dr. Sandy Beal, the chief trauma surgeon on duty at the time of the accident. No blood transfusions were required, and LeMond was fully anesthetized. After the operation he was moved to the intensive care unit of the hospital.

There was some concern about the condition of the injured kidney, according to the spokesman, because LeMond had an accident at age 12 that left the other kidney operating at only 10 percent of normal. But surgeons said the kidney injured in the recent accident should recover fully.

The following day LeMond was listed in fair condition. That was upgraded to good on April 23, when he was able to walk and eat solid foods for the first time since the operation.

In a sense, LeMond was not the only casualty in the accident. Blades was admitted to the Roseville Community Hospital for observation because of emotional distress, according to Newman. And LeMond's wife Kathy, who is in her ninth month of pregnancy, was also admitted to a hospital for observation after the accident.

Doctors originally predicted a hospital stay of several weeks, but LeMond left after only six days.

As of late April, LeMond had still not spoken to reporters about the accident. However, his father, Bob LeMond, held a press conference the day of the incident and said it "possibly means he won't be racing this summer at all."

LeMond is known to enjoy hunting along with his other favorite pastime, golf. Bernard Hinault visited LeMond in 1980 just before LeMond's first pro season in Europe, and the two hunted grouse together. In an interview in *VeloNews* in 1985, LeMond said he planned to spend some time hunting pheasant after a busy season that included more than 100 races.

"I don't understand why Greg is out hunting in April," said Jean-Marie Leblanc, editor of the French sports daily, *L'Équipe,* who flew from Europe to speak to LeMond after the accident. "But I realize his life is not like that of the European rider. He does what he wants when he wants. He is helping us to understand the American lifestyle."

Jim Ochowicz, manager of the 7-Eleven team, said it was "difficult to put the accident into perspective. With his wrist injury, the spring was already shot for Greg. And this spring he was not gearing for the early races anyway. But the Tour de France and the world's — those are the two races it will affect...

"It was tragic it had to happen, regardless of whether it affects racing or not. But he's tough, and he will come back strong. He'll come back with a vengeance. He'll have something to prove."

The accident received wide coverage, including at least two stories on the Associated Press wire service, and notes in *USA Today* and the *New York Times,* Bob LeMond's press conference appeared on ESPN and CNN television, and there were also reports by the British Broadcasting Corporation.

# Irish cycling's finest day

**87**

*In 1987, Stephen Roche of Dublin, Ireland, became the second rider in history (Eddy Merckx for the first) to win the Giro d'Italia, Tour de France and world road championship in the same season.*

**BY JOHN WILCOCKSON**

There was something very Irish about the celebrations in the Gasthof-Pension Piber in the Austrian village of Wernberg on the night of September 6, 1987. The day's main hero, Stephen Roche, still wearing his white, silk racing jersey with its rainbow chest band, was moving from table to table in the hotel's cavernous dining room, talking to each set of friends who had crossed the continent of Europe to support him and the Irish team at the world championships. Between the intermittent popping of champagne corks, Sean Kelly's father-in-law Dan Grant led a raucous rendering of the popular folk song, "In Dublin's Fair City." And the local *burgermeister* made a congratulatory speech before presenting framed pictures of Wernberg to Roche, his Irish teammates and their entourage of French and Italian mechanics, soigneurs, doctors and coaches.

At the end of the burgermeister's list of recipients was the name of Liam Horner. No, he's not a current racer or even a team official. Horner had made the long trip to southern Austria at the last minute, taking a few days off from his job as a carpenter. But this long, lean Irishman in his mid-40s, is held in high regard by Roche and Kelly, because Horner was one of the pioneers of modern Irish racing in Europe. And without his brave efforts more than two decades before perhaps neither Roche nor Kelly would today be at the head of world cycling.

The late Shay Elliott was the first Irishman to make an impact on continental cycling.

He was a top amateur in Ireland before he moved to France to learn his craft and joined the St. Raphaël pro team of French star Jacques Anquetil. At the 1962 world's, in Salo, Italy, Elliott found himself in the race-winning break with Jean Stablinski. And when the Frenchman attacked, Elliott did not chase because the French champion was a senior member of the St. Raphaël squad. Elliott placed second, the first ever medal won by an Irish rider in world professional road championships.

The Dubliner went on to win a stage of the 1963 Tour de France — wearing the yellow jersey for three days, before conceding it to team leader Anquetil. But back home in Ireland, Elliott's exploits made virtually no impact. Cycling was still at a primitive stage. There were few riders and little money for sending teams overseas. And when Horner entered the 1964 world amateur road race championship at Sallanches in the French Alps, it was without any support.

"When I arrived I had nowhere to stay," Horner said over a glass of champagne at the Gasthof Piber. "Luckily, I met (a Belgian) who spoke English, and he sorted something out for me. When I arrived at the circuit for the race they wouldn't let me in. It was raining, and I'd just ridden five miles from the campsite. I started to cry — but they finally let me pass the barrier when I lifted up my cape to show my racing jersey and race numbers. I didn't get too far in the race because I punctured early on and couldn't get a spare wheel. The cars just drove by me."

Horner — who went on to become the first Irishman to win Britain's tough Manx International race in 1967 — stayed in contact with that friendly Belgian, Herman Nys, who continued to help Irish cyclists at world championships. In 1975, one of the youngest members of the Irish team to arrive at the world's in Mettet, Belgium, was Sean Kelly. It was the start of a close relationship between Nys and Kelly, who was a house guest at the Nys home in Brussels for most of his professional career until Kelly's wife Linda persuaded him to buy a house two years ago.

Two days before this year's pro world's the little Austrian hotel had seen a first champagne celebration — for the 60th birthday of Herman Nys. Both Kelly and Roche were relaxed and calm, happy to be away from the crowds that usually follow them. They said that the quiet, smooth back roads winding through a wonderland of lakes, forests and mountains in the province of Carinthia were providing perfect training terrain. And the two Irish stars enthused about the 12km (7.46-mile) course where the championships were to be held.

"It's very fast," commented Roche, "and the uphill finish should suit Sean. I don't think it's a course for me. Argentin will be the big danger. I watched him closely in the race in Italy two days ago, and when he attacked on a hill, none of us could stay with him."

Moreno Argentin didn't win that race, the Tour of Friuli — it was won in a field sprint by another Italian, Guido Bontempi — but the 1986 world champion had prepared for the defense of his title more thoroughly than anyone. After a workmanlike performance in the Giro d'Italia (he won two stages), Argentin raced a few criteriums in July before flying to Hawaii for the start of the Coors Classic in early August.

The 27-year-old Venetian rode an anonymous race and was content to find his form gradually before impressively winning the final stage, a circuit race in the hilly streets of Boulder, Colorado. It was not a sprint victory, but the result of three separate surges on the main climb before he broke clear on his own to win.

Among the other challengers for Argentin's crown, besides Roche and Kelly, were the Dutchman Teun Van Vliet (winner of the Tour of The Netherlands a week earlier), the on-form Kim Andersen of Denmark, Phil Anderson of Australia, and Frenchman Laurent Fignon (who impressively won the hilliest stage of the Dutch tour). Interestingly, the Austrian organizers had been granted permission for parimutuel betting on the championships. They established some surprising odds: Argentin and Bontempi were co-favorites at 4:1, Kelly was quoted at 16:1, and Roche at only 25:1!

Unusually, each of the three road races at the '87 world's were held on separate days. Besides giving the organizers three separate pay days — with an encouraging 15,000 spectators for the women's race (won by France's Jeannie Longo), more than 50,000 for the amateur event (taken by another French racer, Richard Vivien), and upward of 75,000 for the professionals....

There were a record 168 starters from 25 countries for the 23-lap, 276km (171.5 miles) professional championship on the Villach-Faaker See circuit, and it soon became obvious that none of the main teams was interested in opening hostilities until late in the day. A violent thunderstorm had begun in the night, and spectacular sheet lightning and booming thunderclaps were still echoing around the mountains when the race began at 10:30 a.m. More than an inch of rain had fallen, and the wet stuff continued for the first three hours of the race.

Few of the riders were enthusiastic about the conditions. One of the three team colleagues of Kelly and Roche, Paul Kimmage, summed up everyone's feelings. "I feel like shit," he commented. Phil Anderson could probably have added a few more expletives when he rode back to the pits minutes before the start time: His gears and brakes were malfunctioning. He grabbed another bike — one he hadn't raced on before — and transferred the wheels, water bottle and race number from his defective machine. It was incidents like this that disadvantage riders from the smaller cycling countries.

Anderson had found his own hotel and was not being supported by the Panasonic team, which he was leaving at the end of the season.

In contrast, the Italian squad was staying at the secluded Park Hotel in the resort town of Velden, from where they enjoyed morning training spins around the placid waters of the Wörther See, the largest and warmest lake in the region. Most of the fans gathered around the Villach circuit were Italians, many of whom had established mini-villages of camper vans and tents. Even in the wet, they were thrilled to be watching their countrymen in action.

Before the rain stopped on the 10th lap of the pro race, only nine others had joined early crash victim Dag-Otto Lauritzen (of Norway and 7-Eleven) in the showers. Kimmage was almost No. 10, but Roche unselfishly dropped back to speak to his fellow Dubliner during the fifth lap. "Do you want to stay back here and get dropped, Paul?" asked the Giro and Tour de France champion. "Do you want to be regarded as someone who couldn't do as well as Alan McCormack?" The few words helped Kimmage through his bad patch, especially as McCormack, the American-based Irish pro, was not expected to finish the full distance on his diet of much shorter races.

Once the rain stopped, there was still a reluctance for riders to shed their rain gear. There was a distinct chill in the air, and as the clouds began to break up, fresh snow could be seen on the Carinthian Alps that form Villach's backdrop to the west. The pace started to quicken on lap 11, but the first really significant break didn't come until lap 15 (100km from the finish), when the impatient Jaanus Kuum (of Norway and Toshiba-Look) hurtled away from the pack with Johnny Weltz of Denmark in tow. They gained almost a minute and a half, but the Italian and French teams didn't allow them any more rope and the leaders were caught after three laps of effort.

When Kuum and then Weltz were passed, 69km (43 miles) from the end, the three emerald green jerseys of Roche, Kelly and Martin Earley were at the head of affairs among the blues of Italy, the oranges of The Netherlands and the tricolor tops of the French. At last, this race was warming up. Even so, this did not prepare the crowd for the dramatic happenings of lap 19.

With the French looking in control, their Martial Gayant unleashed a vicious attack at the foot of the Mittewald hill, triggering a series of reactions. Notably, Argentin and Van Vliet joined in the action and by the summit, a mile later, these two stars were clear with Juan Fernandez, the Spanish dark horse, and the surprising Jan Nevens of Belgium.

With Argentin and Van Vliet doing most of the work, this foursome gained 51 seconds by the end of the lap, which they completed in 15 minutes and 42 seconds, the fastest of the whole weekend, at 45.9 kph (28.5 mph)! It was a phenomenal speed for a course that included 200 meters (656 feet) of climbing every lap. These men had already been in the saddle for nearly six hours but, with 48km (30 miles) still to race, had they gone too soon?

There was panic behind, with the chase being led by Fignon, almost unrecognizable without his glasses. Going into lap 20, he was joined on the Mittewald climb by a strong-looking Claude Criquielion, the 1984 world champion, and the Belgian's Hitachi team colleague, Fabian Fuchs of Switzerland. The pace was frighteningly fast, and when the leading four reached the first descent the gap had closed to 25 seconds.

Fignon and Anderson were now leading the pursuit, while Argentin and Van Vliet exchanged a few words as they raced toward the Grossattel climb. They obviously agreed to keep on the pressure, as they knew that only the best racers were going to survive this increase in pace, but they couldn't have expected their demise to come so soon....

The man who caused them to be caught just before the lap end was none other than Roche, who powered his way out of the saddle up the Grossattel hill, with Italy's Emanuele Bombini and Earley right behind. Over the top, Earley gallantly picked up the baton for the Irish team, completing the job started by Roche.

The immediate result was a score of riders wheeling into the pits, including a subdued Fignon, joined by teammate Charly Mottet, who U-turned halfway up the Mittewald climb. In the middle of the chase after the Argentin breakaway, there was a spectacular crash on the corner before the finish straight, with both Roy Knickman and U.S. teammate Bob Roll being transported to the hospital. The impact of the crash snapped Knickman's bicycle frame in two.

Only three laps were left and it seemed that everyone now wanted to get into the action. Those three laps produced probably the most intense 48 minutes of attack and counterattack that any world championship has seen. It was difficult to keep a check on the action, because as soon as one attack had been launched, another would already be launching itself from the pack. The event had come alive. The umbrellas had come down and the crowd had taken up the best positions for the finish — sitting in the finish straight bleachers or watching the giant TV screen that could be clearly seen from the hill above the finish area. The sun had yet to make an appearance, but the road had dried out except for damp patches beneath the trees.

Trying to keep a record of who was attacking was like trying to report a fast-bidding auction sale. On lap 21, there were at least eight distinct breaks, notably by Criquielion and Jef Lieckens of Belgium, Gayant and Gilbert Duclos-Lassalle of France, Steven Rooks and Gerrie Knetemann of the Netherlands, and Rolf Gölz of West Germany. The three remaining Irishmen — McCormack and Earley had quit by now — remained close to the front, with Roche again making a significant effort to bring back the attack by Criquielion and Duclos-Lassalle.

Into lap 22, with 24km (15 miles) to go, Lieckens was leading by 10 seconds, but he was quickly caught by Erik Breukink, the talented young Dutch rider, Gayant and Andersen. Then Breukink went clear on his own. But, as other attackers had found, the pace was too high for a small break to sustain its lead. Approaching the end of this lap, the most active riders at the front were Criquielion (tracked by Italy's Roberto Pagnin), Guido Winterberg of Switzerland (shadowed by Roche and Rooks) and Gayant (tagged by Czeslaw Lang of Poland).

Despite all the activity, there were still 70 men together approaching the bell, with sprinters Eric Vanderaerden and Guido Bontempi waiting menacingly near the head of the pack. Through the pits, Jörgen Marcussen of Denmark went to the front, followed by Gölz — but then Roche came storming to the front on the Mittewald climb.

"I went up the hill on the (53-tooth) big ring," revealed Roche. "I was trying to get rid of the sprinters and hoping that we would get a small group away with Kelly."

The plan worked to perfection because with the Tour de France champion went Criquielion, Kelly, Gölz, Winterberg, Breukink, Rooks, Steve Bauer of Canada, Rolf Sörensen of Denmark, and also three members of the day's previous best break, Argentin, Van Vliet and Fernandez. This group of 12 came together along the flat roads through the alpine-like village of Drobollach — and they were joined by a 13th rider, Jörg Müller of Switzerland, on the subsequent steep descent.

Argentin was tracking Kelly very closely, knowing that the Irishman was the biggest danger in a sprint finish. The Italian had no team support now so his choices were limited, whereas Kelly still had Roche to close any gaps. On the Grossattel hill, Roche went commandingly to the front, followed by Bauer and Kelly, attempting to discourage any breakaways. But over the top of the hill, Gölz, Bauer, Sörensen and Rooks counterattacked after a short effort by Breukink.

No sooner was this group brought to heel then another move was unleashed. Winterberg counterattacked, Sörensen chased him, and then Van Vliet and Gölz reacted, followed by Roche. These five came together, and suddenly they had 200 meters' advantage.

Kelly summarized the feelings among the eight riders left behind. "When Stephen (Roche) went away, I could have closed the gap, but I had Argentin on my wheel, and I wasn't going to lead him up. I thought Criquielion would chase, but he didn't," he said.

Criquielion was tired by his earlier efforts; Fernandez and Bauer were watching Argentin and Kelly; while the other three had teammates in the break. But Roche was still not thinking like a winner. "I didn't ride (hard) in the break because I thought Kelly would get back to us and I could lead him out for the sprint," he commented.

The two groups were now racing downhill toward the final left turn only 600 meters from the finish. As they sprinted out of the turn, there were attacks from both groups, 15 seconds apart: the ambitious Sörensen sprinted away from the first group, Bauer from the second. The two moves both brought reactions from the Irishmen, the two best professional cyclists in the world.

Sörensen was about 15 meters clear of the front four when Roche made his move about 450 meters from the line. "I went through on the left of the Dane and gave it everything I had," said Roche. "When I was clear I changed up [to a gear of 53x13], but it was getting harder and harder to turn the gear as I was climbing."

Incredibly, Roche was racing away unopposed. What was happening to Van Vliet and

Gölz, the recognized sprinters in this group? It wasn't revealed until later that this pair had been pursuing a personal vendetta ever since they had a dispute in the Tirreno-Adriatico stage race last March. Van Vliet was leading that race, but needed to gain more time before the final time trial. On one stage he got away from the best time trialists with Gölz, but the West German refused to work with him, saying, "I don't want you to win."

It was all part of the running battle between the rival Dutch squads — Panasonic (of Van Vliet) and SuperConfex (of Gölz) — while Sörensen went on to win that Italian stage race on the final day. Now, in this breathtaking finale to the world championships, Van Vliet was asking himself, "Who do I want to win? Roche, who is the outstanding rider this year? Or Gölz, who doesn't deserve the rainbow jersey? I opted for Roche."

Kelly commented, "I could see that Stephen had broken away at the front. And when Bauer attacked from the corner, I went after him. I had Argentin behind me, and he attacked from the back. I would have beaten him if it had been a sprint for first place."

The spectators were on their feet watching these final, exciting developments of a fascinating race. Was the winner of the Giro and the Tour really going to take the world's as well? The few Irish fans — including Messrs. Grant, Horner and Nys — were shouting themselves hoarse, while the thousands of Italians were screaming for Argentin, who was weaving his way through the riders ahead and hoping that Roche would die. But the Dubliner was still moving well.

"I was looking under both (my) arms, but I didn't see anyone," said Roche. "And suddenly I knew I was going to win. That was the most wonderful feeling in the world."

As he crossed the line with arms held high in unexpected triumph, 20 meters back Kelly was not bothering with the sprint. He, too, was holding both arms aloft. "I felt so happy for Stephen. I wasn't a bit jealous," he said during the celebrations at the hotel. After a season of bad luck, Kelly was happy to be involved with this famous victory, even though he was only in fifth place himself.

Yes, it was a historic day for Irish cycling. Stephen Roche had achieved what only Eddy Merckx had achieved before him: victories at the Giro, Tour and world's in one season. After everyone had gone to bed that night at the Gasthof Piber, Roche went back downstairs, unable to sleep. It was finally sinking in what he had done, and he was probably thinking back a year when he did not ride the world's because he was awaiting an operation on his knee ligaments and wondering if he would ever ride at the top level again. But his glorious 1987 season was better than anyone could have expected — especially Liam Horner.

**1987 WORLD PROFESSIONAL ROAD CHAMPIONSHIP. Villach, Austria. September 6.**
1. Stephen Roche (Irl), 276km in 6:50:02 (40.386 kph); 2. Moreno Argentin (I), at 0:01; 3. Juan Fernandez (Sp); 4. Rolf Gölz (G); 5. Sean Kelly (Irl); 6. Steven Rooks (Nl); 7. Teun Van Vliet (Nl); 8. Rolf Sørensen (Dk); 9. Erik Breukink (Nl); 10. Claude Criquielion (B), all s.t.

# Phinney: 'I had a tremendous fear'

BY PETER NYE

It takes more than smashing head-first into a parked car at 50 kph — resulting in a broken nose and cuts to the face and arm that needed at least 150 stitches — to keep Davis Phinney from trying to be the first U.S. rider to win the prestigious green points jersey in the Tour de France.

Injuries suffered April 17 during the Liège-Bastogne-Liège classic in Belgium put Phinney on the operating table for two hours. A surgeon broke his nose, reconstructed the left side of his face (which took the force of the collision), and put a cast on his right wrist and forearm. Ten days later Phinney was back racing with his 7-Eleven team. Another 10 days later he scored a third-place finish in the final stage of the Tour of Trentino in northern Italy.

"I want to keep my focus in preparing for the Tour de France," Phinney explained May 8 while in Washington, D.C., for a rare 24-hour excursion. He flew in from Europe to ride in the 60km Gore-Tex National Capital Open, held as part of a weekend of activities during which his wife, 1984 Olympic gold medalist Connie Carpenter-Phinney, was honored.

"A crash like that really takes it out of you," Phinney admitted. "It had a big effect on me. I had a tremendous fear of riding again. In the first several races I was really nervous, but that was something I had to face, and I wanted to start back racing as soon as I could." Phinney gestured as though pushing fear aside. "After a while, you get back to where you want to be."

America's premier pack sprinter, who won a stage in each of the last two Tours de France, described his accident in the 260km race.

"There was a big field crash after about 100km. About 80 of us went down. Laurent Fignon, Andy Hampsten, Roy Knickman were involved. I was one of the last ones to get back up. What happened was that there was a big trench in the road about eight inches deep and three or four feet across. Maybe 10 guys made it over, then there was a big crash....

"I wrecked both my wheels. When we finally got going again I figured we were out of the race, but at that point we had nothing to lose and I wanted to finish. Two days before, I had a fourth in a semi-classic race in Belgium. I had won the field sprint and I felt I was going well.

"After the crash Alex Stieda and I were together. We rode in a paceline, working pretty hard. Riders were spread out everywhere. We were catching a lot of guys.

"We kept hammering away. Alex fell back. I caught the tail end of the caravan behind the peloton and worked my way through. I passed Roy. Boom — just flew by. Then I saw the tail end of the peloton. The riders were bunched up. I was within about 200 meters of the peloton in the gap between the peloton and most of the support cars.

"I put my head down to really go for it to regain contact. At that point, though, I was really tired. I had been out there hammering for quite a while. One of the team cars had stopped at the side of the road for a rider. It was my fault because I had my head down, going for it, moving about 50 kph. When I looked up there was the car right in front of me. I was a little too tired. There was no way that I could do anything to avoid what was going to happen.

"My front wheel hit the rear bumper of the car — a European station wagon. I flew over the front of the bike and hit the rear windshield dead on, with the left side of my face. I completely shattered the window. Then I slid down the back of the car and fell on the street.

"I was conscious the whole time. The doctor came along and put a compress on my face."

Stieda went in the ambulance to the hospital with Phinney, who was operated on immediately.

"I spent about two hours in surgery," Phinney said. "I had a good surgeon. He reconstructed my face. He broke my nose and put everything back together. I don't know what the count was on the stitches in my face — between 120 and 150 — plus another 30 stitches in my arm. I had hurt my right arm and wore a cast on it for a week. The cast got in the way when I rode, though, and I had it taken off early."

Despite the accident, Phinney remains on course for a rigorous season in the sport's major leagues. He said he'll spend nearly all year competing in Europe.

Before the sun went down in Washington, Phinney was back on a jet crossing the Atlantic. Two days later he started the Tour de Romandie in Switzerland, where he won the final stage in a bunch sprint. Then it was on to the Tour of Italy, the next step in his quest for the points jersey at the Tour de France.

*The Gavia stage of the 1988 Giro d'Italia has gone down in history as one of the epics of road cycling. It also happened to be the day Andy Hampsten became the first American to take the Giro's pink jersey.*

# Hampsten: 'I was so happy to survive'

## BY JOHN WILCOCKSON

Not in half a century has there been a stage in a major tour as dramatic and decisive as the 14th stage of the Tour of Italy on June 5. Three factors contributed to the drama: an unseasonable day of continuous rain that turned to snow above 6000 feet; the horrifically steep climb and descent of the 8600-foot Gavia Pass (with long stretches of dirt road); and the wide-open state of the race. Going into the stage, just three minutes covered the first nine riders on overall time.

At the heart of this drama was a 26-year-old American named Andy Hampsten. He eventually placed second in the stage, seven seconds behind Dutchman Erik Breukink. But more importantly, Hampsten ended the day clothed in the fabled *maglia rosa*, or pink jersey, as leader of the Giro — the first American to do so.

What was it like to battle the worst conditions possible on a mountain pass that is regarded as the toughest in Italy — maybe in all of Europe? The morning after the epic stage, in his hotel room in Bormio, Hampsten described the day, one that has already entered the legend of bicycle racing.

**VeloNews** What did you know about the conditions on the Gavia Pass?

**Hampsten** Coming down the first descent we were told that the pass was open. I wouldn't have been surprised — although very disappointed — if it had been closed. I was already cold coming down the first descent. I think everyone was. Although that was nothing — nothing — compared to the Gavia. So I started to prepare myself for the conditions. Nobody told me it was snowing up there, but I was certain it was as bad as it was. And I've certainly never raced in anything like yesterday.

I even told Bob [Roll] to prepare himself for an absolute epic. He thought I meant that the climb was going to be so hard, but I wasn't concerned about the climb. I was really looking forward to it, because I heard it was dirt and steep. We train on that [terrain] all the time on our beat rides [in Boulder]. Also Massimo [Testa, the team doctor] has gone skiing here a lot, and he told me about the road. I was more concerned about the descent and the summit, because I knew it was fairly flat at the top. And I was certain the conditions were going to be bad.

**VeloNews** Is that why you put Vaseline on before the stage? Whose idea was that?

**Hampsten** That was Mike [Neel, the team director's] idea. It's a big team joke — you've got to grease up. I had anti-cold cream and Vaseline everywhere on my body, even my face. I didn't wear too many clothes. All I wore was a long-sleeve polypropylene shirt and my wool jersey and a raincoat over that. Coming down the first descent I decided I wasn't going to get rid of too many clothes because it was going to be so cold. Also, we were very well prepared. Not only did Mike have extra clothes in his follow car, we also had Jim Ochowicz at the top with a musette for the descent.

I changed my mind again and I decided — even though I knew the descent was more important than the climb — I was going to get rid of all extra clothing. Bob took back my rain jacket, wool hat, and shoe covers. They gave me an extra rain jacket and rain hat, but I even threw those away on the climb. The only thing I kept that was warm was my neoprene gloves, because I knew that starting the climb I'd be fairly warm, but toward the top my hands would be too cold to put on my gloves. So I kept them on.

At the top, after Jim had given me the musette, I managed to get on a balaclava, a wool hat, and a plastic rain jacket. I lost a lot of time trying to put it all on and Breukink caught me. It was windy and I was pretty uncoordinated and clumsy. And it was hard riding. But [the extra clothes] absolutely saved me. On the descent I was hoping to catch [the rider leading the stage, Johan] Van der Velde and descend with him. But I didn't even worry about that. I was going really hard on the climb, but the summit wasn't my goal. I was just thinking, "Stay in control." I tried to shut out everything and [I said to myself], try to put some clothes on and make it down the descent.

I think I've blocked out most of yesterday. Descending is a very vague image, because if I try to visualize it, all I see are clouds anyways. It's kind of sad, because I've almost blocked out the greatest ride of my career.

It was absolutely shocking what I did. I think if I ever ride or drive back up the Gavia Pass and realize how fast I went down it in those conditions, I'd scare myself silly.

**VeloNews** Were you using your brakes much?

**Hampsten** I was controlling my speed with the brakes, but I wasn't really [using them much]. I was looking for road signs and marshals. Everything was fairly blurred together. I couldn't see where the road was going to go until 100 or maybe 50 meters before me.

I was looking for road signs. So every time it said *tornate* [turn], and every time it had a radical arrow, I would slow down.

My bike was working beautifully. I did have brakes. But really, I let the bike go, just led it, and really went on automatic. I didn't have the vision to look for potholes, even though it was a gravel road with rocks all over.

It's hard for me to say, but maybe I didn't go that fast. But nothing passed me. It was really weird. For a while I thought I was on the wrong road because there were no lead vehicles. There was no frame of reference. Everything was stationary. There were no clues that there was a race as I was coming past. I remember a Carrera support person with a pair of wheels on the gravel part of the descent in a parka. He was just walking up the road against the storm. It wasn't a race anymore. I was going by spectators with umbrellas just walking down the middle of the road. They didn't know I was in the race. I was passing policemen on motorcycles going 10 kph. I was just going — whoosh — past them.

**VeloNews** What about Van der Velde?

**Hampsten** He was with me for a while. I caught him just when the descent started, with Breukink. The three of us were together. Then Van der Velde disappeared. I think he pulled over. He had nothing on. It was insane.

I can remember being behind Breukink for maybe 500 meters at the beginning, even drafting with him. I was thinking, this is great, maybe we can work together and put on some time. But right away I wanted to get ahead of him. I was pedaling as hard as I could just to get my legs moving. And after those 500 meters I forgot about him. I wasn't really racing against him. I had this camaraderie with him, like "Is there some way we can help each other down?" But there wasn't. It was every man for himself. And I didn't want to fall prey to one of his mistakes. I'd rather take my own risks. So, as fast as my bike wanted to go down the mountain, I let it go. I think I probably got a pretty good gap, because at 15km to go — I saw the sign — it was still terrible conditions, still snow everywhere. And somewhere before 10km it changed to rain, and then my vision was fine.

**VeloNews** Did you have glasses on?

**Hampsten** I had glasses, which really saved me. Whenever I dared — when the road wasn't too bumpy — I'd wipe the crust of snow off. And then I'd have to pull them away from my face a bit so they wouldn't fog up so much. The balaclava I had on caused the heat to rise. I put clear lenses in. Once I thought maybe I shouldn't wear them and I pulled them down. And the snow just sand-blasted me. My glasses were fogged over on the side, which I couldn't clean. They had grease from my gloves, which were greasy from my legs. There was a terrible film on them, so everything was a blur.

**VeloNews** Had you put shoe covers on again?

**Hampsten** No, I took those off on the bottom of the climb. My feet were cold on the way up. And on the way down I remember on one of the hairpins in the snow on the paved road — before it turned to rain — I looked down at my legs. I couldn't get a clear idea of what they were like. I knew they were going around, and that they stung a bit, which I knew was good. They weren't totally numb. I made sure I kept spinning. But they were bright red and they had chunks of ice everywhere. Just that one glance terrified me. I'd never seen my body look like that and I refused to look down after that. I remember coming out of a hairpin — I couldn't feel my feet at all — but I flipped my ankles as I was pumping my gears out of the corner just to make sure they weren't locked shut. I really had no idea what had happened to my lower body.

And then on the fast downhill part I was pedaling as hard as I could, just with the fear that if I didn't my legs would just lock up. I didn't have a huge force. I tried to do my Roy Knickman imitation and tuck down the hill, and I think Breukink thought that out quicker than I did and passed me. I couldn't respond at all when he came by. This was about 6km to go.

I was thinking the whole way down, for 25km, each kilometer it's warmer. So get down there as soon as you can. And at this point I'm starting to think about the race. I'm starting to think, "Wow, I might actually win this race." And it wasn't until 6km to go that I thought that I was in a bike race instead of just trying to survive the most wretched thing I'd ever done. And then I just [thought], "Goddam, I want to win this race." But that was just a momentary thought. I was just so, so happy that I'd survived it. It's not as if I could have gone any faster.... I'm just so proud of myself, as I am of everyone who finished, just to make it to the line.

**VeloNews** What happened in the last 6km?

**Hampsten** Breukink went right past me. I never saw him.... Then [race director Vincenzo] Torriani came out of somewhere in his car. And there were motorcycles. And it was, "Oh yeah, this is the Giro." I had no snap at all to go with Breukink. He passed me at maybe 5 kph faster than I was going. There was nothing I could do. But I just took a few breaths and made sure I didn't crack. I just went as fast as I could a little ways behind him. I was really happy in the final little uphill. I kept it in the big ring and maybe a 19 or so in the back. I was just happy that I could force my body to ride, happy that my body was functioning.

After the race I was just an emotional ruin. I went up to the podium to try to do the TV interview and I just left. I couldn't handle it. I went back to the car and hyperventilated — the car was nice and hot — and sat there. Emotionally I was on fire. I cried. I dried myself off a little bit and put on some more clothes. And after 10 minutes I was okay.

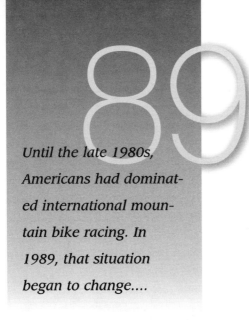

*Until the late 1980s, Americans had dominated international mountain bike racing. In 1989, that situation began to change....*

# Le mountain bike invades Europe

**BY JULIA INGERSOLL**

Something very strange is happening in Europe. Old bistros and boutiques are closing down to be replaced by Pizza Huts and 7-Elevens. Even the politicians are Americanizing the Old World, planning to turn it into a United States of Europe. But most amazing of all is the way in which the Europeans have embraced *le mountain-bike*. Not since the French invented *vélocipede* racing in Victorian times has a new form of cycling so gripped the imagination of the public.

*Le mountain-bike*, according to the French off-road magazine, VTT (*Vélo Tout-Terrain*), is *trés* fun. Parisians are even racing their fat-tire machines in the Bois de Boulogne, the birthplace of bike racing 120 years ago. This time, the French are not setting the style, they are following it. And the style is "Born in the U.S.A."

"We're setting the trends for once," agreed Gary Fisher, one of the originators of the modern mountain bike. While the European racers' bikes aren't quite as sophisticated as the slick machines powered by our own top riders, Fisher said, "They're coming along. Last year, the Europeans were four years behind." He added that while the Americans have a distinct technological edge, the Europeans outdo us with their Technicolor garb and paint jobs.

It's not surprising that the sport should progress so quickly given the enthusiasm behind it. According to VTT, at least 200 competitors line up for every mountain bike race in France, and Italian off-road proponents claim as many as 600 per race. Spectator support is also reported to be tremendous. In Italy, where mountain bike races often pass through towns, crowds of 10,000 people are said to line the streets.

The European mountain bike racing schedule is highlighted by national championship point series similar to our national off-road circuit. It is promoted in several countries including France, which will host five events in 1989. The schedule also lists a world cup series called the *Championnat d'Europe.*

The World Cup will comprise four events this year, and teams from France, Italy, Switzerland, Germany, Austria and Great Britain are expected to compete. Fortunately, the embarrassing problem of having two world championships in one world will be avoided in 1989. The European racing calendar, as published in VTT, states that the organization of a world championships will be left to the Americans, making the August 6-10, Mammoth Lakes, California, race sole bearer of the world title. The event will be sanctioned by the USCF as the world championships of mountain bike racing, although it will not be recognized by the UCI until 1990.

Many American mountain bike manufacturers, including Fisher MountainBikes, Specialized, MS Racing and Klein, have extensive distributorships abroad and plan to send their U.S.-based teams to compete in selected European events. Fisher MountainBikes sponsors teams in Britain, New Zealand and Canada, while Specialized supports squads in seven overseas countries.

American riders have not had much opportunity to race against foreign teams, but the international events they did contest in 1988 clearly showed them to be stronger. Although Peugeot-sponsored cyclo-cross racer Tim Gould of England placed third in the European version of the 1988 world's, the event was otherwise dominated by U.S. riders.

The level of competition on the Continent is expected to be higher this year with the formation of sponsored teams featuring former cyclo-cross stars and professional road racers. Patrice Thévenard, French national off-road champion and veteran of 18 years of pro road racing, will captain the Peugeot team in 1989, along with France's top female rider, Sophie Eglin. Rival French team MBK will feature former French national cyclo-cross champion Bruno Lebras.

Two-time world amateur cyclo-cross champion, Mike Kluge of West Germany, intends to race mountain bikes in 1989, and anticipates competing in America. In Switzerland, Team Ferraroli features former pro road racers Jean-Marie Grezet — 13th at the 1984 Tour.

Mountain bike racers on both sides of the Atlantic share a common passion for the friendly and free-form atmosphere of their sport. Thévenard told VTT, "All those who come to mountain biking from road racing agree. This is most of all an ambiance thing, a convivial movement, while road racing is the school of individualism, egoism if you like."

America still leads the field in off-road racing, but the sport's phenomenal popularity has spurred competition to ever higher levels, and it may not be long before the intense Euro' scene pulls even with ours, or even leaves us in the dust.

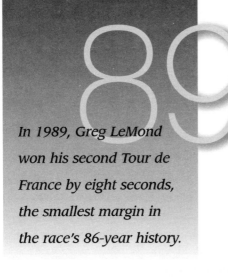

*In 1989, Greg LeMond won his second Tour de France by eight seconds, the smallest margin in the race's 86-year history.*

# LeMond's dramatic Tour comeback

**BY JOHN WILCOCKSON**

U nforgettable moments in sports are rare, extremely rare. That is why Greg LeMond's defeat of Laurent Fignon in the 76th Tour de France, just before 4:42 p.m., July 23 was particularly special. It was a moment full of suspense and emotion. When LeMond crossed the finish line of the 24.5km Versailles-Paris time trial, he knew that he'd won his third stage of the race. But was it good enough to win the Tour?

The whole of France believed the Paris time trial would be a wonderful apotheosis for Fignon, their much maligned favorite.

But LeMond is a fighter, and he would never lie down and die. Without him this could have been just another Tour de France, not one of the most dramatic in its history.

The race had been billed as a duel between Fignon and defending champion Pedro Delgado, but all the theories meant nothing when LeMond equaled Fignon's time in the prologue, a few seconds behind Erik Breukink, another possible race winner.

The American was happy to be back among the leaders after more than two years among the also-rans. And after the tense, high-speed stages through Luxembourg and Belgium, LeMond was sounding optimistic, even talking of a place in the top 10 in Paris.

Then came the Dinard-Rennes time trial, which brought LeMond his first international victory since winning a stage of the Coors Classic in August 1986. "I knew after my second place in the time trial at the Tour of Italy that I could win the Rennes time trial," he said. "I'd felt good since the prologue. But I was so nervous the night before...."

**Back where he belongs**

Those close to LeMond never doubted that he would come back. But on a humid, electrifying evening in Rennes, it felt as if the clock had been turned back three years. Race followers remembered a dramatic time trial at St. Étienne, near the end of the 1986 Tour. LeMond, wearing the yellow jersey, crashed, but still finished second to Bernard Hinault. It clinched the race for LeMond. As the first American to win the Tour de France, he was mobbed by the media — even the U.S. networks sent reporters to cover the story.

Now, in July 1989, here he was again, in the ancient Place des Lices at Rennes, in the eye of another media storm. LeMond came to a halt 50 meters beyond the finish line and immediately dismounted from his low-profile Bottecchia. He knew he was about to be swamped by radio and newspaper reporters, photographers and television cameramen.

As he unbuckled his Giro helmet, there was a twinkle in his soft, blue eyes that shone through the sweat, grit and mucus covering his race-hardened face. He'd ridden most of his time trial in heavy rain.

Before the TV cameras honed in on LeMond, a journalist told him he'd won the stage and probably the yellow jersey. "You beat Delgado by 24 seconds," he was told.

"Is that all?" he asked mischievously. He then looked up and with a small grin, whispered, "It's the bars...." referring to the Scott clip-on triathlete handlebars fitted on his bike.

LeMond decided to test this latest addition to a cyclist's technical armory after seeing the efficiency of these handlebars at the Tour de Trump in May. The European teams were still skeptical, however. And the only others to use the bars on this stage were Andy Hampsten, Sean Yates, Ron Kiefel and Gerhard Zadrobilek of the 7-Eleven team.

While the American was testing his bike on the calm, sunny morning, Delgado was already eating his prerace meal. The Spaniard was lying 134th on overall classification, and with two-minute starting intervals he began his time trial four hours before the race leaders. The 1988 winner knew that a good performance was essential.

Delgado began this 73km Dinard-Rennes stage as fast as anyone. In perfect, dry conditions, he went through the 22.4km mark in 29:52, almost a minute faster than any of the 60 men ahead of him. The three kilometers before this checkpoint at Dinan were the most difficult of the course. Still damp from an overnight thunderstorm, the back road turned sharply to the right, crossed a small, stone bridge and emerged beside the Rance River. Here, the riders raced along the ancient quayside, with fishing boats to their left, before turning left over a hump-backed medieval bridge. Another left turn, and they had to climb a straight 600-meter-long, 10-percent grade to the Dinan checkpoint.

Delgado, riding two disc wheels and a low-profile Pinarello, was throwing everything into his effort. Roy Knickman of 7-Eleven also used two discs, and he reported about the conditions, "There's not much wind so the front disc is good. You lose a little on the uphills, but I was Mr. 12 (-tooth) on the downhills, doing 60 kph."

The American recorded a respectable 1:46:17, but Delgado was on a much more elevated schedule. Making optimum use of the dry conditions, the Spaniard blasted through the middle section of the course faster than anyone; and when he arrived in Rennes at 12:42 p.m. his time of 1:38:36 improved the previous fastest time by almost four minutes.

At about 2:20 p.m., a light rain began falling. The worsening conditions soon caused problems. The 1987 winner Stephen Roche, who was within a second of Delgado at the first check, was more than two minutes slower over the next 27km, and finished in the rain with a time of 1:41:34. The next good ride came from Steve Bauer, who was level with Roche at 50km, but put in a storming finish to move into third place with 1:41:02.

The rain was now falling steadily from a black sky as a storm blew in and worked its way north toward the start point. With the rain came a wind that slowed everyone's times, particularly in the first 20km.

Charly Mottet finished in a disappointing 1:41:55. Then it was Hampsten's turn. The 7-Eleven leader's 50km time was poor, two minutes back of Roche and Bauer, after catching the worst of the wind; but Hampsten made great use of his Scott bars in the final 23km, which he rode faster than Bauer, Mottet, Roche and even Delgado, to finish with 1:42:40.

Two minutes later, his teammate Yates came thundering home. Slower than Bauer at 50km, Yates finished much faster and moved into second on the leader board with 1:40:18. It was a magnificent ride by the tall Englishman who raced close to his best despite some bruises and open wounds down the length of his left leg. The rain had washed grit into the cuts, but Yates downplayed the pain.

The crowd now looked down the finish straight toward the giant TV screen to see the approach of LeMond. Delgado still had the best time, and the American was not expected to approach it: He was still 1:08 down on Delgado at the 50km check.

The storm was at its height when LeMond was negotiating the tricky section before the Dinan checkpoint. But he was obviously moving well, and caught the favored Breukink by the halfway mark. The Dutchman stayed 50 to 100 yards behind him the rest of the way, but this didn't bother LeMond.

The former world champion and Tour winner had the scent of victory. His arrival in the streets of Rennes reminded us of another former champion, Hinault, and when he crossed the line to stop the clock at 1:38:12, we knew that LeMond was back.

There were other dramatic stories. A sick Sean Kelly vomited on his bike several times after the 20km mark, and lost five minutes to LeMond. And Fignon came in third, just missing the yellow jersey. But no one could upstage LeMond.

**Riding on inspiration**

His time trial win earned LeMond the yellow jersey by five seconds from Fignon, while Delgado moved up the overall rankings to 28th. "At the time, we didn't think

Delgado was dangerous (on general classification) because he was so far down (6:53)," admitted LeMond. "The main person I was concerned with was Fignon. But I still wasn't really thinking I could go well overall. I was happy to have the jersey, and then keep it."

On three stages down the west of France, where wind and rain presented potential danger to LeMond, his modest ADR-Agrigel-Coors Light team rose to the challenge of defending the yellow jersey. LeMond's roommate and constant companion, the gentle Johan Lammerts, protected his leader from the wind. The Belgian veterans Eddy Planckaert, Rene Martens, Frank Hoste and Ronny Van Holen are wizards at echelon riding. And the less experienced Johan Museeuw and Philip Van Vooren always rode to their limit.

LeMond himself was riding on inspiration. "Since winning the time trial I slept only five to six hours a night," he said.

The general consensus was that the mountains would kill LeMond's chances of keeping the yellow jersey. But Fignon was weaker in the Pyrénées ... until the Frenchman attacked at the very end of the final climb to Superbagnères, to displace LeMond by seven seconds from the yellow jersey. But the American knew that another time trial was coming up, which could give him the opportunity of regaining the lead.

That mission was accomplished on the uphill stage to Orcières-Merlette, regaining the yellow jersey with a 40-second lead over Fignon, while Delgado was now 2:48 behind. Delgado was still a potential threat, but it finally looked as though LeMond was going to win his second Tour, especially when Fignon showed signs of weakness on the critical stage over the Vars and Izoard passes to Briançon — where Fignon eventually lost 13 seconds on the short, steep climb to the finish.

The roles were reversed the next day at L'Alpe d'Huez, when Fignon retook the yellow jersey with a 26-second advantage. Twenty-four hours later, LeMond found himself again being dropped by Fignon on a climb, on the stage to Villard-de-Lans. Fignon's impressive solo increased his overall lead to 50 seconds, and everyone presumed that the Tour was over. Lesser riders might have believed the consensus, but not LeMond. During an interview that night, he said the Tour was still there to be won in the time trial.

LeMond gained strength from the presence of his family. Also in the group was his close friend Fred Mengoni, whose 65th birthday was the next day, the stage to Aix-les-Bains. LeMond promised he'd try to win the stage for Fred....

"I was suffering a little on the first climb," LeMond said in Aix after winning the stage from Fignon in a five-man sprint. "But I knew if I took Fignon's wheel, I'd win.... Afterward, Fignon came alongside me and said, 'Congratulations, and thanks for a good race.'"

Fignon's gesture perhaps reflected his confidence that the Tour was over. But LeMond said, "Fignon's going to have some sleepless nights before Sunday." The Parisian also had a physical problem, which became apparent on the next stage. He was having trouble sitting on his saddle because of a soreness around the perineum. This caused him problems urinating, and the express train taking the riders to Paris after the stage had to wait for the yellow jersey, who'd been at medical control for more than an hour.

When a film crew from the French TV network, Le Cinq, tried to obtain some words from the race leader, Fignon spat at the camera. This was broadcast nationally that night, and did not improve the Parisian's growing unpopularity. Indeed, none of these things helped Fignon's preparations for the most important time trial of his career....

### An irresistible LeMond

Before this breathtaking finale, from the Palace of Versailles to a sun-drenched Champs-Elysées, only one person in a hundred thought LeMond had a chance of winning. That person was LeMond. His task was to beat Fignon by more than 50 seconds, the margin separating the two protagonists after three weeks and 3244km of superb racing.

The difference in their approach to this final challenge reflected the character of each man. Fignon was hypernervous, and could not relax. The whole world was expecting him to win with the yellow jersey on his back, racing into his hometown.

In contrast, LeMond was focused on the task ahead. "When I rode over the course this morning," he said, "I thought it wasn't difficult enough for me to beat Fignon by more than 20 to 30 seconds. There was a lot of downhill and a strong tail wind. But I felt very, very strong. I thought I could win the stage, but it would be tough to win the Tour."

There were also differences in their equipment. Fignon stayed with his tested technology: a steel-framed Raleigh time trial bike, cow-horn handlebars, and two disc wheels (risky in the windy conditions). But no helmet, because of the 90-degree-plus heat.

LeMond again used a low-profile, carbon-fiber frame, with Scott clip-ons (made more upright to increase his pulling power) fitted to his Mavic time trial bars. He decided to use a rear disc wheel, a blade-spoked front wheel, and a cut-down Giro Aerohead helmet.

In the protocol of time trials, race leader Fignon was the last man to start of the 138 survivors — 198 racers started the Tour in Luxembourg on July 1. LeMond rolled away down the starting ramp at Versailles two minutes before his rival.

It's considered an advantage to start behind because a rider is then informed of his opponent's progress. But the advantage is nil when the news is bad, as it was for Fignon in this date with destiny. At first Fignon resisted LeMond's onslaught. After 5km, he was only six seconds down. And at 10km, mostly on the smoothly surfaced Route National 10, dropping from 400 feet above sea level down to the left bank of the Seine, Fignon came through 18 seconds slower than LeMond. A quick calculation showed that the French anti-hero was losing less than two seconds per kilometer; at this rate he would finish only 46 seconds behind LeMond. The yellow jersey would be saved.

Fignon was riding at his maximum, but the American's advantage continued to climb: it was 25 seconds at 14.5km as he crossed the Seine to its right bank, and 29 seconds at 16km. Even so, the Frenchman was still alive.

Suddenly, Fignon began to show the signs of this incredible pursuit. Now riding on the riverside expressway, there were three underpasses to negotiate, each with a dip down and a ramp back up to street level. LeMond built up speed on the downhills, kept up the cadence and climbed the other side still in the saddle. Fignon did not have the same power, and had to stand on the pedals. The next time check, at 17km, showed him 37 seconds behind; the yellow jersey was beginning to crack.

Meanwhile, LeMond swept onto the smooth cobblestones of the Champs-Elysées like a whirlwind. The atmosphere was electric. The thousands lining the barriers couldn't believe what they were witnessing.

Two minutes and 44 seconds later, with 3.5km still to ride, Fignon emerged from the Place de la Concorde in obvious distress. For the man in the sweat-soaked yellow skin-suit, the world's most magnificent boulevard had been transformed into a road to Calvary.

As Fignon climbed toward the Arc de Triomphe, LeMond hurtled across the finish line in a time of 26:57, a speed of 54.545 kph. It was the fastest time trial of longer than 10km in the cycling record books.

The digital clock above the finish line now became the focus of attention. To win the Tour, Fignon had to stop it at 27:48. Everyone was looking back up the Champs-Elysées, including LeMond. "I heard the announcer say that Fignon still had 20 seconds in which to win the Tour," the American recalled. "Then I looked up and saw him, just there. I thought then that the worst thing that could happen was that I'd lose the Tour de France by a second."

But the clock continued to tick. Fignon, eight seconds short of his goal, collapsed to the hot road surface, gasping for air. His face was red, covered in sweat and tears. The home crowd was stunned into silence, some even booed; but the rest of the world rejoiced. Exhilaration and despair: the contrast was total. LeMond had won the most astonishing victory in Tour de France history.

What made the events of these July days even more astounding is the depths from which LeMond has emerged. Six weeks before this triumph, he finished the Tour of Italy in 39th place, more than 50 minutes behind overall winner Fignon.

Only 27 months earlier LeMond was lying on a surgeon's table fighting for his life after being accidentally shot in the back while hunting wild turkey. Also in 1987, he'd broken a wrist and had an emergency appendectomy. He began racing again at the end of that year, but a crash in March 1988 damaged a knee tendon. And while the Tour de France was happening, LeMond underwent arthroscopic surgery to cure the problem.

Before the "Star Spangled Banner" brought tears to every American's eyes on the Champs-Elysées, LeMond said, "This was the hardest race of my career, and also the happiest day of my life. This means even more than winning the Tour in 1986."

*Near-misses haunted the career of Canadian Steve Bauer. After placing second at the 1984 Olympics, third at the pro world's the same year, and unjustly disqualified when sprinting for gold at the 1988 world's, Bauer looked like a winner in the 1990 Paris-Roubaix...*

# Planckaert nips Bauer at Roubaix

## BY RUPERT GUINNESS

Victory in the world's greatest one-day cycling classic, Paris-Roubaix, fell one centimeter short for Canadian Steve Bauer, when he and Belgian hero Eddy Planckaert fought out a dramatic sprint finish on April 8. As the mainstay of the 7-Eleven team's assault on the 265km cobblestoned classic, Bauer arrived at the Hell of the North's Compiègne start, 80km north of Paris, desperate for a strong performance. His spring campaign, so far, had been troubled — partly due to bronchitis — and he was ready for a chance to show his best form.

But not even Bauer could have expected the climax that occurred when he, Planckaert (Panasonic-Sportlife) and a second Belgian, Edwig Van Hooydonck (Buckler), arrived at the open 500-meter Roubaix velodrome in front. Not only were the three leaders thrillingly captured on the scheduled lap before the sprint — by Frenchmen Martial Gayant (Toshiba) and Gilbert Duclos-Lassalle (Z), and last year's winner, Jean-Marie Wampers (Panasonic-Sportlife) — but the eventual race to the line was followed by an agonizing 10-minute wait, as the judges closely examined the photo-finish before giving their verdict.

Sitting on the grassy velodrome pit, waiting for the decision, Bauer looked uneasy — and so did an exhausted Planckaert, sitting on the other side of the Roubaix stadium. The only hint that the veteran Belgian ultimately was to be declared the winner came from the comparative sizes of the throngs surrounding each rider.

And yet it was Bauer who looked to be setting himself up as a convincing winner when he came through on Van Hooydonck's inside on the final bend. But Planckaert, on Van Hooydonck's right, and having the advantage of being higher up on the turn, was able to milk that extra acceleration to match the Canadian. Dropping down alongside the 30-year-old Bauer, Planckaert had obviously managed to contain the necessary reserves in the last 15km, when he, Bauer and Van Hooydonck established their break from three others.

To the thunderous roar of thousands of spectators, the two men pedaled with all their fury, neck-and-neck. They were ending a race that was highlighted by bitingly cold winds and whirlpools of dust — rather than the fabled mud and rain the fans longed to see — and by the inevitable punishment of 22 sections of cobblestones over 57km of the route. And they ended this Hell of the North in a drama of tension — it was a nail-biting occasion to see the outcome tested so closely.

With equal anxiety, the crowd watched Bauer endure the sufferance of a delayed verdict which, when it finally went against him, he accepted with remarkable dignity. "To lose by two centimeters [officially one centimeter] is hard, sure. But finishing second in a race like this is great, too," said Bauer.

"I think today, I did my best race. I couldn't have done any better," he continued. "I don't think I made a mistake. I felt pretty strong. I was working more than Eddy in the last kilometers, but I thought that by playing the right tactic, I might beat him. I didn't, but this proves I am capable of winning Paris-Roubaix. One day … I will do it."

For 32-year-old Planckaert, victory marked a remarkable turn of fortune. Just a few months ago, at the start of 1990, he had faced the possibility of not having a sponsor. The decision by ADR — the team he rode with last year — to drop its sponsorship, had left 22 contracted riders stranded. Although team director José De Cauwer recently secured IOC-Tulip's backing, by early February, Planckaert had feared the worst, and consequently took up a sympathetic offer from Panasonic to return to its fold.

Winning at Roubaix also crowned Planckaert's distinguished career, which already boasted wins at the Tour of Flanders and Tour de France green points jersey competition in 1988; stage wins in the major Tours; and a flurry of high placings in Paris-Roubaix itself.

"Ever since I turned professional I have done well here," Planckaert said later, in near-fluent English. "I remember the first year I did Paris-Roubaix, when I finished 13th. I said to myself then, 'This is a race for me, I could win it.' And, since then, it has always been a goal for me."

Certainly, Planckaert's victory was thoroughly deserving. As Bauer honestly and generously confirmed, "Eddy was the best … that's all I can say."

Ironically, earlier in the race, Planckaert's most critical move was not intended as a bid for the win. For when the ponytailed Flemish rider first bade farewell to the peloton — numbering about 90, before the 11th stretch of cobbles at 175km — it was more of a surge than an attack.

"Eddy was not the team leader today. No one was, really. We had four or five riders who were in good form … Wampers, (John) Talen, (Olaf) Ludwig and me. When Eddy went, he was going slowly. It was not so much of an attack," Planckaert's Swiss teammate, Urs Freuler, said later.

Nevertheless, Planckaert had no trouble catching a lone Stephan Joho (Ariostea) of Switzerland, who was the sole survivor of a three-man break that began after only 19km and gained up to 16:33 by the first cobbles (or *pavé*) at Troisvilles, after 100km. This was the same place where Planckaert suffered his one flat tire of the day, and received a wheel from teammate Guy Nulens.

Joho, who had long ago dropped his two attacking TVM companions — Dutchmen Peter Pieters and Rob Kleinsman — was suffering when Planckaert rolled alongside him, on the 11th set of cobbles, 90km from the finish.

As Planckaert swept past the tiring Swiss rider — who quickly retreated to the obscurity of a curiously regrouped peloton — his lead was 1:15. However, the peloton was still full of gusto, thanks to a mighty tail wind that helped it regroup soon after the route's most notorious cobbled path, through the ancient Wallers-Arenberg Forest.

Emerging from the crowd-lined forest road at 157km, the chase group behind Joho and the distanced Pieters looked like the decisive challenge for authority. Twelve riders, including Laurent Fignon, Planckaert, Wampers, Freuler and Marc Madiot (Toshiba), were 10 seconds ahead of a second group of five, which comprised Belgian Rudy Dhaenens and Norwegian Atle Pedersen (both PDM), Frenchman François Lemarchand (Z), West German Andreas Kappes (Toshiba) and Italian Claudio Chiappucci (Carrera).

That group had about two minutes on Italy's Franco Ballerini (Del Tongo) and a fading Kleinsman, and around 2:45 on the main bunch, which included Maurizio Fondriest (Del Tongo), together with the 7-Eleven duo of John Tomac and Davis Phinney. But, under the awaiting tail winds outside the forest, these gaps didn't prove large enough to consolidate the splits, nor prevent the regroupment that preceded Planckaert's solo break.

It was only when two chasers — Gayant and the virtually unknown Belgian neo-pro, Kurt Van Keirsbulck (Isoglass) — joined Planckaert after 201km, that the thought of keeping up the ante to the finish became a serious inclination. "At first, I never really thought about it. Then, here, I started contemplating the idea," reflected Planckaert.

These three were never able to extend their lead beyond 1:28 at 213km, and it was sometimes much less. However, the rearguard tactics of Planckaert's Panasonic teammates — to counter a never-ending series of attacks by Castorama's Laurent Fignon — pegged back the leaders' advantage to between 40 and 45 seconds.

Fignon was now clearly regretting his decision to let Planckaert get away with so little challenge; as every time he accelerated, he found one or two of the Panasonic riders on his wheel — usually Ludwig or Talen, but sometimes even Wampers or Freuler. But Fignon's desperate bids to bridge that elusive 40-second gap split the main field, with one noted discard being Fondriest, who fell on the seventh to last section of pavé, at 218km.

Eventually, Fignon went clear with the four Panasonic riders and 10 others — Duclos-Lassalle, would join this group, after a most impressive chase brought him back from a puncture that had put the veteran French rider one minute in arrears.

With 33km to go — on the approach to the fifth-from-last section of pavé — the first to take advantage of the opportunity opened by Fignon's wrangle with the Panasonic riders was Van Hooydonck. Up on his feet, his long, hefty torso shaking like a tree in a gale, the Belgian winner of last year's Tour of Flanders — twice a top-five finisher at Roubaix — bolted away.

Then, after Van Hooydonck joined the three leaders, along went Dutchman John Van den Akker (PDM) and finally, Bauer. "I think everyone was feeling just as tired as I was when I went up to the lead group," Bauer said later. "But the Panasonics were shutting down the race. There was a Panasonic in front and four in the group. So I figured that if I could get to the break, I had a chance to stay away."

With six leaders now, the deficit for Fignon's group was 20 seconds by the fourth-from-last cobbled section, 21km from the finish. But it soon shot up to 45 seconds, due to the energetic pulling of Bauer, Gayant and Van Keirsbulck — who was reveling in a most extraordinary opportunity, considering he was originally only a reserve rider for the Isoglass team.

Behind the leaders, several notable chases were being made from Fignon's group by Switzerland's Thomas Wegmüller and Dutchman Adri Van der Poel (both Weinmann), and Johan Museeuw (Lotto-Superclub).

However, these all appeared to be belated efforts. And apparent confirmation came when Bauer put his new-found form on the line with a bold, solo attack on the second-to-last sector of pavé, with 15km to go — on the same, slightly uphill track where Dirk De Wolf and Wampers launched their winning break last year, and where, this year, Fignon would collide with a horde of photographers!

Unpredictably, Planckaert was the first to catch Bauer. For the previous 10km, the wily Belgian had done nothing but sit in the wake of his companions, apparently saving himself for either a sprint or to chase just such an attack made by the Canadian. Then, just as predictably, Van Hooydonck surged up alongside the duo.

With their lead still 45 seconds, Fignon was no longer in a challenging position, and knew his day was over. The greatest threat to the three leaders, with 10km still to go, was a new group of pursuers — Duclos-Lassalle, Talen, Van der Poel, Wegmüller, Museeuw and Gayant.

Passing the last cobblestones, just on the southern outskirts of Roubaix's shabby industrial limits, Bauer, Planckaert and Van Hooydonck suddenly seemed to be in big trouble. Just when they needed every ounce of effort to fend off a solo bid by Gayant to join them, Van Hooydonck dropped off the pace in apparent fatigue. Gayant surged forward and was just four seconds short of succeeding in his chase.

Then, miraculously, Van Hooydonck summoned up the energy to rejoin the two leaders who, having witnessed the Belgian's hiccup, were reassured that the decision would be between them — should they stay clear.

Entering the velodrome, with one-and-a-half laps (750 meters) to go, Bauer was the rider most worried about Gayant's chase succeeding. "We knew someone was coming, so I was doing a little bit of extra work in the finale. I thought I could beat Van Hooydonck in the sprint, but Eddy ... I didn't know," the 7-Eleven star later recalled.

The three men were only 200 meters onto the track when a huge cheer from the packed stands heralded the arrival of Gayant and then, just 15 meters behind, the other nine pursuers. Suddenly, it seemed, the crowd was about to witness a mass sprint!

Wampers, justifiably sensing a repeat win, instigated the sprint after a nervous 200 meters of tense positioning for the crescendo. Then, Van Hooydonck shot past him, as Bauer and Planckaert fought to hold a high position going into the final turn.

And when the two protagonists came charging onto the home stretch, no one could tell who was the true winner. Officially, it was Planckaert. But ultimately, it was everyone present, watching a uniquely exciting race, contested by two outstanding riders.

**88th PARIS-ROUBAIX, France. April 8.**
1. Eddy Planckaert (B), Panasonic-Sportlife, 265.5km in 7:37:02 (34.855 kph); 2. Steve Bauer (Can), 7-Eleven; 3. Edwig Van Hooydonck (B), Buckler, both s.t.; 4. Martial Gayant (F), Toshiba, at 0:03; 5. Jean-Marie Wampers (B), Panasonic-Sportlife; 6. Gilbert Duclos-Lassalle (F), Z, both s.t.; 7. Thomas Wegmüller (Swit), Weinmann, at 0:07; 8. Adri Van der Poel (Nl), Weinmann, at 0:10; 9. Rudy Dhaenens (B), PDM; 10. John Talen (Nl), Panasonic-Sportlife, both s.t.

# Overend, Furtado complete gold rush

BY JOHN WILCOCKSON

**90** *The first official world mountain bike championships, sanctioned by the Union Cycliste Internationale, were held at Purgatory Resort, near Durango, Colorado, in August 1990. The Americans dominated....*

N ed Overend has never looked better than he did on the glorious sixteenth of September. Just before 3:30 p.m. on a warm, mainly overcast day, the Specialized team captain and kingpin cruised into the short, finishing straight at Purgatory Resort, 2:36 ahead of his nearest challenger, Thomas Frischknecht of Switzerland, to win the most prestigoius title of the inaugural UCI world mountain-bike championships: the senior men's cross-country.

Before crossing the line, Overend raised both arms high to acknowledge the roar of approval from the large, exuberant crowd. Then, as if for his own satisfaction, the 35-year-old from Durango punched the air with his right fist, then with his left.

Like the other hundreds of off-road racers who had traveled from 25 countries to compete in Colorado, Overend knew that this first official world off-road championship meant so much more than the two, so-called world titles he had won at Mammoth, California. And joining him among the day's cross-country gold-medal winners were three other Coloradans: Juli Furtado and Lisa Muhich, who scooped the two women's championships, and junior Jimi Killen. The only cross-country rainbow jersey that eluded the home contingent was the veteran men's — that went in dramatic style to French champion Patrice Thévenard, from multi-world cyclo-cross champion, Albert Zweifel of Switzerland.

Furtado's victory over Sara Ballantyne in the senior women's cross-country was the biggest upset of the championships — and it was a win based on merit, not luck. Furtado went out fast, as she has often done in the past. But this time, she didn't weaken or, more importantly, crash. The Yeti rider was strong on the climbs, more controlled on the downhills, and showed greater vitality than all her opponents. In contrast, Specialized's Ballantyne, like many of the other off-road stars, had a jaded, end-of-season look.

Of the 10 world championships contested at the Purgatory Resort (there were not enough competitors for the junior women's division), the American riders won eight gold medals, five silver and six bronze — a total of 19 medals. The other 11 medals were divided among Great Britain (one silver, two bronze), Switzerland (two silver, one bronze), Canada (one gold, one silver), France (one gold), Belgium (one silver) and New Zealand (one bronze).

The cross-country races completed a successful week of mountain-bike racing that impressed visitors and captivated many new spectators. Although there were a few loose ends noticed by seasoned observers of other cycling world's, the organization masterminded by Durango promoter Ed Zink operated like clockwork. Events started on time, the rugged San Juan Mountains were majestic, the weather was clear and warm ... and the racing was superb.

**Senior men**

Thc four-lap, 52km cross-country didn't go completely the way of Overend and the American national team. Although Overend (and the other team leaders) had a front-line berth on the starting grid, his teammates Rishi Grewal, Tim Rutherford, John Tomac, John Weissenrieder and Dave Wiens all lined up in the depths of the 130-man field. And when one of the inexperienced Austrian riders fell after 150 meters — just as the grass-covered start narrowed into the first uphill trail — Overend was nearly dragged into the 20-rider pileup.

"I didn't want to get caught in the traffic," Overend said later, "but I didn't get in my toe clips fast enough. So the crash happened in front of me. My front wheel got hit by a guy who went down, but I managed to go wide, to get around."

By the time the men emerged at the top of the first, curving uphill — riding one behind the other like a Tour de France peloton — Overend was back in 18th place. The line was led by Italian roadman Claudio Vandelli, ahead of Belgium's Filip Meirhaege, a fast-starting Grewal, Italian off-road champion Mario Noris, and Britain's Tim Gould. Others who had already worked their way into the top 20 included Weissenrieder (ninth), Tomac (10th), Frischknecht (13th), Italian road sprinter Paolo Rosola (15th), Wiens (19th) and AlpineStars' Mike Kloser (20th).

This fast lap didn't follow the pattern of following laps. Instead of plunging to the right to begin the principal, excruciatingly steep, climb, the riders continued uphill on a broad, dirt trail, to join the climb at the second of its four turns.

By the initial, 9700-foot summit — before the course cut through the trees and headed for the top, far turn — Vandelli was joined by Frischknecht, Gould, Overend and Tomac.

Fiercely determined, Tomac then launched himself into the longest part of the descent — down the terrifyingly bumpy Swire's Gulch — to dramatically take the lead from Frischknecht and Overend.

To make such death-defying downhills, Tomac explained that he "corrals the adrenaline." And contradicting the conventional wisdom, the Yeti-7-Eleven pro clearly wanted to make the downhills more crucial than the uphills on this particular day. Whether he was right we will never know, because Tomac flatted just as he hurtled back to the 8950-foot base level. And as the Durango-based rider spent a frustrating two minutes changing his tube, a dozen riders flashed by him, headed by Frischknecht, Overend and Gould.

These three — the ultimate medalists — were bunched together when they completed their first lap. They were followed across the line by a fading Vandelli, Kloser, Grewal, an emerging Paul Thomasberg (Giant), Noris, Weissenrieder ... and Tomac. Shouting at the riders ahead of him to move out of his way, the demonstrative Tomac was clearly determined to overcome his losses as quickly as possible.

But now, the race was becoming an uphill battle, an exercise that suited the leading trio much better than their pursuers. And for the remaining three laps, the riders would descend the switchbacks from the first uphill, and head across the lower mountainside, before starting the main climb. Overend spun out his granny gear on this vital pitch, while former world junior cyclo-cross champion Frischknecht shouldered his bike and ran alongside the American. Gould used a combination of riding and pushing to overcome the near-30-percent grade.

By the top, the three leaders were 1:30 ahead of a still surging Grewal, who was followed at five-second intervals by Tomac (up to fifth), Weissenrieder, Kloser, Thomasberg and Vandelli. At the front, Overend was still more afraid of Gould than Frischknecht, having finished almost a minute behind the 26-year-old Englishman in the non-championship uphill race, earlier in the week. However, it was now Gould's turn for mechanical problems.

"I dropped my chain on an uphill, and couldn't get it back on," he lamented, later, "I lost about 15 seconds to the other two. But I couldn't do anything about it." That same lap, descending Swire's Gulch, Gould again dropped his chain — but was able to lift it back before emerging into a short, muddy, section of single-track below Purgatory's ski lift No. 6. The two front riders were now 45 seconds ahead of him.

Behind them, Ritchey's Rutherford had emerged from nowhere into fourth, 2:00 down, followed by Coors Light-GT's Grewal, and Tomac, while Vandelli had now been replaced by Noris as the top Italian challenger. Also moving up on this second lap were Tom Rogers of GT (up to eighth), Fat Chance-Campagnolo's Dan Myrah (11th), and Mongoose's Max Jones (15th). The next few minutes saw national team members Rutherford and Wiens both drop out of the reckoning.

Rutherford came to grief on the descent, while Wiens was having all sorts of problems. First, his chain dropped and jammed between his chainrings. "I sorted that out," said Wiens, "and I was only just behind Max (Jones). Then my rear tire flatted, and I was about five minutes down when I restarted. And as I was descending the switchbacks, stuck behind some slow Mexicans, I fell over and broke my pedal...."

While these minor dramas were being played out, the most crucial phase of the whole race was taking place ahead. Now on their third lap, and ascending the ultra-steep part of the principal uphill for the second time, the 35-year-old Overend and 20-year-old Frischknecht were again alongside each other. When the Swiss remounted, he was still with the American. Then, Overend started to open up a slight lead — first one meter ... then two.

He was three seconds ahead at the climb's second turn, and Frischknecht could do nothing about it. "I didn't want to back off on that third lap," stated Overend later. "I was working pretty hard. I suspected I'd be stronger than him (Frischknecht)." Riding in the saddle, with his chain on the middle chainring, Overend was working at his maximum. He was clearly more comfortable in the thin air than either of his immediate challengers.

And at the fourth of the climb's turns, before disappearing into the trees, the U.S. champion was 15 seconds clear of Frischknecht, and 1:10 ahead of Gould. Next came the surprising Noris, with Rogers (at 2:00), followed in the next minute by a determined Tomac, a cool Thomasberg, a gasping Grewal and a consistent Myrah (who had won the three-lap qualifying race, four days earlier).

However, the strongest-looking climbers at this stage looked like the pair riding in 16th and 17th positions: Tom Collins of Marin, and Durango Wheel Club expert, Travis Brown. These two continued to move forward, and passed three more riders on the course's back loop. And before the finish, they would also overtake a fading Weissenrieder, and an exhausted Grewal — who pulled out of the race. Meanwhile, Overend continued to open up his lead on Frischknecht: one minute by the end of lap three, 1:30 by the main climb's summit, two minutes before heading back down Swire's Gulch for the last time ... and 2:36 at the finish.

After completing this final lap, the tired, but happy Swiss uttered, "I almost died," before rolling on his back, and kicking his muddied, cramping legs into the air. Frischknecht then said, "Ned was clearly the best. He's the right champion."

Both Overend and Frischknecht explained that they had taken things easy on the final had held at the top of the main climb, while others closed in. The most notable of these were Thomasberg — who overtook Noris and Rogers to claim fourth place ("My best ever race"); and Jones — who went past Myrah, Tomac, Noris and Rogers, to finish fifth.

### Senior women

Taking the lead on the first climb, and extending it throughout the three-lap, 39km senior women's race, the short, powerful racer in the stars-and-stripes jersey rode to an easy victory. However, the winner wasn't the expected Ballantyne, but her national teammate and Boulder neighbor, Furtado. It was the upset of the championships, and a result that left Ballantyne tight-lipped, and doing her best to put on a brave face.

After finishing 2:27 behind Yeti's exuberant Furtado, Specialized ace Ballantyne hugged her younger colleague, and said, "This is good for you." And trying to explain her own disappointment, the 29-year-old Ballantyne told reporters, "I was waiting for her to collapse. I usually wait until she falls on a pile of rocks — but not this time. She had a good race." However, Ballantyne admitted that, unusually for her, she had some cramping on the inside of her thigh muscles, on the last lap. And friends said that the hot favorite was ultra-nervous before the race, and was able to eat only half a pancake for breakfast. And that nervous energy possibly cost megawinner Ballantyne the victory in the race she most wanted to win.

From the start, where Canada's Elladee Brown made a brief appearance in the lead, the race quickly became a battle between Furtado, Ballantyne … and a third Boulder resident — world road race silver medalist, Ruthie Matthes of Ritchey. These three were well clear by the top of the main climb, on its easier ascent; and by the end of lap one, Furtado had already pulled 45 seconds ahead of the other two, with Susan DeMattei of Diamondback a further minute behind, in fourth.

Matthes surprisingly outclimbed Ballantyne on the second lap, and briefly held second spot, before dropping back again around the course's back loop. DeMattei was holding strongly in fourth, while fifth spot was taken briefly by yet another U.S. national team member, Julia Ingersoll of KHS. Ingersoll overtook both Brown and West Germany's Susi Buchwieser on the main climb on this second lap … but she never looked like catching DeMattei or Matthes.

On the final lap, while Furtado continued to extend her lead, Buchwieser, only 19, showed remarkable stamina. The powerfully built West German recaught Ingersoll, raced by a suffering DeMattei, and was only 30 seconds behind bronze medalist Matthes at the finish. Buchwieser's recovery showed that the Americans may not have everything their own way in future years … although 23-year-old Furtado also has plenty of time for improvement.

Since leaving the U.S. alpine ski team, Furtado has had remarkable success in cycling. She was national road champion last year, and has improved consistently since turning to full-time off-road racing in mid-July. "I've trained really hard for the past month," explained Furtado after her win. And her methods were clearly better than Ballantyne's, who had twice flown to Europe and back to clinch her overall title in the Grundig World Cup. The resultant jet lag, and the pressure from her sponsors and supporters, meant that, for once, Ballantyne had to settle for silver instead of gold.

*The United States had never won a world team time trial championship. That changed at the 1992 world's in Spain....*

# U.S. finally tops in TTT

## BY RUPERT GUINNESS

The U.S. consecrated its long-held status as a rising power in women's team time trialing, by taking the gold medal in the world championships at Benidorm, Spain, September 5. On a technically demanding 50km course, Jeanne Golay, Bunki Bankaitis-Davis, Eve Stephenson and Jan Bolland averaged 46.573 kph, to defeat defending champion France by 13 seconds and Russia by 46 seconds.

Of the participating teams, France was the most disappointed — having come to Benidorm expecting another gold medal.

French star Jeannie Longo later said that a permanent retirement from cycling was her most likely avenue for the future. "I would so much have liked to have finished with a gold medal. But I haven't. Where could I find any incentive to motivate me now?" said the distraught former champion.

But the reality is that the French were always behind the Americans in terms of time, class and determination. The U.S. quartet rode superbly, with only Bolland — racing in her first world's — showing any sign of weakness, and then only in the last 10km. And after finishing fourth in last year's championship at Stuttgart, Germany, it was a new-look U.S. line-up: The only returning members were 22-year-old Stephenson and 34-year-old Bankaitis-Davis — the latter using the world's to mark her retirement from racing.

From the 14 teams that started, the U.S. was always the dominant force. It clocked the fastest split at every interval, and its advantage increased on every occasion. These results reflected the commitment the U.S. team had made throughout the year. Three earlier training camps at Colorado Springs, four days of training on the world's course beforehand, and the luxury of having five riders to choose from for the final team ... all played their part. Another factor was that the Americans never discounted any of their rivals, even though they quickly realized they were on a gold-medal-winning schedule, after receiving splits during the race.

"You can never underestimate the others," said Golay. "In this discipline, there are really four or five countries which are strong. We had to be ready for any of them."

"We were all very strong today," continued Golay. "We rode evenly, although the only one who was a bit weak in the end was Jan Bolland. It's her first world's and she has less experience. We had to get her to drink a bit of Coke at the end."

The Americans didn't find the race an easy one. "It was a very technical course," Golay reported. "The first 10km seemed like a criterium course, with all the turns. And that made it difficult to get into an early rhythm.

"Also, the wind was very fickle. It seemed like a head wind all the way, no matter which way we turned, for some reason. The only time we felt any tail wind was after the first turnaround, after 17.5km."

Another major obstacle was how the race was organized. The original route was altered due to too many traffic circles. But then, nobody knew exactly what the new route was! Finally, after "clarifying" it — as Bankaitis-Davis so diplomatically labeled the Spanish effort to correct their mistakes — the race went ahead without a team knowing the exact details.

"We didn't find out where the turnarounds were until we got to them in the race," exclaimed Golay. "At one of them, it was in a parking lot: It was an especially tricky one, but luckily we had no accident there."

The Americans also overcame all the other problems posed by a quirky organization, but when you have the gold medals around your necks and rainbow jersey on your shoulders, the need to cast blame for those problems is quickly made a second priority....

**1992 WORLD CHAMPIONSHIPS, Valencia, Spain. August 6.**

**Women's TTT**

1. USA (Bunki Bankaitis-Davis, Eve Stephenson, Jan Bolland, Jeanne Golay),  50km in 1:03:30 (46.573 kph); 2. France (Jeannie Longo, Corinne Legal, Catherine Marsal, Cécile Odin), 1:03:43; 3. CIS (Nadejda Kibardina, Natalia Grinina, Goulnara Fatkoullina, Alexandra Koliaseva), 1:04:16; 4. Italy (Antonella Belluti, Roberta Bonanomi, Alessandra Cappellotto, Maria-Paola Turcutto), 1:04:28; 5. Lithuania (Aiga Zagorska, Daiva Cepeliene, Natalia Olsevskaja, Liuda Trebaite), 1:04:40; 6. Ukraine (Tamara Poliakova, Elena Ogouy, Svetlana Gyigyileva, Irina Denisiuk), 1:05:12; 7. Netherlands, 1:05:16; 8. New Zealand, 1:05:39; 9. Spain, 1:06:08; 10. Norway, 1:06:21.

*Nearly 10 years after Francesco Moser put the world hour record "on the shelf" in Mexico City, two British amateur racers improved the record over the course of one dramatic week in July 1993....*

# Boardman tops Moser ... and Obree

BY JOHN WILCOCKSON

A hundred years after Henri Desgrange set the first mark of 35.325km, a half century after Fausto Coppi topped 45km, and almost 10 years after Francesco Moser broke the 50km barrier, the world hour record was shattered twice within a week last month. On July 17, the unconventional Scotsman Graeme Obree, 27, riding his homemade steel track bike, covered 51.596km in 60 minutes around the indoor track at Hamar, Norway. Six days later — three hours before the stage 18 finish of the Tour de France at Bordeaux — Britain's Olympic pursuit champion Chris Boardman, 24, improved the record to an astonishing 52.270km, riding a prototype, Kevlar monocoque-framed Corima bicycle.

Boardman's new record was 1119 meters more than the fabled 51.151km set by Moser at Mexico City, in January 1984. And when compared with Moser's now obsolete, but more relevant record (indoors, at sea level), which he set on his giant-wheel bicycle, at Stuttgart, Germany, in May 1988, Boardman rode a further 1626 meters — a mile more than Moser!

The two new records are not only a reflection of the advances made in sports medicine and preparation, but perhaps more importantly the improvements in bicycle aerodynamics. Obree has a unique, egg-shaped position on his bike — which has an ultra-narrow bottom-bracket, and bars only 30cm (11.8 inches) wide. Boardman, of course, used his hallmark "ski" bars that give him an immensely more aerodynamic position than that available to Moser on his bull-horn bars, a decade ago.

Boardman began his preparation for the July 23 record attempt in January, under the supervision of his long-time trainer Peter Keen, who guided the Englishman to a gold medal in the 1992 Olympic pursuit. Then, Boardman utilized a prototype Lotus Sport machine — with its now famed mono-blade fork and single rear chainstay. The rider and Lotus have since fallen out, and Boardman tested four new bicycles when he first traveled to Bordeaux in May.

The Corima monocoque, made in France, came out the best — because of its rigidity, aero' qualities and the possibility it offered to duplicate Boardman's ultra-low, flat-backed position he had on the Lotus. Some 2000 man-hours later, after constructing a new frame and adapting it to accommodate the British rider's carbon-fiber bars, the world hour-record machine was ready for action.

A week of further tests, mixed with road and track training, preceded the attempt on the Bordeaux track: a 250-meter oval, made from doussie, an African hardwood. Scheduling the attempt before the Orthez-Bordeaux stage of the Tour insured a big media presence and also attracted a crowd of 2000 fans, many of whom had driven or flown over from England.

After 20 minutes of steady warming up, Boardman dismounted — already to loud cheers and applause — and went to his cabin, 10 minutes before his start time. He drank some water, wiped himself down, and then rezipped his skinsuit (in the gold and red colors of his North Wirral Velo club, which is sponsored by Kodak and Reebok). Trainer Keen, a physiologist, then sprayed Boardman and his skinsuit with a mixture of water and alcohol — "to give him some additional sweat" — and the long-awaited moment had arrived.

A remarkably relaxed Boardman walked to the track, like a boxer marching to the ring. The crowd cheered. The Olympic champion climbed onto his golden-colored bike, with its four-spoke, black-and-gold-striped wheels and Continental track tires — which the mechanic had just wiped down, searching for cuts and checking the pressure. Boardman — who wasn't wearing gloves or socks — then donned his clear-lens Oakleys, buckled on a black, tear-shaped Vetta helmet over his closely cropped hair, clicked his uncovered Carnac shoes into Campagnolo pedals, and pedaled away. He slowly circled the track before coming to a halt midway down the home straight, next to the timekeeper and commissaires who would be in charge for the next 60 minutes....

It was exactly 10 a.m. The temperature was 72 degrees and the humidity 75 percent outside, where rain clouds hung heavily over the steel-and-glass-structured velodrome. Because of the dark morning, the stadium lights were on, accentuating the heat. Shirts stuck to the backs of perspiring television cameramen working trackside. As Boardman said later, "These were the worst conditions we could have done the record in."

At the start line, Boardman dismounted and began to compose himself for the intense effort that lay ahead. An official held his bike as he remounted, and Keen quietly gave some final words to his rider. They both knew Boardman's limits; a pulse that would probably rise to 185 bpm, and a power output that would average 470 watts, increasing to 530 watts at times. The scheduled target was 52.5km, dropped because of the humidity from the 53km that Boardman privately hoped to reach. A last word, then Boardman said, "Okay." It was almost time to go.

It was 10:01 a.m. The crowd went silent. Nearly everyone stopped talking, as if they were in a place of worship. But only time, courage, power and preparation would be the arbiters of this hour. The computers and chronometers were ready to roll. Everything was ready, except for a Spanish radio commentator, who was talking loudly and quickly into his mike: People nearby told him to hush.

It was 10:02 a.m. The stadium was perfectly silent. Then, a Scottish voice shouted from the crowd: "Chris, you can do it!" Almost simultaneously, Boardman made the first thrust on his 53x13 gear (at 110 inches, considerably smaller than the 52x12, 117 inches, used by Obree); the crowd began applauding and shouting, whistles blew; and what the racer would later describe as his "toughest-ever race" was underway.

From a standing start, he slowly began, "sprinting" out of the saddle, and holding the stub bars that would only be used for half-a-lap. Then he flattened into his perfected aero' position, sitting on the peak of his saddle and gripping the ski-bars with his bare hands. He was already making the most of his powerful thighs on the 80-degree seat-angle bike. The first lap took 21.93 seconds … and then he was into his rhythm, reeling off successive laps of 16.87, 17.74, 17.96, 17.68 and 17.14 seconds. His 52.5km goal would be achieved by laps times of 17.14 seconds, or kilometer times of 1:08.56.

That was the target, but it soon become clear that this was too ambitious a schedule. The second through fifth kilometer times were 1:08.55, 1:08.05, 1:08.71 and 1:08.70. "It was going well," Boardman later reflected, "but we needed to slow down after a bit because the temperature was too high. I was starting to feel dizzy. I knew I could break the record, so I decided to be more careful. There was a chance I was going to faint."

At 5000 meters, Boardman's time was 5:48.55, almost 1.5 seconds slower than Obree; but this didn't perturb Boardman and trainer Keen, who knew that they had planned a gradual build-up of speed. When the 10km time showed the Englishman was more than two seconds faster than his Scottish rival — the two times were displayed on the velodrome's electronic scoreboard — the crowd roared, and Boardman seemed to physically grow in confidence.

Riding at an even cadence of 99 to 100 rpm, he was showing his skills as a world-class pursuiter (holding his line around the turns, so that he was riding the absolute minimum distance), and those of a champion time trialist (judging his pace to perfection, looking straight ahead and remaining completely focused on maintaining an even speed).

When discussing the qualities of Obree and Boardman, British national team coach

Doug Dailey said, "They're both steady-state riders. They've been doing it all their lives, riding 10s and 25s (10- and 25-mile time trials)."

By the 20th kilometer, Boardman was 15 seconds faster than Obree, having reached an average speed of 52.32 kph. It was clear that barring an unforeseen collapse, the English amateur was well on his way to a splendid new record. He was making it look easy, calmly setting 4000-meter times of 4:34, again and again and again — times that few specialist pursuiters can even record one at a time!

Boardman did show some signs of his awesome task: His head began to rock slightly after 20 minutes; he eased himself back on his seat after 25 minutes; his body was rocking after 40 minutes; and he was sometimes wobbling, coming out of turns, after 55 minutes. By this time, the crowd was roaring, as the French announcer started counting down the minutes, and the 50th kilometer split showed that Boardman was now more than 40 seconds ahead of Obree.

The noisy support, and the realization that the end was near, goaded the Olympic champion to increase his speed a notch on each of the last eight laps, so what had been a 52.20km average after 202 laps became 52.27km by the time the bell was rung at the end of the 209th lap (52.25km), with a few seconds still left to complete the hour. The final distance of 52.27062km was computed after he completed lap 210, as fans banged on the trackside fence, with the rest erupting in a wall of sound; a commissaire fired two shots of his starter's pistol to officially end the ride. "The crowd was so loud," reported Boardman, "that I didn't even hear the gun go off."

The pain was finally over for the pale-faced rider from Hoylake, near Liverpool, in northwest England. He took a long time to wind down, before punching the air three times in triumph, and then riding to the top of the track to slap hands with fans leaning over the fence. After a second loop, followed by a mob of photographers, TV cameras, microphones, reporters and fans, the rider grabbed a helper's hand, and stopped where he had started just one hour earlier — an hour that may change the course of cycling as much as the one ridden by Moser a decade before in Mexico City.

*At age 21, Texan Lance Armstrong became the third youngest rider in history to win the world professional road race title. It happened on a rainy day in Oslo, August 29, 1993.*

# Armstrong takes world's by storm

## BY RUPERT GUINNESS

With arms outstretched in celebration, eyes burning with joy, and a grin as wide as the chasm he has crossed in one year as a professional cyclist, Texan Lance Armstrong claimed his destined glory by winning the 1993 world professional road race championship, on August 29.

The feeling that Armstrong was on the verge of a truly major victory has been present since the very first day he donned the Motorola trade team jersey — after the 1992 Barcelona Olympics. And as each month has passed since then, Armstrong has not just taken consistent steps toward achieving that stardom, but rather, has *marched* his way up the ladder of success.

Yet, as admirable as his earlier successes have been — including his 1993 Tour de France stage win and CoreStates USPRO Championship victory — nothing can surpass his stunning solo success in the 257.6km world championship race at Oslo, in which he finished 19 seconds clear of a 10-man chase group, led by Spanish Tour de France champion Miguel Indurain and Germany's Olaf Ludwig. The American's win was impressive for the calculating, daring and courageous manner in which he won — as well as for the historic significance it immediately took on.

For Armstrong, the poignant moment was his chance to share the victory with his mother, Linda Walling, who flew to Europe to be with him. The feelings between mother and son couldn't be clearer than at his post-race press conference. "I owe everything to her," he said, in a voice strong with emotion. And if anyone really needed more proof, there was the fact that when called upon for a private audience with King Harald and Queen Sonja of Norway before meeting the press, Armstrong shed all intimidation of royal protocol and said he would go only if his mother could, too.

For cycling aficionados, the Texan's victory was meaningful in that it came 10 years after American Greg LeMond won the first of his two world professional crowns, at Altenrhein, Switzerland, at the age of 22. Furthermore, being only 21 years old, Armstrong became the third-youngest world pro road champion — after Belgium's Karel Kaers (1934), who was 20, and Jean-Pierre Monseré (1970), 21.

The pro road championship was raced in abominable conditions. Cold sheets of rain fell all day, and many abandoned because of the shivers. Still others were brought to a halt when the 18.4km circuit became dangerously slippery — awash with rain and wet paint, washed from the signs painted on the road by fans. Crashes were plentiful and in the end, only 66 riders from 171 starters finished.

Armstrong himself crashed twice — on lap one, and then again mid-way through the 14-lap race, which lasted six hours and 17 minutes. "Guys were crashing all around me," the champion noted. This observation was shared by all, including Indurain, the silver medalist who beat Ludwig, Johan Museeuw and Maurizio Fondriest in the sprint.

Armstrong came into the race rated an "outsider" for victory — although he, his teammates and allies had stronger convictions than that. After the previous Sunday's Championship of Zürich, he had traveled to Oslo with his mother to prepare for the event; and as each day edged nearer to the race, it seemed he grew more and more into the role of the U.S. team's undisputed leader.

The U.S. team and Motorola riders (eight of whom were riding for other national teams) were equally convinced of Armstrong's chances. They didn't want to leave anything to happenstance. And, as has been the case all year, team director Jim Ochowicz had all his riders on radio link-up to make sure the battle plan was acted out as perfectly as possible.

Most pundits were labeling the course as too easy, simply for the fact that the two climbs were not selective enough ... or so everyone thought, until Armstrong made his winning attack with 10km to go.

Certainly, the dry conditions for the previous day's amateur men's and women's road races heightened such belief. However, Armstrong's words minutes before the gun fired for the start indicated otherwise.

"I'm not so sure the course will be that easy," said the Texan, as he stood in the drizzle alongside the top-billed Italian, World Cup leader and race favorite Fondriest. All around them, the mass of nervous riders, all draped in rain jackets, heightened the tension the two men must have been experiencing.

Hindsight makes you wonder if Armstrong's comment was a threat rather than speculation! But he was quick to clarify it: "I didn't think it was hard enough at first. But really, with the rain, crashes and all the other variables, it was a very hard course."

One of the key factors of Armstrong's success was his calm demeanor throughout the race. He didn't overextend himself and attack at every moment's notice, as has often been the case in past races. Rather, he held onto his resources until the crucial moment.

"In the past, I haven't been like that as much as I should have," he admitted. "But today, I was trying to be patient and control myself. I knew that if it was going to happen (a winning break), it would happen on the last lap."

Racing in the early laps saw the traditional escapes by little-known riders. And the most significant trait of the event up until lap seven was the abundance of spills. For these, there were three key locations on the two descents. The first was at the foot of a steep one-kilometer drop from the summit of the first 4km climb at Ryenberg, after 5.5km, where the route suddenly swept up to the left for a 2km rise to the Ekeberg, where the course reached a plateau.

The second danger point was on a gradual left turn, midway down the 4km-long descent from the top of the second climb, where yellow lane markings were as slippery as ice — no matter how deliberately riders tried to take the turn.

The third and most obvious crash location — whether wet or dry — came with 4km to go, on a very tight dogleg turn, at the foot of the final descent, where hay bales lined the curb in anticipation of some nasty crashes. Among the early victims with Armstrong were Germany's Jens Heppner and Denmark's Jesper Skibby (lap one); German Kai Hundertmark and Frenchman Philippe Louviot (lap two); and Frenchman Jean-François Bernard and 1986 world champion Moreno Argentin of Italy (lap three).

On lap seven — at the front end of the peloton — the 1987 world champion Stephen Roche set the action going with a burst off the front. Riding the last "serious" race of his career, the Irishman charged up from the left of the peloton and went clear. But he wasn't given more than 50 meters' grace before the bunch swept him up. Still, his move certainly sounded a call for the real race to begin, even if it had little effect on the race speed, which had averaged a steady 40 kph — a considerable pace in such foul and conditions.

The attacks became more frequent after Dutchman Erwin Nijboer's solo move provoked a chase by four, and saw the event's first serious assault. The next lap saw Armstrong's teammate Frankie Andreu attack as well. Although the Motorola rider was chased by local hero Dag-Otto Lauritzen — who was also supposedly racing for the last time — his move was effective in shedding driftwood from the back of the pack and leaving the race with a drastically diminished front group.

The first member of the star-studded Italian *squadra* to break away was Tour de France stage winner Fabio Roscioli, who attacked toward the end of lap nine, with almost 100km to go. The Carrera veteran was given a few seconds of grace before the chase began, and he entered the 10th lap with 34 seconds on the peloton. One of the key discards here — however temporarily — was Ludwig. At 1:03 to Roscioli, he was in the throes of being helped back onto the peloton by teammate Gerd Audhem.

Roscioli was finally caught on the climb to Ryenkrysset, after a series of chases by Bruno Cornillet of France, Spain's Marino Alonso, and then Lauritzen. By the top of the climb, the peloton was once more all together. But a crash involving Mexican Raúl Alcalá on this lap's final descent ended any hope of a respite. In his spill with seven others, Alcalá was thrown over a road barrier and onto the parallel tramlines. He was not seriously injured, but his dazed look as he was helped back up was all one needed to realize that the Mexican's championship hopes were over.

Meanwhile, the crash also saw the peloton split in two, with its front group numbering 14 riders — none of whom were Armstrong's teammates. In it were Frenchmen Richard Virenque, Charly Mottet and Jacky Durand; Italy's Claudio Chiappucci, Marco Giovannetti and Roscioli; Switzerland's Heinz Imboden and Rolf Järmann; Germany's Christian Henn; Australia's Scott Sunderland; Dutchman Adri Van der Poel; Moldavia's Andreï Tchmil; and Belgium's Museeuw.

The peloton, including Armstrong, was at 30 seconds by the end of the lap. And up front leading the chase were Spain's Pedro Delgado and Javier Mauleon — Banesto teammates of Indurain. By the start of the first climb on lap 11 — and with the average speed up to 41.5 kph — the lead group was back with the peloton.

It was the 12th of the 14 laps that saw the race really take shape, though. Chiappucci let loose with an acceleration, which Danish Tour de France star Bjarne Riis snapped up and used to launch himself onto a brave solo attack. The Dane, riding with the confidence he showed in his fifth-place Tour performance, powered away and took a 22-second lead by the lap's end. However, with two laps (37km) still to go, it was clearly a premature move.

Riis's break — and the ensuing chase that saw the lap speed climb to 42.5 kph — took its toll on the peloton, too. Among the abandonees was Roche, who had done all he could to make a fight of his farewell, yet clearly lacked the spark needed to finish.

Riis was wound in on the first climb of the 13th lap by three others — Chiappucci, Frenchman Gérard Rué and Dutchman Frans Maassen. And then, following a solo chase, Indurain joined them on the second climb. And it was here that Armstrong first took the offensive, as he followed Indurain's move. Suddenly, the race had five leaders, although they would be caught shortly before the end of the lap.

Meanwhile, numerous aspiring contenders were throwing in the towel. Defending champion Gianni Bugno of Italy stopped at the pit area one lap earlier, as did Switzerland's Alex Zülle and France's Mottet. And after this 13th lap, they were joined on the sidelines by Dutchman Erik Breukink, Colombia's Alvaro Mejia and Australia's Sunderland.

Up front, Lauritzen was the force in the leading five's arrest. He threw everything into his descent, and when he moved up alongside the five leaders, he just motored past. Only Maassen had the initiative to jump on his wheel, and this pair rode past the finish line — where the clanging bell denoted one lap to go — with a four-second lead. But the chorus of cheers greeting them was like thunder, as Norwegian fans sensed a possible home victor in Lauritzen. And with the Norwegian monarchs watching, the event looked on the verge of having a true fairy-tale ending....

Lauritzen and Maassen could have done without Ludwig's chase, though. Having done so well in chasing back to the peloton earlier, the German now charged like a mad-man through the finishing area — in desperation to reel in the two leaders before the main climb. The 1988 Olympic champion did make it ... and the immediate effect was to cancel Maassen's commitment to ride hard.

Lauritzen now had no choice but to attack again on the Ryenberg. The peloton was closing in, and when he did go, Ludwig and Maassen didn't oppose his attack. But behind them, Armstrong was getting very antsy. He feared Lauritzen's gap and sensed the danger of the peloton becoming reluctant to chase. So he set off on his own.

"The peloton was racing negatively. I knew that I had to go then," recounted Armstrong, who still found the cunning Maassen on his wheel. The pair caught Lauritzen near the top and then plummeted in full flight down the Ryenberg's descent to the foot of the Ekeberg, where the American's launch pad to success was waiting.

"I just gave it all I had then, on that last climb. When I got with them, they were not organized. At first, I didn't want to go too fast ... but once I got the gap, that was it," said Armstrong, who fled unchallenged and by the top was 10 seconds clear.

By the end of the long and final descent, with four kilometers still to go, the gap had grown to 20 seconds. And the peloton, still making its descent with total caution, was now thinking only of silver and bronze ... as Armstrong realized that the gold was his.

"I turned around to see if the peloton was there," he recalled. "But I couldn't see them, and with three kilometers to go, I knew I had won." So, too, did everyone else who saw Armstrong ride so confidently down the finishing straight. His flurry of victory salutes, the bowing of his head and blowing of kisses to the crowd began with 700 meters to go!

Some may see this as a sign of arrogance. But to those who were there it was a champion's true way of sharing the elation of a world championship win with as many people as possible, and most of all with his mother, Linda.

**1993 WORLD PROFESSIONAL ROAD CHAMPIONSHIP, Oslo, Norway. August 29.**
1. Lance Armstrong (USA), 257.6km in 6:17:10 (40.979 kph); 2. Miguel Indurain (Sp), at 0:19; 3. Olaf Ludwig (G); 4. Johan Museeuw (B); 5. Maurizio Fondriest (I); 6. Andreï Tchmil (Mld); 7. Dag-Otto Lauritzen (N); 8. Gérard Rué (F); 9. Bjarne Riis (Dk); 10. Frans Maassen (Nl); 11. Marco Giovannetti (I), all s.t.; 12. Claudio Chiappucci (I), at 0:24; 13. Andreas Kappes (G), at 1:17; 14. Adri Van der Poel (Nl), s.t.; 15. Laurent Jalabert (F), at 1:47.

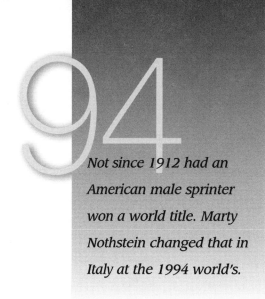

*Not since 1912 had an American male sprinter won a world title. Marty Nothstein changed that in Italy at the 1994 world's.*

# Nothstein the toast of Palermo

**BY RUPERT GUINNESS**

In the history of track cycling, the Paolo Borsellino Velodrome in Palermo, Sicily, will be remembered as the site of a long-awaited emergence by the United States as a world power. After the 11 men's and women's events were fought out August 14-19, the U.S. placed third on the overall medal tally — after winning two gold medals, two silvers and a bronze.

Sprinter Marty Nothstein was the master of the meet, taking his two golds in the men's sprint and the keirin — after overcoming the German colossus Michael Hübner in both events. The other Americans to medal were a brilliant Erin Hartwell, who was second in the kilometer time trial; Dirk Copeland, Mariano Friedick, Adam Laurent and Carl Sundquist, who earned silver medals in the team pursuit; and perennial bronze medalist Janie Eickhoff, in the women's pursuit.

No records were set on the bumpy concrete of the outdoor 400-meter oval, but there was plenty of excitement, especially in the men's sprint....

Not only did Nothstein and fellow finalist Australia's Darryn Hill put an end to Germany's modern domination of the sprint — as Hübner and Jens Fiedler were relegated to the race-off for third and fourth places — but Nothstein's win also marked the first world's gold-medal win by an American sprinter in 82 years. In 1912, American Frank Kramer won the professional title and compatriot Donald McDougall the amateur crown, at the Newark, New Jersey, velodrome.

The 23-year-old Nothstein easily took out the final from the 20-year-old Hill, winning the first two of three scheduled race-offs, in last-200-meter times of 10.887 and 10.965 seconds. For Nothstein, it was a formidable feat, for he was still recovering from a broken foot, which led him to arrive at Sicily with limited ambitions of doing better than top six. "My foot is really hurting ... even now," he said after the final.

Because of a knee injury, Australian Gary Neiwand — the 1993 world champion — abandoned his hopes of defending his title on the eve of the qualifying round. The Victorian's ailment was a split bursa in the right knee, which he sustained at the team's training camp at Colorado Springs in July.

The fastest qualifier from the 200-meter, flying-start time trials was Hill in 10.321 seconds, followed by Canadian Curt Harnett, 10.330, and Italian Roberto Chiappa, 10.359. Fiedler was fourth in 10.402, while Nothstein was only seventh fastest in 10.472, followed by Hübner, 10.586.

Nothstein's run to the semi-finals saw him defeat Slovakia's Jaroslav Jerabek in round one, Italian Federico Paris in round two, Russia's Igor Shelinskyi in the eighth-finals, and Chiappa in the quarter-finals. As for Hill, his final berth included wins against Slovakia's Martin Hrbacek and then Jerabek, Latvian Viesturs Berzins and, finally, Paris.

The series' highlight really came in the semi-finals, in which Nothstein came up against Hübner, and Hill battled Fiedler. Fiedler took Hill to three matches: The German won the first in 10.965, but lost the second and third in respective times of 11.173 and 11.006.

Then the drama came in Nothstein's battle against Hübner, who also took the American challenger to three races. Hübner won the first in 11.117. Then Nothstein kept his flame alive by winning the second in 10.931. And in the third, he crossed the line first in 11.092 — but was amazingly relegated to second place, for allegedly blocking Hübner's path in the final turn.

The Americans quickly appealed the seemingly unjust relegation. And after 15 minutes, the news came through that they won! After a spate of irregularities by the UCI race jury during the previous days, the success of an appeal caught many by surprise — even though consensus agreed with Nothstein's plea of innocence.

In many ways, judging by Nothstein's efficient and almost surgical elimination of Hill in the final, the semi-final was indeed the American's biggest hurdle of the series.

"In the final also, Darryn made several mistakes," Nothstein later recounted. "There is no love lost between us, so when we go out there we go at it. This time, I took advantage of his errors and won."

*Mountain biking entered a new era in August 1995, when the first off-road version of the Tour de France — the Tour VTT — was won by Dutchman Bart Brentjens.*

# Bart's breakthrough

BY **JULIA INGERSOLL**

Launched into the great unknown, the brand-new realm of multi-day, point-to-point mountain-bike racing at the highest level, the 120 starters of the first-ever Tour de France VTT demonstrated just how tough the European fat-tire peloton is. This off-road tour proved to be a savage echo of the "big Tour," as the famous road version of the French race is called in the off-road camp. And on the eve of the final time trial, after 430km in eight days of racing, 103 racers arrived in La Bourboule to contest the finale on August 30 — to the astonishment of the organizers, who had said at the beginning of the Tour that they would be happy if 35 riders made it to the end.

No one quite knew what to expect. From the scorchingly fast opening prologue, in which steep, slippery climbing and treacherously technical downhills were attacked as if this were to be a one-day race, it was evident that the riders had arrived in superb condition. And by the finish of this nine-day-long tour, one thing had been discovered without a doubt: This was certainly among the most hotly contested mountain-bike races ever held.

Despite the quantity and difficulty of the obstacles faced — long distances, repeated World Cup-level efforts, lack of recuperation time due to liaison stages over challenging, off-road terrain, and bivouac (camping) in group tents at night — the average race speed equaled the toughest rounds of the Grundig World Cup. Furthermore, the *maillot Volvic* — the blue-and-gold jersey of the overall race leader sponsored by Volvic mineral water — changed hands four times, with no rider able to retain the lead for more than two stages.

Crashes, unfortunately, played a major role in the men's race, with the first two race leaders — Peter Van den Abeele of Belgium and Jean-Christophe Savignoni of France —

both being forced to abandon after untimely spills. In the end, last year's Grundig World Cup winner Bart Brentjens (American Eagle) of the Netherlands came through to win by just 51 seconds over one of the many French sensations, Christophe Dupouey of the Sunn-Chipie team. In third, was Dupouey's 19-year-old teammate, Miguel Martinez, the reigning world junior champion. The women's classification was taken by German upstart, Hedda Zu Putlitz, the one female member of the successful American Eagle formation.

At the Tour's closing dinner, winner Brentjens was given an 84-pound wheel of cheese in addition to the crystal cup presented by Tour de France director Jean-Marie Leblanc ... *and* his prize for the overall win of 80,000 French francs — about $16,000.

This was the richest mountain-bike race ever held, with the total Tour VTT prize list equal to about $200,000 — paid out in stage prizes, overall classification, team classification; plus the women's stage and overall prizes, and the special Best Young Rider competition taken by Martinez.

A cool, humid morning greeted riders for the Tour VTT prologue, held on the mist-shrouded flanks of Métabief's Mont d'Or ski station. Ever since the popular success of the muddy 1993 world's, this resort has been the mountain-bike capital of France. And the fiery prologue time trial initiating this first off-road Tour gave the waiting crowd a mighty dose of action. For while the course was only 4.5km, it included a substantial amount of steep climbing, two technical descents, and a fast finish. Although such a short, super-intense effort was unlikely to have major consequences on the overall results, the pace was electric, setting the tone for the days to come.

It was former Belgian national cyclo-cross champion Van den Abeele of the Espace Card team who turned the fastest time in 12:24, beating by only one second the newly crowned European champion, Savignoni of LaPierre-Kona. Savignoni's performance surprised all, including himself. "I'm not a short-race specialist at all," said the French rider, who had traveled for 15 hours to the start of the Tour VTT from the Czech Republic, where he won the European title in a grueling race only two days before. "For me, 12 minutes feels as hard as three hours! But that unfortunate little second won't matter a few days from now."

Among the women, it was Savignoni's LaPierre-Kona teammate, French national champion Nathalie Fiat, who won in 16:15 — 10 seconds faster than her compatriot Sophie Eglin-Hosotte of Gitane.

Exhilarated by this tonic preamble to the most important mountain-bike stage race held to date, Savignoni was lucid about the adventure ahead: "We're heading into the unknown," explained the Frenchman.

The first point-to-point stage, from Métabief to Les Rousses, was anxiously awaited by all, not only because of its grueling length, but even more due to the lingering mystery as to what the *true* character of this stage race would be. "It'll be more clear after today," British hope Barrie Clarke mused before the start on a dark, cloudy morning. "We just can't be sure what the courses will be like ... bunch racing or real mountain biking."

But from the very start of this arduous stage — across the forested crest of the Jura mountains, made wet and slippery by the overnight rains — it was obvious that this was to be a hard-core mountain biking contest; and the intensity of the pace and competition were astonishing, considering that there were seven demanding stages still to come.

Coming out on top in this confrontation was Van den Abeele. The Espace Card rider pulled off his second win in as many days in a sprint finish, at the top of a steep one-kilometer grind. On his heels — or wheels — were France's 19-year-old phenom, Martinez, and Brentjens.

Mud-coated and pale from the strain of racing for each precious second, all the way to the line, the riders streamed in, now well aware of just how demanding this stage race would be. "It was unbelievably hard," Clarke said, just after crossing the line in 14th place, 2:40 behind the leaders, "like a proper cross-country."

Almost entirely off-road, the course passed through villages on short paved stretches that hardly offered a respite from the technically demanding terrain — the asphalt was slick as ice and saw many crashes. The notable casualty of the day was the unfortunate Van der Poel, who crashed on his face into an unseen gully on a high-speed descent, and was forced to abandon due to his injuries.

Racing the same challenging distance as the men — as they would throughout the Tour VTT — the women's race was surprisingly close. In a duel to the finish, Zu Putlitz beat Eglin-Hosotte by 17 seconds, after attacking on the final, cruelly steep climb. After leading with Eglin-Hosotte early in the race, Nike's Dany Bonnoront was third, 1:19 down, while race leader Fiat faltered in the final kilometers, dropping back 3:38 and forfeiting the yellow-and-white Volvic leader's jersey of the women's competition to Eglin-Hosotte.

After awakening in pre-dawn darkness to rain pelting the tents of the first night's bivouac, the riders were soaked during the morning's 32km liaison that was diverted onto paved roads to avoid the mud. It was an ominous beginning to what would be the toughest day of the Tour. The profile of the 57km stage from Nantua to Hauteville-Lompnes promised a brutal test, starting with the nearly 3000-foot climb up massive limestone cliffs in the first 7km of the race. Lining up beside a lake in the mountain town of Nantua, the riders could contemplate the rocky crest looming menacingly above them in the dripping, cloud-shrouded forests.

Undaunted, LaPierre's Savignoni rode like a man possessed, stunning the field by simply riding away in total domination from the very first hill, as he headed toward a brilliant solo victory — over four minutes ahead of his nearest challenger.

"It was just unbelievable," Clarke, who finished fifth, later reflected. "Savignoni rode away 400 feet into the race. When we got to the top, he had two minutes and the bunch was going well — we were at Grundig pace, which means all out.... It's tough recovering from these long days — especially sleeping in a tent. I don't think many people got much sleep last night."

When the European champion looked back, 5km after topping that formidable climb, he saw that Sunn-Chipie's Dupouey was not far behind and waited for the lean 126-pound climber, in order not to ride alone. Dupouey — a top amateur road racer who only began mountain-bike racing in March — seems to be on the fast track to the top of the mountain-bike ranks.

The two Frenchmen together increased their lead over the nearest chase group, which included Dutch Giant rider Marcel Arntz, Raleigh's Clarke, Brentjens, Belgians Van den Abeele and Arne Daelmans, Sunn-Chipie's Martinez, and Optex-Hawk's Jan Wiejak.

The field was shattering into mud-coated clots of riders battling the epic course that traversed bogs of shin-deep mud, ultra-slick forest single tracks, and uncountable steep climbs.

Just before the second feed zone, with 25km left to the finish, Savignoni left Dupouey behind, looking nearly as fresh as when he started more than two hours earlier. Dupouey commented at the finish: "Savignoni so impressed me, it felt like following a motorcycle. Even in World Cups, I've never been dropped, left behind like that."

When the wiry Martinez learned that his Sunn-Chipie teammate had been dropped, he started an amazing surge through the chasers and eventually finished second, 4:24 behind the superb Savignoni, and 31 seconds ahead of Dupouey, who hung on for third.

With race leader Van den Abeele finishing seventh, more than 10 minutes down after a puncture, Savignoni took over the Volvic leader's jersey.

The women's race became a long-distance duel between overall leader Eglin-Hosotte and her German rival Zu Putlitz, on loan for the Tour VTT to American Eagle, from her full-time sponsor Schwalbe. The pair battled each other for over three-and-a-half hours, until the French rider finally escaped with two male members of her Gitane team, in a tricky wooded section two kilometers from the finish. Arriving 1:29 ahead of a fading Zu Putlitz, Hosotte-Eglin retained the leader's jersey, to the delight of the crowd in Hauteville.

After two days of rain, it was decided that it was too soggy to unfold the 1300 square meters of tents to bivouac in a lonely cow pasture, and the teams were berthed instead on cots in elementary school classrooms.

The 6 a.m. wake-up call came painfully early for the riders, still exhausted from the late-finishing stage two; and before beginning the 31km morning liaison stage from Le Bois d'Oingt to Marchampt, there was a 100km car transfer. But clear dawn skies lifted morale, and spirits were high as the more fortunate teams started off at intervals.

The route immediately began climbing steeply, however, to the wild and forested crest of low mountains that traverse the region. Indeed, the very hilly, technical route proved rather merciless for a liaison stage, and the leading riders were informed that they were well off the pace to make the time limit at the finish. This caused a mass panic and subsequent high pace down the rugged descents of the Beaujolais hills, into the manicured vineyards surrounding the idyllic village of Marchampt-en-Beaujolais.

With no time after the lengthy liaison stage to preview the demanding course, there were many crashes in the afternoon time trial, which was held on a challenging, hilly 17km course through the famous vineyards. And one disaster or another befell nearly all of the favorites.

Beginning with a steep 5km climb that passed through the courtyard of an 11th-century château, the course also featured fast, twisting descents, a water crossing, and a rough, undulating stretch before the sharp climb to the finish in the village square. For such a comparatively short stage, the race against the clock had a heavy impact on the overall standings: The seemingly untouchable race leader, Savignoni, took a disastrous fall and gashed open his left knee, after clocking the second-fastest intermediate time (behind Martinez) at the top of the course's main climb, 5km into the race. According to his coach, Savignoni crashed while reaching for his water bottle. Losing 40 seconds, the race leader resumed his torrid pace, only to puncture a few kilometers later, at the very spot where Martinez was stopped, changing his own flat.

Second on G.C., the small Sunn-Chipie rider had sped past his minute-man Savignoni, as the latter got up from his painful crash. The two rivals restarted together, with Martinez sprinting into the steeply uphill finish ahead of his wounded countryman.... But moments before the ill-fated duo, a bullet-fast Dupouey had arrived, wearing a fabulous grin, and beating the best previous time — 39:50, clocked by Brentjens — by 1:20. Dupouey's smooth ride moved him into second place overall, ahead of Brentjens and teammate Martinez.

Although the bloodied Savignoni retained the leader's jersey by 2:48, and vowed to be back the next day, his knee was open to the bone and required 10 sutures, forcing the race leader to abandon.

Dupouey — winner of the day and race leader by default — later reported that he, too, crashed twice, but was unhurt. Another unlucky rider was Van den Abeele, who punctured twice in the time trial, dropping to seventh overall and losing three more minutes. On his way to the showers, the talented Espace Card rider quipped, "I put new tires on for tomorrow, and tomorrow, I'm gonna have revenge!"

Starting before the men, the women racers had barely two hours to rest between the taxing, two-hour-long liaison stage and the start of the time trial. Eglin-Hosotte was again fastest with 50:25, her smooth descending style outpacing Zu Putlitz by 37 seconds. In third was French champion Fiat, in 51:20l.

After double-flatting in the time-trial, Van den Abeele got the revenge he sought: He claimed his third stage win in a dangerous 50-kph sprint that ended in the town of Noiretable, in the center of France.

A rare sunny day and a relatively short, 24km course sparked a spirited race, animated by French university champion Thomas Dietsch, 20, of the Gitane team. The 6-foot 3-inch blond pulled at the front for almost the entire race, and *still* finished third in the sprint, just behind race leader Dupouey. "Dietsch gave us a hell of a race," the Sunn-Chipie leader proclaimed, relieved to have defended the jersey successfully.

When Zu Putlitz came flying along a farm track early in the race, it took a second look to see that this was indeed the head of the women's race — the German rider looked so smooth and powerful. Meanwhile, Eglin-Hosotte, race leader and winner of the last two stages, was having a nightmarish day. After 13km, she had already lost two minutes to her rival, who took over the Volvic leader's jersey at the finish.

A dominant Brentjens claimed his first stage win of the Tour VTT in the rapid fifth stage that began in pine forests, high atop the Col de la Loge. And yet, he was unable to gain a single second's advance on determined race leader Dupouey, who shadowed him down the perilously fast 10km descent to the finish at Ambert.

Although there were several short climbs early on, and a longer, challenging ascent about 30km into the race, the course had a notorious drop to the finish, almost 2000 vertical feet lower than the start, which was reached in the morning's steeply climbing liaison stage.

After traversing an extremely rocky ridge that forced many riders to dismount and run, a group of 14 had formed at the head of the race. Notably missing from the lead group was Clarke, who had punctured. Both the group dynamics and the dry course contributed to dangerously fast descending, especially considering that no one had seen the course before. "We were smashing through branches — it's amazing we survived. I'm all covered with cuts and scratches," Dupouey said.

On the climb preceding the long, rocky drop to the line, Brentjens began attacking Dupouey on steep sections, which splintered the group, but the Sunn-Chipie rider responded each time.

Behind the two leaders, the riders spread out on the taxing descent, which claimed at least one notable victim: Van den Abeele broke his shoulder just 6km from the finish. He finished the stage while holding his arm in great pain, and he was then forced to abandon.

Downhill specialist Fiat made a brief appearance at the head of the women's race, before flatting twice on the rocky descents ... and allowing the super-consistent Zu Putlitz to claim yet another stage win, consolidating her overall lead.

After a much-needed rest day spent in bivouac, beside the town of Ambert, the last cross-country stage was awaited with apprehension by those in contention for the overall title. With only the final time trial remaining, the leaders realized that the prestigious first Tour VTT could easily be decided on this day. And so, despite its grueling 63km length, the race averaged an amazing 27.52 kph, and turned out to be the fastest and most turbulent of the Tour.

Dariusz Gil of the Polish Optex-Hawk team emerged the powerful — and lucky — winner, as the strongest man who escaped misfortune; while the rivalry between an unlucky Dupouey and new leader Brentjens — second in the stage — brought them closer than ever. Only 59 seconds now separated the two, and the Volvic jersey passed from the Frenchman's slight shoulders to those of the on-form American Eagle rider, after a frenetic battle fraught with unexpected twists.

The strategy for race leader Dupouey — surrounded by his powerful Sunn-Chipie team that also counted the little Martinez in third place overall — seemed simple enough: follow Brentjens, who, at just 1:29 behind, was the Frenchman's only true threat for the overall crown. Almost from the start, however, the well-organized Sunn-Chipie team was plagued by incidents: Super-domestique Sanders crashed and flatted, and Martinez felt ill with stomach problems ... leaving Dupouey — who himself crashed and had his chain tie in knots — all alone to chase the flying Brentjens, who had attacked when the race leader crashed. "I got a handlebar stuck in my thigh," lamented the French rider after the finish.

Brentjens looked indomitable as he led for most of the race with Dutch compatriot Arntz. As the gap stretched to five minutes, the race looked to be over for the beleaguered Dupouey, until Brentjens's luck suddenly ran out and he flatted — losing three minutes in repairs — while Arntz powered briefly on ahead, before becoming a puncture victim himself.

Passing through the sparsely populated forests of the Haute-Loire region and on to the peculiar volcanic mounds of the Puy-de-Dome, the dry course had many sharp, short climbs, and the high-speed, rocky descents were the scene of scores of punctures.

"I was taking a lot of risk," Brentjens later reported. "I hope my lead is enough. But that's mountain biking: You can flat anytime, there's no telling what might happen to you."

While the leaders were halted, the 22-year-old Gil, who had been chasing over two minutes back with MBK's Olaf Candau, surged powerfully over the remaining 15km to win the stage.

Behind Gil, the gaunt Dupouey was ably cutting his losses in a desperate attempt to keep the Volvic jersey. Working alone as he sped through small groups of riders unwilling to aid him, Dupouey fairly flew up the steep final climb to the hilltop village of Nonette, taking back a full minute from Brentjens on the way up.

Long legs churning up the steep, grassy goat track leading to the finish in the village square at Nonette, women's leader Zu Putlitz took yet another stage win, to put a lock on the overall title. The veteran Bonnoront took second on the stage, three minutes back, while — after a disastrous stage, Eglin-Hosotte conceded more than 11 minutes and any hope she had of displacing the German from final victory.

It seemed incredible that after seven days and 430km of mountain-bike racing, it would come down to the final 9km time trial to decide the winner of the first Tour VTT. Incredible, but true. For while Brentjens held the advantage with a slim 59-second lead over Dupouey, the Dutch rider admitted that "anything can happen. It's an interesting time trial with a steep and dangerous downhill. We will see it in this afternoon's liaison stage, and I'll practice."

Over the previous two days, the American Eagle leader had shown increasingly good form and confidence, and the ball was certainly in his court going into the final test. It would be up to the challenger Dupouey to overcome a minute's deficit. "If this were a road race, it would be over," Dupouey said on the eve of the time trial. "But here, the whole thing can still be played out. If I had problems today, why not him tomorrow?" And considering the course, which climbed over 1000 feet in the first 7km, before dropping down 2km of hyper-technical, steep descent through the trees, there was a chance the determined Dupouey could, as he put it, "pull off a LeMond-style win."

It was raining lightly on the morning of the time trial in La Bourboule, making the course's infamous descent even more dangerous and slick than usual. Beginning in reverse order of G.C., the anxious leaders had to wait all morning for their duel. Meanwhile, the crowds were rapt watching the dramatic descending that included drop-offs, slick stair-steps, and cruelly glistening paving rocks that had many top contenders dismounting to run.

"It's do-able," Dupouey believed all the more after his morning preview of the treacherously slimy course. Later, after the race, he would recount, "But at the midpoint, when I learned I'd only gained 10 seconds on the climb, I knew all was lost." Far from cracking under pressure, however, the slender Sunn-Chipie team leader finished in 28:26, the second-best time.

For his part, Brentjens said the blue-and-gold Volvic skinsuit of race leader made him feel stronger than usual. "The downhill was dangerous," he recounted. "When I heard I was equal with Dupouey, I took no chances." Brentjens placed fourth in the stage with 28:36, and his overall win was secured.

But no one looked happier at the finish of this first Tour VTT than Martinez: Third overall and the darling of French mountain biking, he earned a victory in this final time trial with 28:02, cementing his position as a rising star in the senior ranks at only 19 years old.

Fiat was the day's fastest woman, acing the steep climb and descent in 35:55 — 2:16 faster than the runner-up, America's Leah Garcia, who was followed by Louise Robinson of the English Raleigh team. After clocking the fastest time on the climb, overall leader Zu Putlitz rode a conservative descent, relieved to have such a comfortable lead over her nearest rival, Eglin-Hosotte.

The shy Brentjens was quietly thrilled to have won, and noted that "it wasn't as hard as I thought it would be. The pace was nearly World Cup rate each day, but I'm in a good shape and recovered well each day. The first three days in the rain and mud were very hard on us, but when the weather's good and the stages not too long, we could go more than eight days, I think."

TECHNICAL and TRAINING

*By 1977, Eddy Merckx was nearing the end of his phenomenal career ... but he was still an amazing athlete.*

# The 'phenomenon of the century'

## BY WOLFGANG GRÖNEN

Dr. Josef Assenmacher knows Eddy Merckx inside and out. He is the great rider's personal physician, in addition to his duties with the Institute for Cardiovascular Research of the German Sports University at Cologne. Assenmacher, 55, has worked with world-class athletes in many sports, having served as an Olympic physician in 1964, 1968 and 1972. He has been the physician for German world championship teams since 1956. His cycling patients include such riders as Rik Van Steenbergen and Patrick Sercu. In this interview for *VeloNews*, Assenmacher tells the inside story of Merckx's physical make-up.

**VeloNews** How long has Eddy Merckx been your patient?

**Josef Assenmacher** For several years now — I acted as Merckx's personal physician during the 1974 Tour de France and Giro d'Italia, and the Tour de France and Tour de Suisse in 1975 and 1976.

**VeloNews** How would you compare Merckx with athletes in other sports?

**Josef Assenmacher** I consider Merckx the greatest athletic phenomenon of the 20th century. I don't believe there's an athlete alive with whom he could be compared.

**VeloNews** What's your opinion of Merckx?

**Josef Assenmacher** Merckx is an exceptional character, intelligent and eager to learn. As an athlete, he has an inflexible will to win, and all the ambition he needs. He's also a man of faith — a religious man of unusual modesty.

**VeloNews** Merckx rode a number of "world 30-minute ergometer records" under your supervision at the Institute of Cardiovascular Research, culminating in a ride of 450 watts. World-class athletes from other sports have yet to score much above 400 watts. How can we put Merckx's unusual ability in a familiar perspective?

**Josef Assenmacher** A 450-watt ergometer performance corresponds to an all-out effort on a second-category climb in the Tour de France, for 30 minutes without stopping. The ergometer which Merckx rode doesn't register higher than 450 — I'm convinced he could do better if we had the equipment to record higher performances.

**VeloNews** It's common knowledge that Merckx has unusual lung capacity and heart volume. Does this account for his performance capacity?

**Josef Assenmacher** Not entirely. These factors are not decisive. His lung capacity is less than Fausto Coppi's, and though Merckx's heart volume is 1500cc, the greatest heart volume measured to date was Van Steenbergen's at 1700cc. World professional road champion Rudi Altig has a heart volume of 1200cc.

**VeloNews** What is the physiological explanation for the phenomenon of Eddy Merckx?

**Josef Assenmacher** To begin with, I know of no athlete besides Merckx who trains and prepares for competition with such complete earnestness and consistency. His cardiopulmonary (heart-lung) system is optimal, too. But the "miracle of performance capacity" that is Eddy Merckx can be surmised from his body's metabolic activity. Just after his 450-watt performance, Merckx had a lactase (lactic acid) reading of 4.0. This means he could not yet have reached the upper limit of his maximal performance capacity. After a short break, he could have continued — he was still to a large extent in the aerobic state.

**VeloNews** What are some typical lactase values for rowers and track-and-field athletes, for example, after a 400-watt performance?

**Josef Assenmacher** Most other athletes finish the test with lactase values around 20.0, which means total acidification, total fatigue. Anaerobic metabolism begins at 4.0, and total exhaustion occurs at 20.0.

**VeloNews** What's your main function as Eddy Merckx's personal physician?

**Josef Assenmacher** My main task is to monitor his blood metabolism values and blood mineral levels. But obviously, there's an element of psychological consultation as well.

**VeloNews** Merckx suffered a severe fall on September 9, 1969, while riding behind a Derny pace machine in Blois, France. His pacer died in the crash. There is the feeling that Merckx never completely recovered from this fall, that he is still having physical troubles — constantly varying his riding position during races and so on.

**Josef Assenmacher** You touch on a problem that has finally been resolved. Two years ago Merckx was wanting to end his career because of these difficulties. As a result of the crash, not only his lower spinal vertebrae but the musculature of his upper left thigh were so damaged (atrophied) that he could scarcely sit on the machine at all. I initiated rehabilitative treatment and succeeded in strengthening the muscles in question. By the time of the Tourmalet climb in the 1974 Tour de France, Eddy was in physical condition comparable to his pre-crash state.

*Four years before the heart-rate monitor and Conconi Method revolutionized cycling, VeloNews published a column that discussed the principles of anaerobic-threshold training.*

# Cross anaerobic threshold to find endurance

**BY EDMUND BURKE**

aximal oxygen consumption (Max $VO_2$) is one of the values found during an all-out test of cardiovascular fitness. Testing is done on a bicycle ergometer, normally beginning at a low level of work and increasing in regular increments until the cyclist can pedal no more.

There has been much discussion about the worth of Max $VO_2$ test results. It has been found that highly trained cyclists have levels between 70 and 80 milliliters per kilogram per minute. (Note that oxygen consumption, measured in liters per minute, is converted to milliliters and divided by body weight in kilograms to standardize the value for body size.) Lesser trained cyclists usually have values of 50 to 60 ml/kg/min. Now the questions: Can Max $VO_2$ values tell us which persons can ride faster or longer than others? Can one definitely say that a cyclist with a Max $VO_2$ of 60 is more highly trained than one with 50 ml/kg/min? These and similar questions must be approached with great care.

It would seem that cyclist A with a large Max $VO_2$ should be able to maintain a faster pace than cyclist B, who has a smaller Max $VO_2$. If cyclist B tries to keep up with cyclist A, he will probably have to supply part of his energy by anaerobic means, which will lead to the build-up of debilitating lactic acid. Why is it, then, that some national and world-class cyclists do not have exceptionally high Max VO$_2$ values?

The answer lies at least in part with the anaerobic-threshold concept. This term refers to the work-load intensity during progressive steady-state riding at which lactic acid in the blood begins to rise significantly above normal resting levels. It is well-known that lactic acid will begin to accumulate even during work that requires less than maximal oxygen uptake. This is based on certain muscle fibers contracting anaerobically, and the body's capacity to remove and resynthesize the lactic acid. Factors include things such as fatigue, terrain changes and increased wind.

Recently, it has become apparent that a person's anaerobic threshold is a critical factor in determining potential to perform prolonged physical exercise. In cycling, two events that require a high anaerobic threshold are individual and team time trials.

Let's look again at the finding that good performance in cycling does not always relate to a high Max VO$_2$. Suppose that three cyclists (A, B and C) have respective Max VO$_2$s of 75, 70 and 70 ml/kg/min. Cyclists B and C have high anaerobic thresholds of only 45. In a long distance race, cyclist A can maintain a pace requiring 60 ml/kg/min and build up very little lactic acid, whereas B and C, in order to keep up, must work anaerobically and therefore produce more lactic acid.

How do you know when your anaerobic threshold has been reached? When you begin riding, ventilation increases rapidly and then climbs linearly with the increase in oxygen consumption (VO$_2$). As the effort goes from moderate to intense, a point is reached where ventilation increases more rapidly than VO$_2$.

The graph shows the ventilatory response of two cyclists to a Max VO$_2$ test on a bicycle ergometer. Cyclist A has a lower Max VO$_2$ and anaerobic threshold than cyclist B. It can be seen that the breakaway point of ventilation is at a higher absolute and relative workload in cyclist B. For example, at a workload requiring 4.5 liters/min of oxygen, cyclist A's ventilation would be approximately 25 liters/min higher than cyclist B's. Over a long period, this extra work to simply breathe would eventually take its toll on cyclist A.

This breakaway point of ventilation is a result of the buffering action of lactic acid in the blood. Excess carbon dioxide is generated from the reaction of sodium bicarbonate and the lactic acid that is beginning to accumulate. In simple terms, you are beginning to hyperventilate in order to blow off the excess carbon dioxide.

The cyclist with a lower anaerobic threshold is also at a disadvantage when it comes to using fats as an energy source. Lactic acid in the blood has been shown to interfere with the mobilization of fatty acid. The use of fat plays an important role in endurance exercise since fats release 9.45 kilocalories of energy per gram compared to 4.1 for carbohydrates. Fat stores equal 50,000-70,000 kilocalories in an athlete compared to 2000 kilocalories of stored carbohydrates (glycogen).

In a road race, the highly trained cyclist who can operate at 80- to 85-percent of his Max VO$_2$ while accumulating very little lactic acid is capable of obtaining a relatively great amount of energy from fat stores. On the other hand, a less well conditioned rider can complete the first 75 percent of the race with some ease, but then experience the "bonk" in the final miles. Remember, when glycogen stores are depleted, muscular effort becomes nearly impossible.

The question facing the coach and rider is what form of training can best improve anaerobic threshold. Most of the current research has focused around the "duration" of the training load and the "intensity."

Before using endurance training to increase anaerobic threshold, you need to know your best time for a 25-mile time trial on a level course. (If, for example, you recorded 60 minutes then your pace is 2:24 per mile.) On days you designate for anaerobic threshold training, ride your miles at approximately 10-15 seconds per mile faster than your TT pace. Initially go 10 miles and work your way up to 15. Don't be in a hurry to increase the mileage — give your body a chance to adapt to the stress. When you reach 15 miles, then quicken the pace another 10-15 seconds and go back to 10 miles, eventually working up to 15 again.

If you are more inclined to interval training or are limited by time, try this: Perform work intervals of two to three minutes at intensities equivalent to 90- to 100-percent of Max VO$_2$, spaced with equal intervals of moderate pedaling. Begin with a comfortable amount and increase as the season progresses.

In summary, your potential to be a successful endurance cyclist appears to be related to your anaerobic threshold. When racing pace exceeds your anaerobic threshold, lactic acid and ventilation increase and there is diminished capacity to use fats after muscle glycogen stores are depleted. Hard-paced endurance training and interval training are excellent methods for increasing anaerobic threshold.

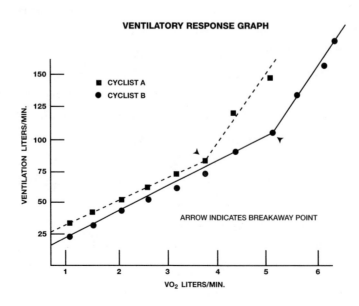

VENTILATORY RESPONSE GRAPH

*The U.S. Cycling Federation's 1985 decision to make hard-shell helmets compulsory in American races caused a huge controversy.*

# Leather hairnets out, hardshells in

**BY GEOFF DRAKE**

On September 21, the board of directors of the U.S. Cycling Federation passed a rule that effectively requires the use of hard-shell helmets in USCF events. The rule, which takes effect January 1, 1986, states that helmets must meet or exceed the Snell Memorial Foundation or American National Standards Institute Z-90.4 standards. Leather hairnet-style helmets have consistently failed such tests.

The movement toward a hard-shell helmet rule gained momentum last year after both ANSI and the Snell Foundation came out with their standards for bicycle helmets. Both organizations had previously been involved with the regulation and testing of motorcycle headgear, but had no bicycle standards.

"That was a large stimulus to the members of the board," USCF executive director Dave Prouty told *VeloNews*. USCF president Phil Voxland cited advancements in helmet design and concerns over the influx of new, inexperienced riders as other reasons the rule passed this year.

"(The helmet issue) has been a matter on the minds of the board of directors for over a year," Voxland said. "It's not a new issue. It was part of an evolution. Les Earnest was working hard with the technical background, and circulated a position paper, and (USCF technical director) Ed Burke wrote articles in *Cycling USA* on the topic.

"There were newer people on the board, too. They could have been more open to new ideas, or they might have been more willing to go against tradition or the visual aspect (of helmets)."

Reportedly, a large majority of the board voted in favor of the rule. "I was surprised it passed as easily as it did," said Prouty.

Prior to 1984, the rule specified the dimensions but not the protective ability of helmets. Last year, the rule was changed to emphasize personal choice in selecting the best helmet possible. "That was not satisfactory to the board of directors," said Voxland.

The rule applies to all USCF-sanctioned races that are not also on the calendar of the Union Cycliste Internationale. This means the regulation does not apply to the Coors Classic or to next year's world championships in Colorado Springs. U.S. riders competing abroad will not be required to wear the helmets.

"It is what the UCI calls a domestic regulation," Voxland said. "It's for national races only." He noted that riders from other countries wishing to race in USCF-sanctioned events must follow the rule.

Riders who start a race without a helmet that displays a Snell or ANSI sticker will be disqualified. The rule also specifies that the stickers may not be removed or placed in another helmet.

What will the reaction to the new rule be from riders? "Everyone expects some agonizing from people who have been in the sport for a long time," said Voxland. "But I think any club, once they took the overall problem into mind, would find they had no choice but to accept the ruling.... The thing I regret the most is that we didn't bring it specifically and at this moment to the attention of the clubs. They have every reason to be surprised."

Said Prouty, "I would suspect — and someone brought this up the other night who is a lot closer to the riders than I am — that a lot of riders would like to wear an ANSI or Snell helmet, but were kind of afraid to, due to peer pressure. So there may not be the reaction that we think. There may be just as many or more people saying, 'Oh, good — now I can race, have fun, and have the best protection available for my head.'

"We are getting ready to go through what several other sports have already done. I was playing baseball as a kid when Little League went from cheap plastic things to foam liners and things like that. Hockey has gone through it — auto racing has always had helmets, but they've had other improvements — and football has seen a lot of improvements in helmets. I think most people when they think about it are going to say, 'Hey, we have people going 30 to 40 mph on the track, 25 to 50 on the road, with no padding, no protection, and people in other sports where the impact is not as great wear a lot more equipment. So the time has come.' At least I hope that is the reaction."

"People are sitting back wondering about the backlash of this whole thing," Burke said. "I'm tired of hearing about accidents. I know of seven people who have been killed or seriously hurt. Could those have been prevented by a helmet? I'm sure it would have in many cases, although it won't stop them all. Within 18 months, I think it will be as accepted as it is in football and hockey."

A possible effect of the new rule may be the development of new helmet designs. "We are hoping that the rule change stimulates even further research," said Prouty. "The technology appears to be available to produce safer helmets that also take into account weight and heat build up."

Both the Snell and ANSI standards were developed independently of the USCF. ANSI deals with many different types of standards — such as thread pitches on bolts — but does not do any testing itself. The Snell Memorial Foundation — so named after an automobile driver who died of head injuries — deals exclusively with helmet testing.

"Snell acts as a watchdog," said Burke. "They test helmets off the shelf. ANSI provides information on what is needed in a general way, then it's up to the individual helmet manufacturer to meet the standard. The Snell standard is tougher."

Burke said he plans to develop a list of helmets that pass one or both of the standards, to be distributed to clubs and district representatives." We hope to keep as up-to-date as possible. But unless there is a law to register helmets, there is no way to find out about every helmet that comes into the country. We will try to have the manufacturers tell us about their helmets, and then somehow alert officials and members."

Voxland and Prouty noted that the use of hardshells may also put the USCF in a more favorable position with insurance carriers.

"The insurance industry — from everything I read — is in its worst depression since 1906," said Prouty. "It's an insurance problem way beyond just helmets and bicycle racing. The liability costs are just getting out of hand.

"Many carriers are leaving the amateur sports scene. Not only cycling, but to my knowledge, 10 or 12 other national governing bodies (of Olympic sports) lost their carriers last year. And that's related to the general depression in the insurance industry.

"If we can make the sport safer — and there is no absolute guarantee that this is going to do that, but logic takes us in that direction — yes, we ought to have an easier time with insurance."

Said Voxland, "At this time there are 12 lawsuits outstanding against the federation. In my recollection, it has never been higher. And several of those involve allegations concerning helmets.

"It wouldn't surprise me if in Europe the same action must be taken. Insurance is a global issue. Delegates and presidents of other federations are faced with the same problem.

"The good news is the application of technology to the design and production of helmets. The downside is the increased risk of injury. The decision was not easy, but it was inevitable."

*After bicycle technology stagnated for two decades, it started to change in the mid-1980s. By June 1989, clip-on aero' bars were the hot new product. Two VeloNews editorials discussed the subject....*

# High technology: innocence lost?

**BY THE EDITORS**

In 1984, Laurent Fignon won the Tour de France on a bike remarkably similar to the machine used by Eddy Merckx to win his first Giro d'Italia 16 years earlier. Both bikes were made from steel, used essentially unchanged Campagnolo components, 73-degree frame angles, 32-spoke wheels, and toe clips and straps. Both weighed about 21 pounds. For two decades and more, there had been little change in the look or performance of the professional racing bicycle.

That all changed on January 19, 1984, when Italian Francesco Moser used a new contraption called a disc wheel in his successful world hour-record attempt in Mexico City. The Union Cycliste Internationale technical commission's approval of Moser's aerodynamic disc wheels forever changed the technical development of bikes and equipment.

In effect, the UCI ruling opened a Pandora's box of technical innovation. In short order, the professional cycling world was introduced to rubberized suits, disc wheels, aerodynamic frames, small-front-wheeled funny bikes, teardrop helmets, and razor-sharp bladed wheels with as few as 16 spokes each.

With the post-Moser technology era came a development that had not been seen before: the use of technology as a tactical element in pro racing. Whereas in the 20 years prior to 1984, almost every cyclist had access to the same equipment, such was the cost and exclusivity of the new technology that it was introduced strategically by well-equipped teams at important times. Such is the case with the new Scott-type narrow-section time trial bars, introduced to triathlons in 1987. When these bars were used by triathletes like Scott Molina and Scott Tinley, times for the time trial leg of Bud Light USTS triathlons fell by about two minutes over the 40km distance. That translates into a three-seconds-per-kilometer advantage. However, the first generation bars were not suited to European-style time trial courses with numerous corners, hills and tricky descents.

That changed with a second-generation clip-on bar that could be added to the cow-horned bars of a funny bike. Now a time trialist theoretically could make almost the same time savings as with a first-generation bar, but had more options for corners and hills. The 7-Eleven team picked up on this and planned to strategically introduce these new bars at the 1989 Tour de France. Its team manager, Jim Ochowicz, wanted to keep the bars under wraps because he knew that other pro teams would soon get the bars once they were proven by 7-Eleven in Tour de France combat. But by then, so 7-Eleven thought, the bars would have already helped them win the Tour.

However, the strategy went out the window at the Tour de Trump, in which 7-Eleven's Dag-Otto Lauritzen had to do well in the final time trial to preserve an important home-soil victory for the team. Not only did the narrow-section bars speed Lauritzen to one of the best time trial performances of his career, but the first five stage finishers all used narrow-section time trial bars.

Other pro teams took note of the bar's excellent results, proven for the first time in high-level pro competition, and wanted them. Scott DH bar developer Boone Lennon reports inquiries from the Panasonic, PDM and ADR teams. Profile for Speed reports similar interest. And the tactical advantage that 7-Eleven hoped to have at the Tour de France looks to have gone by the wayside. Other teams have taken the approach of lobbying the UCI to ban the bars from international use. Lennon, who has been in touch with the UCI, told *VeloNews* that the UCI technical commission would meet shortly before this year's Tour de France to decide if the new bars will be allowed in the race.

Despite allowing Moser's disc-wheeled records to be approved, the UCI has in many cases hindered new technical innovations. At the end of the recent Giro d'Italia, Dane John Carlsen was disqualified for using tri-spoked composite wheels in the final Prato-Florence time trial. The reason? The UCI had not yet approved this new development.

It is clear that the UCI does not have the support of all its members in interpreting its rules. The U.S. Cycling Federation takes a far more lenient attitude toward what is allowable in domestic competition. Spoke covers, tri-spoke wheels and narrow-section bars are all allowed in USCF events, but are not approved for international competitions.

The question is this: What constitutes fair play in sport? Is it fair that 7-Eleven has secret equipment that could affect the outcome of the world's biggest bike race? Could Andy Hampsten win the Tour de France and technically use less horsepower than his competitors? Or is this technological free-for-all a wave of the future that will steadily introduce aerodynamic and equipment advances to the advantage of us all?

As spectators and participants, the *VeloNews* staff expresses a certain romantic fondness for the old days when a bike was a bike. Admittedly, it is difficult to turn back the clock once a new innovation has been introduced to widespread use. And if the UCI bans narrow-section time trial bars, such a move would be a backward step for all of us.

### LeMond: The latest champion of innovation

Not only did Greg LeMond show tremendous willpower and physical excellence to win the Tour de France last month, but he also displayed a technical awareness that has been a hallmark of all great cycling champions.

Looking back over the past 50 years, six names stand out from the pack: Fausto Coppi, Louison Bobet, Jacques Anquetil, Eddy Merckx, Francesco Moser and Bernard Hinault. Besides leaving their names in the record books — they won a total of 20 Tours de France, 15 Giri d'Italia, and seven world road titles — each of them greatly influenced how cycling is practiced today.

When Coppi came into the sport just before World War II, bicycle technology and training methods had remained largely unchanged since World War I. One reason for the stagnancy was the attitude of the Tour de France founder and organizer Henri Desgrange.

In 1930, Desgrange ordained that all 100 starters in the Tour de France would ride identical bikes, all painted yellow, and supplied by the organizers. This rule remained in force until illness forced him to retire in 1936. And only in the following year were the Tour men allowed to use derailleurs, which had been in fairly common usage for a dozen years.

Coppi had helped the Campagnolo company in the development of its parallelogram derailleur, and the Italian champion became one of the most adept users of the new gear mechanism. He was also an innovator in terms of physical preparation.

At the time, cyclists were expected to live like monks, eat steaks every day, and ride their bikes at every available moment. Coppi questioned this philosophy. He hired his own trainer, who gave him daily massage; he experimented with more balanced diets; and he adopted training methods that allowed him to peak for certain events.

The world hour record of 45.871km that Coppi set in 1942 remained unbeaten until Anquetil added 288 meters to the figure in 1956. But both these champions, who were aged 22 when they set their hour records, are best remembered for their exploits in the major tours.

Until Anquetil came onto the scene, Bobet was the Tour de France record holder with three successive victories from 1953-55. The son of a baker from rural Brittany, Bobet was not the most talented cyclist of his generation. But he studied Coppi's training methods, and further developed them to become one of the most resilient athletes in the sport.

After a frightening car crash forced him to retire from cycling, Bobet used his knowledge of physiology to establish a chain of thalassotherapy centers: where patients with muscular problems are treated with seawater.

Anquetil was a more talented athlete than Bobet, which allowed him to ignore some of the athletic norms. (It wasn't unknown for Anquetil to sit up all night drinking champagne and playing cards — and then go out to win a tough race the next day.) But he was an innovator in other ways.

In his five Tour de France victories, Anquetil was unbeaten in 11 of 12 individual time trials (losing only an uphill mountain test to the exceptional Spanish climber Federico Bahamontes). Besides his natural talent for time trialing — he won the prestigious Grand Prix des Nations time trial nine times out of nine — Anquetil was the first to see the advantage of big gears. His use of a 52x13 gear in the early 1960s brought gasps of astonishment from the traditionalists.

At the end of his career, Anquetil often competed with a youthful Merckx, who was to become a champion in every respect. Not only did Merckx train harder, ride faster and win more races than anyone before him, he was always fine-tuning his bicycles and equipment.

Merckx was obsessed with weight; and he began the 1970s' fad for drilling holes in chainrings, gear and brake mechanisms to make a bike as light as possible. He matured hundreds of inflated tires in his basement to reduce the likelihood of flats in races, and constantly experimented with different frames, seat heights and handlebar positions to obtain optimum streamlining.

Before Merckx broke the world hour record in 1972, he simulated the humid, thin-air conditions of Mexico City while training on a stationary bike in his garage. His Colnago bike, made from special manufactured tubing, was the lightest ever used in a record attempt.

Another 12 years passed before Merckx's record was beaten by Moser riding a state-of-the-art low-profile bike fitted with two disc wheels. It was one of the heaviest machines used by a record breaker.

So programmed was Moser — he had three months of preparation using the heart-monitor training methods of Dr. Francesco Conconi — that he was able to improve his record only four days later. That same year, 1984, Moser went on to win, for the first time, both Milan-San Remo and the Giro d'Italia. Cycling would never be the same again.

Hinault was not as big an innovator, but he was a perfect example of the coaching methods of his Renault team director Cyrille Guimard. They made use of the Renault car company's wind tunnel to perfect Hinault's riding position, and also to develop the famous Delta bike, with its razor-sharp handlebar, as well as the team's Smurf-like helmet.

Ironically, Laurent Fignon was using this same (dated) equipment, less the helmet, in the Tour's historic Versailles-Paris time trial on July 23. In contrast, LeMond wore a 1989 aero' helmet, and the Scott clip-ons that he'd had inventor Boone Lennon modify to give him more power. LeMond is the latest of the champion innovators. We wonder what Henri Desgrange would have thought....

*After winning the Tour de France for a second time in 1992, Miguel Indurain was being described as a super-man. French journalist Guy Roger spoke to the people who helped mold Indurain the athlete.*

# Indurain the indestructible

BY GUY ROGER

To put into perspective the remarkable physical qualities of Miguel Indurain, we need only recount two moments recalled by Eusebio Unzue, the man who first "discovered" the two-time Tour de France winner. The first incident happened 10 years ago. "It was the day that Miguel became the amateur road champion of Spain," Unzue reported. "He'd joined our club, Reynolds, three months earlier, and I didn't know much about him. After he won the race, I ran for 200 meters to join him. I found him not even out of breath. And a minute later, he was completely calm, as if he hadn't even raced."

The second memory is much more recent. This time, Unzue was driving the Banesto team car, following Indurain in the time trial stage of the 1992 Tour de France, at Luxembourg. "Never had I been so ill at ease," Unzue revealed. "I thought Miguel had gone crazy. For the first 20km, he'd turned his 54x12 at more than 62 kph. If he'd had a 56 chain-ring, I believe he would have averaged more than 70 kph. He was gaining four to five seconds per kilometer, on everyone."

That performance — in which Indurain beat his main rivals by four minutes or more — made Indurain a phenomenon, a robot, a Martian, in the eyes of the public. His seemingly effortless strength astonished people. And the reality is almost as amazing — if you listen to José-Miguel Echavarri, the Banesto team director, who has one guiding rule: knowledge.

Every year, Echavarri makes Indurain go for tests at the University of Navarra, at Pamplona. And every year, Professor José Calabuig — a heart specialist — is astounded by

Indurain's powers of recuperation, his resistance to effort, the volume of air pumped by his lungs, and the liters of blood that his heart can circulate in a minute. "Ignoring all that," Echavarri exclaimed, "Miguel is not a superman. I've seen him stop in a mountain stage, his face twisted in pain. I know that he suffers ... and that he has exceptional willpower. He knows how to 'surpass' himself."

Echavarri, of course, has reason to portray Indurain through his virtues: Courage, free-spirit, humility and pride lend a more *human* dimension to his rider's exploits. But genetically, his star racer is undoubtedly a special case ... a gifted individual ... yes, a phe-nom-e-non!

Calabuig's test results of the champion's anatomy take your breath away: chest capacity: 8 liters; resting pulse: 28 beats per minute; generated power: 550 watts. And that's not all. His heart — with a seven-centimeter (2.75-inch) diameter for the left ventricle alone — is capable of circulating 50 liters of blood per minute, during a prolonged effort, like a time trial. Furthermore, Indurain's cardiac capacity is such that it allows him to maintain an oxygen consumption of more than 80cc per kilo per minute, and to have one of the highest VO2 max readings in the athletic world. His heart rate, which rises to 150 bpm by the summit of a mountain climb, drops back to 60 bpm, within 30 seconds of descending.

What did Indurain *do* to join this world of giants? As Echavarri explained it, "I've simply molded Miguel as I wanted, without any pressure on him.... There hasn't been anyone like him before, and there won't be anyone like him again."

Ten years separate Indurain's first tests from the last. When he started as the leader of the Reynolds amateur team, in 1983, Indurain was not even 19, and had never extended himself in a bike race. He just knew that he enjoyed cycling more and more, having come into the sport due to a particular set of circumstances. At high school, he could run 400 meters in 55 seconds, showed talent as a mid-field soccer player, and won regional-level cross-country races. Living nearby were three cousins, all older than him, who were into bike racing. Their closeness, complicity and regular group rides around Villava (Indurain's hometown) pushed the five Indurains — Miguel, his younger brother Prudencio and their three cousins — to continue their adventures, Sunday after Sunday ... until the day when Unzue introduced Miguel to the *juvenile* class of racing, the juniors.

Indurain was 17 years old, in his last year of an electromechanics course at the Pamplona High School. "He didn't have anything to show me," admitted Unzue, "but I had an intuition that he had exceptional potential as a cyclist."

So, in 1983, wearing the Reynolds jersey, Indurain took part in the pro-am Tour of the Asturias. Two weeks later came his breakthrough: At Alicante, under a burning sun, he became the Spanish national champion. The victory brought tears to the eyes of Unzue — who called Echavarri with the news: *"Es un fuera de serie!"* — "He's a super-gifted one!" There's one minor detail to add to this story: The "super-gifted one" weighed 10 kilos (22 pounds) more then, than he does today.

Such demonstrations of Indurain's amazing class — when he would play with the opposition — would continue in the following years. As a 20-year-old neo-pro in 1985, he became the youngest-ever leader of the Tour of Spain — wearing the *amarillo* jersey for four days (although he finished the three-week race in only 84th place). A few months later, Indurain won two stages of the Tour de l'Avenir (the pro-am version of the Tour de France) — taking the 30km time trial by a clear half-minute, from Frenchman Jean-François Bernard. After that performance, Echavarri uncharacteristically proclaimed, "Indurain will be the next Moser." (Francesco Moser, of course, is the holder of the world hour record.)

The following year, Indurain was on the point of winning the Tour de l'Avenir, when he faced a stage over the Col d'Izoard: his first major mountain climb in the Alps. With the race leader's yellow jersey on his back, and after 16km of climbing, the Spaniard crossed the 7200-foot summit in fourth place. "Ever since that day," Unzue confessed, "Miguel stopped being a normal rider. The Izoard revealed his true class, just as Mount Everest proves the true status of a mountaineer."

In those early years as a professional — riding alongside such race-hardened pros as Pedro Delgado, Angel Arroyo and Julian Gorospe — Indurain was not fully committed to his cycling career, but spent just as much time on his activities outside the sport. "That doesn't mean that he was doing things half-heartedly," explained Unzue. "He just wasn't making racing his entire focus. Miguel isn't a romantic, a bike-crazy guy who sacrifices everything for his sport." Those who were with him at that time sensed that Indurain was happy with his life, and that was sufficient. His time had yet to come....

During these years, Echavarri's credo — "To be patient is to be intelligent" — started to make sense. "Miguel's greatest quality," Echavarri said, "is that he knows how to be second, how to wait, not making excuses or accusations against those who beat him. He's always at ease, except perhaps in airplanes, where his legs swell up...."

It's difficult to argue with Echavarri's description of Indurain — who doesn't make mistakes with his diet, never makes a tactical error, and is a perfect athlete, according to every quality required. Even at age 22, the first physical tests at the Pamplona clinic showed that Indurain possessed an exceptional physique. During one of those early tests, on an ergometer, starting at 250 watts, the scientists incrementally increased the load by 50 watts, every three minutes. And Indurain continued to pedal the stationary bike for a half-hour, developing as much as 450 watts. (Today, it's 550 watts.)

"At that time," confessed Unzue, "his body was still 'green.' After three days of racing, Miguel always had some aches — a tendon, his back, a knee. That was another reason not to push him too hard, then."

So Echavaarri and Unzue polished their raw diamond, without making a lot of noise about it. Sometimes, they dreamed of what might be possible — asking themselves some disturbing questions: Was their jewel a real one, or was it made of paste? The day came when they just had to find out: Echavarri put his protégé in his car, and set off for Ferrara, Italy, to the university of Professor Francesco Conconi (the medical scientist who had prepared Moser for his world hour record attempts).

They returned home with an interminable list of prescriptions and schedules. But Echavarri was comforted — Miguel wasn't a lemon. Of this trip to Italy, Echavarri still remembers one important thing: It was absolutely essential that Indurain lose weight, without losing any muscle mass. They began this process slowly....

Indurain has unpleasant memories of this period, early 1988: "The training schedules of Conconi were too severe, his regime too strict. I didn't agree with him, but he made me realize that I had to be more disciplined. I knew when and how I should train, when and how I must eat. But at the time, Conconi — who had given everything to Moser — was asking too much of me."

Nevertheless, Echavarri's perseverance, talent, science and patience all combined to create the desired results. Slowly, the prodigy buckled down to training harder. More recently, another man has come into Indurain's life: Sabino Padilla, a doctor of physiology and sports medicine, who graduated from the University of St. Etienne, France. Like Echavarri, Padilla follows, step by step, everything that Indurain does — he observes, takes notes, and reacts. Top secret: His champion "is a man with his weaknesses, that you have to constantly correct, to stay the best." And that's Padilla's goal — to keep Indurain "the best." In three years, the doctor has become indispensable....

Also now in Indurain's shadow is Vicente Iza, his masseur for the past 12 years, who travels with the Banesto rider for 200 days a year. "From the soles of his feet to the backs of his ears, I work on him for an hour each day," Iza stated. "I only need to touch his heels for me to know in what condition are his veins, his vertebral column, ... and all the rest. And his legs, I could pick them out from among a thousand pairs, with my eyes closed. I don't know of any weaknesses ... but he is fragile — like the engine of a Formula 1 car."

For example, Indurain, the indestructible champion, takes a long time to build up his form in the springtime. And three years ago, he had to have surgery for a deviated septum, to overcome persistent sinusitis. So, is Indurain still a phenomenon? Echavarri smiles: "His real strength, I repeat, is his mental toughness. If he still has as much enthusiasm as now, he could continue enjoying himself in cycling for another seven or eight years. Now, his turn has come. And he's in charge."

But once they again start talking about the Luxembourg time trial, Echavarri and Unzue have the same adjective in their mouth: bestial. That day last July, Indurain was neither Robocop, nor The Terminator. At the height of his effort, his heart-rate never passed 190 bpm ... and less than a minute after the finish, it was again beating at 58! A beautiful beast, indeed!

*Electronic gear-shifting was brought to the market in 1993.*

# Mavic reinvents the derailleur!

### BY LENNARD ZINN

Mavic's ZMS 8000 electronic, rear derailleur — the world's first electronic derailleur — will finally be widely available in mid-June, and in a *VeloNews* exclusive, we tested the new system on its whirlwind tour through the United States. I'll go into detail, but I can sum up the test in one sentence: I was impressed.

Nicknamed "ZAP," the electronic derailleur has already been winning races in Europe — including Erik Breukink's victory at the Critérium International, where it was also on the bikes that took second and third places. And if it's performing that well in race situations, the product about to be released in the United States is already meeting high expectations.

Mavic calls the system "electro-mechanical." The "mechanical" part is represented in the derailleur itself, which, like a standard mechanism, moves the chain from cog to cog due to side pressure on the chain, supplied by the jockey wheels. The new Mavic system is "electronic," though, in that the command moving the derailleur is an electrical impulse.

To initiate this electrical impulse, the rider pushes a rocker button on the handlebar. Mavic makes certain that the rider can shift from a variety of hand positions by supplying two rocker button sets, to be set up anywhere on the bike. Each rocker button set is about the size of a four-bump by two-bump Lego brick — and weighs about as much. A push of one of the set's two buttons causes the derailleur to move one way, and the other button moves it the other way. If necessary, further button sets can be spliced into the two-conductor wire, so that the bike can be shifted from even more than two positions.

The entire system relies on a microprocessor to send the information to the derailleur, and this is handily located inside a handlebar-end plug, which also contains a Kodak K28A (or equivalent) six-volt battery. The wire that connects the microprocessor and the two button sets runs under the handlebar tape, along the frame, and back to the rear derailleur, where it attaches with a waterproof plug-in connector. Mavic plans to offer a handlebar-end plug for the other side, to hold a spare battery and wire.

The derailleur itself looks fairly similar to a standard rear mechanism, except that it has a gray plastic blob extending from its side, and away from the bicycle. Inside this gray Delrin shell is the column that translates the communication from the microprocessor into derailleur movement. This column looks like a hollow, aluminum bar, with lengthwise slots on two opposite sides and notches running up the length of a third. The notches are on the underside of the column, and are spaced the same distance apart as freewheel cogs. A spring-loaded pin, or détente, clicks into each notch, to center the jockey wheels under each cog.

Inside of the column is a plastic ratchet, with steps on either side of it, visible through the two slots. The ratchet is connected through a gear-and-cam linkage, to the upper jockey wheel. When the jockey wheel rotates, it drives the ratchet back and forth in continuous reciprocating motion. Two solenoids — one to engage each set of ratchet steps — are located at the base of the Delrin housing, on either side. Receiving an impulse from a shift button, the solenoid corresponding to that button moves inward. Each plastic step has a flat top, and a bottom that angles away. A solenoid can only engage a flat top, and it will slide off an angled bottom, to the next flat top. The two sets of steps are oriented opposite one another, so that the flat stair tops face toward the bicycle on one side, and away from it on the other.

When the rider shifts to a larger cog, by pushing the downshift button on either button set, the solenoid on the side with the stair tops facing away from the bicycle moves in, to engage a step. Once the solenoid has engaged it, the step is held fixed during the outward portion of its reciprocating motion. Bound from moving outward, the ratchet stays in place, and the entire aluminum column moves inward one notch. As the bar is connected to the jockey cage, the cage moves in one cog width, and, voilà, the shift is accomplished. Vice-versa accomplishes an upshift.

Multiple gear changes are accomplished by simply hitting the button as many times as shifts required. And simply holding down the button results in the derailleur moving through *all* of the gears. An especially nice feature is the system's one second of memory — which allows you to push the button while coasting or standing still, and still consummate the shift, if pedaling commences within one second.

The shifts are limited to pedaling only, since the energy to perform the shifts is provided by the rotation of the upper jockey wheel. Pedaling also affects the frequency with which the stair steps move back and forth — because this is directly proportional to the speed of rotation of the jockey wheel.

Battery life is expected to be for about 4000km — the distance of the Tour de France

— since the microprocessor is only sending "yes-no" messages, like a calculator. There is no servo motor, or anything similar, driving the derailleur; only the upper jockey wheel acts as the drive motor. Furthermore, the type of batteries used are widely available and usually cost less than $8.

Derailleur installation and adjustment is simple. After the derailleur is mounted to the dropout hanger, a plastic knob is turned by hand to line up the jockey wheels under the first cog. The electrical wire is then plugged in ... and that's it — unless you want to change from eight- to seven-speed operation. But even this is a simple adjustment. The ratchet has eight steps on either side, and if a screw on the end of the aluminum bar housing the ratchet is turned a quarter-turn, a plastic flap covers the eighth, downshift ratchet step. Turning the screw back to its original position opens the step again and allows the use of eight cogs. The only time-consuming step of installation and adjustment is removing the Delrin cover to get at the seven- or eight-speed adjustment screw. Other than that, there are no adjustment screws to set end stops, and there is no cable tension adjustment to perform — you don't even need to turn the pedals once when setting up!

As with all of its components, Mavic promises that this unit will be easily serviceable, and that replacement parts will be inexpensive and easily obtainable. Furthermore, rubber accordion seals on the new derailleur are intended to keep water and dirt out, to help minimize service.

Derailleur capacity is 28 teeth, more than most top-end racing derailleurs. This means it will handle a 12-28 cogset with a 53-39 chainring set. But it's *not* intended for mountainbike use yet — both because of insufficient capacity, and because the derailleur isn't designed to withstand banging on rocks.

The problem with much new technology is that it weighs too much, but this system weighs within about 10 grams of Mavic's down-tube-lever system — and it's hundreds of grams lighter than either Shimano's STI or Campagnolo's ErgoPower brake-lever shifters.

Initially, the system will only be available as a complete group. There's no word on exact price yet; Mavic only will say that the group price will be comparable to Dura-Ace STI and Campagnolo ErgoPower. Once again, the groups are scheduled to be in dealers' hands by mid-June.

As for the question of possible problems on the road, Mavic offers some solutions. If the battery goes dead or the wire breaks, the derailleur will remain on the same cog (unlike spring-loaded ones, where a broken cable results in the derailleur moving to the smallest cog). If for some reason you can't use the replacement battery and wire, you can still stop and manually move the rear derailleur to any cog you wish.

Assuming that durability or availability issues don't plague the new derailleur, Mavic can expect to have enthusiasts flocking to buy this newest gruppo.

94

*Suspension forks on road bikes first appeared in 1993. A year later, a large section of the Paris-Roubaix peloton opted for this mountain-bike-developed product.*

# Top four at Roubaix used suspension

**BY MARTI STEPHEN**

Rock Shox introduced suspension to the European peloton at last year's Paris-Roubaix, and the stunning result — a win for suspension-fork equipped Gilbert Duclos-Lassalle — convinced even the most powerful teams that suspension could help Paris-Roubaix riders outfitted with Rock Shox. In 1993, the results were much the same — with a modified-Mag 21-equipped Duclos-Lassalle repeating his win. Furthermore, second-placed Franco Ballerini (GB-MG-Bianchi) used a suspension stem from Softride, while the third- and fourth-placed riders also had suspended bikes.

The winner's Rock Shox fork utilized air-oil damping and weight-saving technology, such as a magnesium brace, Easton aluminum upper tubes, and titanium steerers and fasteners. At 2.2 pounds, the special edition is substantially lighter than the three-plus pounds that Rock Shox forks usually weigh.

All Rock Shox forks allow riders to dial in damping adjustment while on the bike — via knobs on top of the crown — so Duclos-Lassalle was able to significantly reduce the suspension action on smooth portions of the course. Extra tuning ability was provided by a new line of high-viscosity-index, performance shock oils, just introduced by Rock Shox — whose new, eight-weight oil was used at Paris-Roubaix.

Rock Shox's success was not limited to first place: Both Telekom's Olaf Ludwig, in third, and GB-MG-Bianchi's Johan Museeuw, in fourth, also used the U.S. manufacturer's forks. Other riders using Rock Shox included Greg LeMond of GAN, Sean Kelly and Thierry

Marie of Festina, Dirk De Wolf of Gatorade, Marc Bouillon of Collstrop, Christian Chaubet of Chazal-Vetta-MBK, Museeuw's teammate Mario Cipollini, and Steve Bauer of Motorola. Teams using the fork on all their bikes included Castorama, ONCE, Telekom and Subaru-Montgomery.

In fact, Rock Shox was so successful in supplying forks to racers that it was difficult to convince European teams that there was any other kind of suspension. This was not the case for Ballerini, however.

Softride supplied "front suspension systems" as they call the stem, to four riders besides Ballerini — his teammate Eros Poli, Motorola's Frankie Andreu and Bjørn Stenersen, and Telekom's Brian Holm. The racers used the company's standard 135mm aluminum stem, and a prototype 120mm stem — both modified with a side lever that could lock out the suspension for smooth sections, climbs and sprints. The 135mm version weighs 590 grams.

Two days before the race, Ballerini expressed some concern about the length of the stem and its height. In stepped expatriate American David Silva of Bianchi, who proposed a bike with a sloping top tube, which would lower the head-tube height and leave the stem height equal with Ballerini's usual stem height. Ballerini liked the idea, Silva got on the phone with Bianchi's *Reparto Corse* factory in Treviglio, Italy, and the bike was built and shipped to France within the space of two days. The top tube had also been shortened, so that the stem's 135mm length was closer to Ballerini's usual 130mm.

After two wins, and one second-place, at Paris-Roubaix, mountain-bike suspension is now a legitimate technological contribution to certain aspects of road racing. Both Rock Shox and Softride have suspended the peloton's disbelief.

*A new training device, developed in the late 1980s by German engineer Ullrich Schöberer, was the hottest coaching gadget by Olympic year, 1996.*

# Look who's using the SRM!

**BY JULIA INGERSOLL**

What do the leaders of almost every Italian pro team, the gold-medal-winning Australian pursuit squad and world champion time- trialist Karen Kurreck have in common? They are all training according to data collected by the SRM Powermeter system.

The SRM system is the most advanced training monitor in the world: The heart of the system is a replacement crankset unit that allows a cyclist using his or her own bicycle to simultaneously measure, display and record power output, heart rate, cadence and speed.

That mysterious red box you may have seen lately, mounted on the handlebars of many of the world's best racers, is the system's computer display unit. And it is giving these riders and their trainers access to groundbreaking knowledge of performance on the bike. The SRM takes training science a step further than heart-rate monitoring by providing the first and only objective measurement of how much power a cyclist is actually producing — independent of physiological variables — using the cold, hard fact of wattage.

The applications of this versatile tool are wide-ranging. Just a sampling of what the system can be used for includes equipment tests (e.g. does a rigid mountain bike require more or less power than a full-suspension bike for a given speed?); aerodynamic tests (finding cyclist-bicycle set-ups requiring less power for a given speed); and defining the racing demands of any discipline, thereby allowing course-specific training preparations.

In laboratory situations, the SRM allows use of the rider's own bike, instead of an ergometer. The Australians have even developed a pursuit test that compares a would-be champion with world record pace, based on measuring how much work is required to achieve that pace.

Although the SRM Powermeter has been used extensively — and with a high degree of success — by the German and Australian cycling programs since the early 1990s, it did not initially meet with widespread acceptance. A general perception of the system was that it was esoteric and intimidating. Indeed, the innovative Greg LeMond was on the cutting edge when he began training with the SRM in 1993, under the guidance of Dutch physiologist Adrie Van Diemen…. But his life circumstances prevented LeMond from reaping the benefits, and the SRM's tremendous potential remained relatively undiscovered … until very recently. According to Dean Golich, a physiologist formerly with USA Cycling and a leading authority on the SRM, the reason that the system wasn't understood for so long is that it was way ahead of its time. "It still is, actually," says Golich, who is based in Colorado Springs, Colorado. "The SRM was ahead of coaching. Many coaches didn't understand how to use power as a unit of measurement. Now, most top pros are being coached by physiologists who have studied power intensively."

According to Golich, riders need not be intimidated by the wealth of information supplied by the device, because, as with heart-rate monitors, you can learn to use the data, and experience will relate it to your personal use. In fact, he warns, "those who resist the SRM will fall behind very quickly. Remember the first time you heard about heart-rate monitors? There was some resistance. Now we talk about lactate threshold like it's the babysitter — and we know just where to get one."

The reason that the SRM is so great a tool is actually simple, Golich maintains: "You get a real-world measurement of what you are actually doing. It is a definitive way to measure your work, your fitness, and your racing, that is not subject to the whims of heart rate or perceived exertion. "There is error in using *only* physiological variables such as heart rate, lactate levels, or 'how hard you were going.' Heart rate is affected by too many things other than just fatigue: for instance, humidity, altitude, dehydration, adrenaline. We want to correlate high heart rates with strong performance, and low heart rates with poor results, but since heart rate is a physiological variable, there is a low rate of correlation."

There are two major ways in which the SRM has revolutionized training science: It establishes the demands of racing in any cycling discipline, and it clarifies what training to do to meet those demands. "Whether it's mountain biking, time trialing, road racing or track, the first thing the SRM did was identify the physiological demands of the sport. And each has different power requirements," Golich reports. "Before the SRM, no one really knew what the demands of cycling were."

Previous work in this regard has relied on the *general* relationship between heart rate and bicycle power as determined in the laboratory, and a comparison with heart rates measured during racing. For example, if a cyclist produces 240 watts at 160 bpm when tested in the laboratory, heart rates near 160 bpm recorded during racing are assumed to indicate that the cyclist was working at a bicycle power level near 240 watts.

But during tests of U.S. national team members during the 1994 Tour DuPont, the SRM revealed that without direct measurement of power, significant errors are possible: "We found that heart rate does not accurately reflect effort level in long races," Golich says.

SRM data has also demonstrated that heart rate doesn't always reflect how much work a rider is capable of performing in training. These findings go against the conventional thinking on this subject, that if high heart rates are not being achieved, it's time to back off and rest.

"The SRM is more accurate in determining how hard you are going," says Golich. "You can't be sure what the work load really is with heart rate alone, and could potentially be undertraining because you're doing less than you realize — or overtraining.

"A major principle of training is overloading: You must accumulate a level of stress that's greater than racing — in specific physiological systems. And to get maximum gains, you have to achieve optimal overloading in training.

"We have experience of elite riders producing higher power outputs on the second day of intervals, and maintaining that level the third day, while heart rate continually declines — as does mood, the psychological state of perceived effort. "The question we ask is: Should we have stopped the workout after the first day when the heart rate went down? No, because the overload is not there — muscularly, nor in other physiological systems."

Thanks to SRM measuring, sports scientists such as Golich have shown that even with a lowered heart rate, if a rider is still capable of producing a given workload, that rider's capacity for work can be increased. And this work can be targeted very specifically. "Power recordings during racing tell you what power outputs to shoot for in training," Golich says. "Take the time trial for instance. You do a really good one, and say you averaged 300 watts for 40km. You can take this information to improve to a 310-watt average by trying to accumulate a higher level of work in your training."

The SRM has also provided some surprising data concerning the true power nature of mountain biking. "Many people say mountain bikers need a lot of power," Golich reports, "or that it's like a road time trial, only you produce more consistent power compared to road. But it turns out that both assessments are wrong. We have monitored mountain biking and found that both average and maximum power output is not nearly as high as has been thought, nor was it sustained.

"You don't need to produce huge power for mountain-bike racing, you need *accelera-tory* power. Because you can't maintain your momentum, you can't produce as much power and still recover, in a mountain-bike race. You need the ability to accelerate many times over, instead of just maintaining. For instance, in a standard 40km road time trial, the acceleration is from the start line, then momentum allows the rider to maintain a high watt output — which for an elite man averages 350 to 470 watts. On mountain-bike courses, however, the speeds are so slow and the courses so resistant to them that you must go from 20-

30 watts to 350 repeatedly. Both types of effort are equally taxing, but in a different way."

While training science has already made great strides with the SRM, Golich is the first to admit that "we are still at the primitive stages with this. But already the 'art' of SRM interpretation is a lot more accurate than the 'art' of heart-rate interpretation."

USA Cycling coaches have been recording SRM data for two years, while some national teams have been using SRM for four years.

Golich emphasizes that experience with the device is priceless: "The sooner you start accumulating data recordings, the sooner you will get a major advantage in your training."

**How it works**

The SRM system is composed of three parts: the Powermeter, the Powercontrol, and the computer software program, "Ergo." Together, these three elements measure, store and evaluate the data produced on the bike. An integrated serial interface is included in the package, but the system requires an IBM-compatible PC on which to download the data files.

***How it functions***

1. Power measuring by the Powermeter: This is a computer-designed torque transducer machined in high-precision 7075 aluminum. Driving power is measured by strain-gauge strips inside the chainrings, which measure the deformation of the metal under torque. The change in resistance measured by the strain gauges is digitized and transmitted continuously to the sensor of the handlebar-mounted Powercontrol computer.

The Powermeter operates on a lithium battery and takes no rider power away in measuring. It is completely dirtproof and waterproof, temperature compensated, and extremely accurate. There are both road and mountain-bike models available.

2. The Powercontrol computer: It simultaneously displays and stores power, cadence, speed and heart-rate (compatible with Polar Electro heart-rate sender) data. You can choose the storage interval from between one and 60 seconds, and the unit's storage capacity is 72 hours of training at the 10-second storage interval.

The display shows current, average and maximum values for all functions: heart rate, power, speed and cadence. The Powercontrol battery allows 25 hours of continuous training. All data can be downloaded to an IBM-compatible PC, and statistical evaluation of training data can now be seen without a personal computer — directly on the LC-display of the Powercontrol.

3. "Ergo" software: It evaluates training data and can represent the information in graphs, statistics or tabular form. The evaluation possibilities are too numerous to list, and applications of the information are virtually limitless. Among the options offered by the software: It stores 20 training units with date and time, and can analyze each training file in a spectrum of ways. It can graph each function separately or together; can perform a Conconi test; mark segments of workouts; export data of completed training or marked ranges; and accommodate a personal comment line for every training file.

*97*

*An interview with UCI president Hein Verbruggen in February 1997 discussed the latest developments in bicycle design and drug controls.*

# Bikes, drugs and the media

BY CHARLES PELKEY

He has been president of the Union Cycliste Internationale since 1991. Hein Verbruggen came to the post as a reformer, ushering out some of the most established members of cycling's "old guard." And yet, the 55-year-old Dutch business consultant has his own decidedly conservative outlook on some aspects of the sport.

A recent example was when Verbruggen became the driving force behind rule changes that he says will put an end to the use of bicycles that "resemble airplanes more than they do bicycles" in track and time trial events. Verbruggen often cites last year's Atlanta Olympics as the final straw — when it became clear that an over-emphasis on technology only leads to "uncontrollable costs, unequal access to technology (and) wild innovations" that cause great harm to the integrity of cycling. On January 31, Verbruggen, with the full support of the UCI's management committee, "put a stop to this headlong rush" by adopting a set of stringent controls on bicycle design.

Meanwhile, the past few months have also been marked by controversy surrounding the alleged use of performance-enhancing drugs, especially EPO, by professionals in the European peloton. Articles in *La Gazzetta dello Sport* and *L'Équipe* suggest that the use of EPO is pervasive. Verbruggen, in turn, argues that the problem has been exaggerated by both journalists and a small number of less-than-successful riders.

Verbruggen spoke with *VeloNews* about these and other subjects during this year's world cyclo-cross championships in Munich, Germany.

**VeloNews** The UCI technical committee, the management committee and you made a pretty significant decision regarding bicycle technology yesterday (January 31). Can you outline that rule change and explain the reasoning behind it?

**Hein Verbruggen** We decided yesterday that as a follow-up to what we had discussed and decided in Lugano in October, we really do want to get back to basics. That's the best description.

We have decided that we will re-introduce the double-diamond shape. We will allow everyone who has other equipment to continue to use that until January 1, 2000. As of that day, every bike is to have that same basic shape. Second, we want to have the same-diameter wheels on the bike. Again, everyone who has something else will be able to use it until January 1, 2000. At the Olympics in Sydney, everyone will be at the line with essentially the same equipment.

We have also confirmed our decision to stick with the 65cm (between the bottom bracket and the front hub) and 15cm (from the front hub to the tip of the handlebars) limits, with a small exception here or there in those cases where a bike might have a 67cm (dimension). There we would limit the bars to 13cm. We have also decided that over the next few months we will look at making this rule more applicable to differing physiologies, rather than just using a single number for all riders. But that could come later.

I know that especially for the Americans and the Australians, this decision is a little difficult to understand, because they have a desire to always see in a sport something that is glossy, flashy, glitzy. They say that these things are advantageous for the sport. Perhaps it is true, but I have yet to see proof of that.

**VeloNews** There are those who believe that (such technology) generates popular interest in the sport — not necessarily among enthusiasts, but rather among members of the general public. I still hear people mention the funny bikes of the '84 Games.

**Hein Verbruggen** Okay, that's one side. But on the other hand, you have to ask how many people are put off from the sport because of the enormous costs involved. Cycling has always been a class-equal sport, a popular sport. It might be true also that all of this equipment and technology puts people off from the sport. We have serious questions about whether it is better from the standpoint of the participant, especially the youth.

The great majority of the management committee feels that the bike must be — and this is the key word — secondary. Look at what happened in Atlanta. I won't say that medals in Atlanta were won by engineers, that would go a little bit far, but one could ask: "Who won? Was it the rider or was it the bike?" I don't want to have that question hanging over our sport. For me, that's okay in motor sport, in car racing, but not in bicycle racing.

I have never, ever heard in road cycling that at the end of a great performance people ask was it the bike. On the road, you don't hear that except....

**VeloNews** Excuse me, but didn't that question immediately come up after the 1989 Tour?

**Hein Verbruggen** That's what I was about to say. The only exception is with the time trials.

I was referring to normal stages. Something like L'Alpe d'Huez. There, it is obvious that it is not the bike, it's the man.

Yes, we have had these big discussions about cases like Greg LeMond and with the time trial. We have those questions out there and we don't want that. It shouldn't be the equipment that wins the race, it should be the man.

**VeloNews** Okay, with that example in mind, do you ultimately want to eliminate the use of time trial bars and disc wheels?

**Hein Verbruggen** There are certain things that you can't go back on. If you were to ask just me, I would say yes. That would be the idea. But there are certain things that are now so accepted and, unlike the Superman position, do not pose a danger to riders or seriously affect the handling of a bicycle.

Using these bars in time trials or on the track, they are relatively safe. But these long bars simply don't allow you to maneuver a bike safely. I think we would have seen a lot of problems with safety as far as these were concerned.

As for the wheels ... not yet. But there are certain medical specialists who are not too happy with the use of those wheels, because they do not allow any compression like a spoked wheel. They are, some say, too rigid and therefore could cause problems for a rider's back.... It was raised in the discussions, and I think we will look carefully at any potential problems.

**VeloNews** Looking back over the years, where is it that the genie was let out of the bottle?

**Hein Verbruggen** Moser.

**VeloNews** The allowance of Moser's disc wheels in 1984, confusion about LeMond in 1989, the example of Graeme Obree in 1994 and the Americans at the 1986 world's.... Do these represent a weakness and lack of clarity in the regulations?

**Hein Verbruggen** Yes. I am not a technician, but I know that it seems to be an extremely difficult subject to put into rules. But I think we are getting closer.

Take, for example, what we did late last year. When we set the handlebar extension limit at 15cm, we forgot about an old rule that had been around since 1939 that allowed a full 75cm between the bottom bracket and the front hub. So, very quickly, we got indications from not only Obree, but other people, that they would just build bikes as long as was legal, getting around the 15cm rule. So we made a very quick decision to cut it back to 65cm, because we know that with very rare exception, there are hardly any bikes out there that are longer than 63cm.

The only discussion now is how to go about eliminating from the sport those bikes that look more like airplanes than they do bicycles. And I think we managed to do that yesterday.

I find it interesting that over the past few days many of the specialists — the engineers, the biomechanicists — believe that these bikes don't really have that much of an impact. So why then are these federations spending zillions of dollars when it seems that it is only a marketing tool for the manufacturers?

Whatever the impact of the bike — be it insignificant or major — our goal is to ensure that the next time the Olympics rolls around, the riders will have, more or less, comparable equipment.

**VeloNews** What role do you see for innovation, for invention, for the development of technology?

**Hein Verbruggen** As long as it is secondary to the rider and widely available, I have no problem. Again, with the Olympics, those who support this high-tech stuff said this year there were 17 countries who came to Atlanta with such bikes. That means, they say, that it is now available to everyone. But I say that it means that only 17 countries can afford such technology. We want to stop this technology race from going to the extremes it did last summer, with, for example, the Americans talking about their "million-dollar bicycle...."

Of course, there can and should be innovation; they can continue what they do, but not to the detriment of our sport. They should concentrate on other things like, for example, the things we have seen in the past — the clipless pedal, improvements in brakes, gears, safety improvements — but not this stuff anymore.

**VeloNews** So, you now have an hour record achieved on a bike that will soon be illegal, by a rider using a position that you believe is unsafe and have, therefore, banned. Nonetheless, his record stands. How do you reconcile the establishment of rules that, for the moment, make it extremely difficult to attack that record?

**Hein Verbruggen** There is no need to try and rewrite the record books. We know, and our specialists have confirmed, that the world hour record will be broken. I know it will be difficult, but it is still possible. We are pretty much convinced that even with these rules in place, it is still quite possible with advanced training methods to break it. It is especially likely that the record will be broken by someone who *specifically* trains to do it.

**VeloNews** Beyond the fact that the wheels were of different sizes, Rominger's hour bike would still be legal, correct?

**Hein Verbruggen** Yes. He was on a bike that, in my opinion, would be legal. Once again, I am not a specialist, but that's my perception.

**VeloNews** There are some who would say that your emphasis on technology is misplaced, especially if you are trying to level the competitive playing field. They would argue that far greater inequality exists because of the use of banned substances, EPO for example, than from an aerodynamic bicycle. I know that you met on January 24 to discuss this subject. Are you taking as aggressive an approach toward EPO as you are toward technology?

**Hein Verbruggen** First of all, EPO is on the list of forbidden products. Can you be more aggressive than that?

**VeloNews** Yes, through aggressive testing, perhaps.

**Hein Verbruggen** Yes, but that's something that is out of our control. The only thing is that we can rely on laboratories. If it can't be detected....

Secondly, I think it is an extremely unfair statement to make. We are doing a lot. It's only that many of your colleagues that are writing, in my opinion, in completely irresponsible ways — stupid ways, if you allow me to say that — about this issue. The coverage has given a completely inaccurate picture of this issue.

The problem lies often with the journalists. I know journalists and nothing wrong is ever righted. Once it is written, no matter how incorrect it is, it is never retracted or corrected.

**VeloNews** The meeting on January 24 ... you did decide to begin blood testing, a series of hematocrit tests....

**Hein Verbruggen** Before EPO came on the market, we had already done a great deal of work on studying the hematocrit levels of riders. The hematocrit levels of riders are normally between 40 and 52, with an average of 43.

We've seen for years stories about the dangers, even deaths from EPO. The news reports also say that up to 90 percent of the peloton is riding with levels up to 60. Well, at last year's Tour of Switzerland, we conducted voluntary blood tests on 77 riders. Out of the 77, there were two with a hematocrit higher than 52. One was just barely over 52 and the other was at 55. Please take into account that these levels fall well within normal parameters. These two exceptions could be from dehydration, it could have been a Colombian from a high altitude, whatever. The point is that of these 77 riders, only two exceeded 52. The average was slightly higher than the figure we got before. I think it was still under 44, but I can't recall.

So all these stories about riders doping themselves up to a hematocrit of 60 are bullshit. I don't have any other word for it, so please write that. They are bullshit.

You might believe that certain riders are using EPO, but from looking at the hematocrit, there is no indication. Of course, at this point, we cannot detect the drug, so we have to rely on the hematocrit test; but that suggests that the problem, if it exists at all, is not nearly as extensive as certain colleagues of yours are saying.

**VeloNews** But your argument is based on a set of *voluntary* blood tests. It's not likely that you will get many volunteers from the ranks of those using the drug.

**Hein Verbruggen** Would you think so? Out of 90 riders who rode in the Tour of Switzerland, we got 77 to volunteer. Sixteen of 17 teams volunteered.

We got a slightly higher hematocrit average than our first sample, you might believe that it is from EPO, I don't know. But to suggest that 90 percent of the peloton is raising their level up to 60....

It is important to recognize that the health of the riders in today's peloton is much better than it was 20 years ago. I mean the overall health. That is because of the close medical attention they receive, the specialized training, the diets.

**VeloNews** So, you will be testing hematocrit levels this year?

**Hein Verbruggen** We will be testing hematocrit levels this year for the health of the riders. What we are doing is an incredibly revolutionary thing. I would go so far to say that if we can really put it through with the help of the riders and the teams, we might just have a final solution to the doping problem.

What we will establish, and it is outside of our doping control, is to make the teams responsible for the health status of the riders. What we will do is to check the riders for many things.

We know that it is unsafe and unhealthy for a rider to have too high a level of iron in the blood. There are vitamins that can be too high. So, what we are installing is a health control. In addition to the doping control, we are establishing a health control. We will be checking, for example, hematocrit levels. You should note, however, that from the very moment we can detect EPO, it will immediately go over to the doping control. At the point when it becomes detectable in the urine, we can expect its use to disappear. But the problem will remain. EPO comes, EPO goes, people come, people go, and new products come and go. This is always something that happens in sport. We just try to do what we can to control it.

For now, our approach is based purely on the interest of the riders' health. We consider a hematocrit level above 50 to be unsafe for anyone practicing our sport. So, we conduct tests. When we find a rider who is at 51, he doesn't start. He's not punished, because at this point, we don't know where that high level comes from.

Sure, all these journalist will say, 'Oh, sure, it comes from EPO,' but we don't know.

That's another point about journalists. You know the story that we've had 24 dead riders already from EPO. But there is no evidence of that. There were in the Benelux countries seven sudden deaths among riders, some of which pre-dated the introduction of EPO. But that happens regularly in sport. It happens also in other sports. Now from those seven, we know for sure that four riders died of cardio-myopathy. They shouldn't have been riding in the first place. The other three, we still don't know, but it doesn't mean that it was from EPO. We just don't know. And again, if you don't know, you should shut up.

Because of the riders' heart problems, we have also now for three years invested heavily in cardiological studies of riders. If we determine that there exists a propensity for such a problem, the rider will not be allowed to start. We also do that in the case of serious visual problems, and now we add to that excessively high hematocrit. We might also add this year a maximum allowable level of iron. It may also be in the future that the allowable hematocrit level will be adjusted down to 49 or up to 51. It is all based on what we believe to be safe.

FEATURE STORIES

*On the road to the 1978 world's, two American cyclo-cross riders, Laurence Malone and Clark Natwick, raced in Switzerland for five weeks.*

# Cyclo-crossing Switzerland

## BY LAURENCE MALONE

It has been said that 400 years of democracy has brought Switzerland a good banking system and the cuckoo clock. Less celebrated is the level of cyclo-cross competition which, like the others, may or may not be an outgrowth of such a regime.

Cyclo-cross is practiced by most cyclists in Europe at one time or another. Unforgettable is the sight of a wiry old Swiss person pushing a bike across hill and dale, through detours, around snow banks, two-wheel drifting ice-patched roundabouts. The observer is struck by what appears to be a native ability to ride a bicycle in the elements.

These elements are periodic only in the sense that they occur between September and February, which for a Californian is six months too many. This is when the European cyclo-cross season takes place.

A gnarled veteran of 40 cyclo-cross seasons might just look upon the youngsters who participate in these weekend frenzies as mere apprentices, greenhorns. Not yet experienced enough to test their mettle against all the elements, they have well-designed, roped-off courses, which they circumnavigate 10 or 11 times before crossing what's called the "finish line."

All the veterans of seasons past and present come out in droves to cheer the apprentices on, exhorting them to go so fast as to imperil life and limb. Some even jump out of the crowd to give the apprentice a push, perhaps remembering how rough life was during the pre-titanium days of the Depression. Juniors may not be as strong or rugged as the veterans used to be, but with advances in communication he sure knows a lot more. With that in mind, it's hard to say what brought two American apprentices over to Europe to engage in the people's sport of cyclo-cross.

As far as the cyclo-cross *tifosi* here in Switzerland are concerned, the two apprentices, Natwick and Malone, came first because they qualified, and second, being amateurs, they wanted to more appreciate the range and meaning of that Hellenic expression: Amateur, for the love of....

Upon arrival, everyone asks about form — *goot?* — slapping a leg muscle for emphasis. An American is never quite sure whether the answer should be yes, no, or okay. Now we know how the first girl to break the sex barrier in Little League must have felt when asked about her chances.

Noteworthy about the Americans are their clothes — their civilian ones. The racers here tend toward the patent vinyl look, matching shoes and jackets, tight sweaters and tighter pants. That this is *de rigueur* for a bike racer is lost upon the Americans, who insist on their Levis, Ben Davis work shirts, favorite sneakers and general West Coast casualness.

Organization of races, particularly in Switzerland, is exceptional. At the registration table lies a stack of race numbers with safety pins neatly attached. Category A, B or C walks up, flashes license, is duly registered, receives number and program. Inside program is itinerary, starting times, map of course, roster of riders with corresponding patrons. Each patron, whether local bank, insurance company, restaurant or grocery store, has donated a bit for the privilege of sponsoring a rider for a given race. The bigger, regular sponsoring heavies fill the remaining pages of the program.

The races invariably start on time — Swiss watches didn't get their reputation for nothing. Before the start, the assemblage of riders is introduced to the crowd, amid much fanfare and horn-blowing. The Category A race starts at three o'clock. Of the 35 or so entrants, some 12 or 15 are given a one-minute head start. Among these are the two American apprentices. When all is said and done, this means a difference of less than three or four places in the outcome, but it's embarrassing nonetheless. The Swiss hosts are too kind. Such chivalry won't be afforded in Bilbao for the world championships.

Cyclo-cross was once termed by an American as "essentially a gambler's sport," and in some ways it is. But looked at in terms of consistency of placings, it is less so than road racing. The same people finish in the same order, give or take a couple of places, in nearly all the Swiss races. There is no wheel sucking here. Until American cyclo-cross courses cease being bike or back breakers, or until Americans reach the apprentice stage in bike-handling abilities, it will continue to be perceived as a "gambler's sport" in the U.S.

Here, as in any 'cross race, a good start is essential. Each turn, each obstacle of the course, requires a pause in the momentum, or "pause squared," as it were, for the trailing riders ... the fifth car at the red light doesn't start moving until the first car is well on its way — same idea. With the added problem of uneven terrain, the increased visibility afforded the leader is considerable. The one-minute handicap suddenly assumes more importance.

You go as fast as you can but, like happiness, there come times when you only *think* you're going as fast as you can. You demand a bit more output, possibly chide yourself for holding back. Can there be any doubt that you are holding back when the first wave of super apprentices sweep by? You grimly "latch on" to their wheels, using them as some sort of psychological pacing devices.

The first wave usually consists of reigning world professional champion Albert Zweifel, silver medalist Peter Frischknecht, German pro Klaus-Peter Thaler, world amateur champion Robert Vermeire of Belgium, and one or two of the Czech Varsity team. They soon pull away, out of sight, and nearly out of mind.

Even the gnarled veterans on the sidelines admire today's riders' finesse, their raw power, the promptness of the bike changes. The Swiss were not always top dog in the world of cyclo-cross, but since the successes of Zweifel and Frischknecht, enormous popular interest has been generated. Odd though it may seem to many in America who prefer watching little balls being kicked, thrown, batted, whacked, and sliced around on television, people here actually pay $4 a shot to come out in sub-freezing weather to watch others do something they do, and have done, nearly all their lives — ride a bicycle in the elements.

Covering the last kilometer is hard; threading a route through the finishing area mob and back to the dressing room is an art. It would be nice to hose down the filthy bikes before showering, but the pro mechanics already have dibs on the next 24 cleanings, so you shower first. Dog tired, you stumble into a dressing room where a man shoos you away — it's Zweifel's masseur, waiting for the podium act to end, and the room is *reseviert*.. Well, these Swiss doors all look alike. You finally find the right room where a warm shower and the togs for civilian identity await.

Outside the dressing room, a mob of kids, armed with pens, waits for autographs. "Those goofy looking ones must be the Americans," whispers one, and suddenly they're upon you. Sometimes you can sneak out the back, but that's not playing fair. You have to set an example for these kids, you know, assure them that what you do keeps you off the streets.

Evening has already fallen, tripped, stumbled and cursed its way in when the American apprentices find the assembly hall for the award ceremony. While elves are printing result sheets and arranging start money envelopes, the public is busy eating, drinking and generally hob-nobbing with the apprentices. Few sports allow such spectator-participant contact and rapport.

The drive back to the hotel is anti-climactic. The American apprentices talk about home and their common front-porch view of the Pacific Ocean. Spoiled Californians, they expect to see sunlight in winter and miles-per-hour signs. When will they understand that one franc isn't 50 cents, or that 10 kilometers isn't six miles, but that each is the sound of one hand clapping?

# Alcalá es el héroe

BY SUSAN EASTMAN

*Raúl Alcalá was at the height of his fame in the fall of 1987. His home-coming was described in this previously unpub-lished story by VeloNews specials editor Susan Eastman.*

The Mexican city of Monterrey sits in a desert valley amid the craggy, 5300-foot-high Sierra Madre mountains. Chiefly industrial, it is that country's richest and third largest metropolitan area and boasts the production of cement, crystal, textiles, steel, and *mucho cerveza* — such as Tecate, Carta Blanca and Bohemia.

Monterrey is also the home of Mexico's greatest bicycle racer, Raúl Alcalá, a member of the 7-Eleven team and his country's only registered professional cyclist. After four non-stop months of international competition in 1987 that included a ninth overall and the pres-tigious white jersey at the Tour de France and the overall title of the Coors International Bicycle Classic in the U.S., the prodigal son was finally returning home in September.

On his flights from Denver to Houston, then on to Monterrey, Alcalá knew that a reception of some kind was planned for his arrival, but he wasn't sure what, and he fidget-ed and squirmed all the way. Nervous, Raúl? "No, just so happy and excited!" he answered as he reached over to playfully slug Louis Viggio, his manager, translator and confidant. "He's nervous," confirmed Viggio, with whom the 23-year-old Alcalá had lived while in Boulder, Colorado, for the past two years. "He's afraid that no one will show up."

He needn't have worried. While waiting to board the plane in Houston, Alcalá had a hint of what was to come when other Mexicans scheduled for that flight recognized him and asked for his autograph. When he disembarked at the gate in Monterrey, blinding television lights and camera flashes documented his surprise as he was mobbed by the media, fami-ly and friends.

Mexican sports are run by the government, and department officials whizzed Alcalá through customs like royalty and into a press conference where approximately 75 reporters and friends awaited. Professor Cesar L. Faz, director of sports and recreation for Mexico, crowned him with a laurel wreath and presented him with a commemorative medal. The media pushed and shoved and hollered questions about his 7-Eleven team sponsorship, his views on international cycling, and what his plans were for the future. Alcalá assured them that he was staying with his American sponsor for another year, because they treated him well and it was best for his long-term maturation as a pro cyclist.

Despite his dark, swarthy complexion, Alcalá looked very American. He was dressed in a Ralph Lauren cotton polo shirt, a wool blazer by Emmanuel Ungaro, khaki slacks and tan Bally loafers. He had been promised a 150-percent increase in his 1988 salary, and he was looking like a million bucks.

After the 20-minute press conference, Alcalá was again led through the airport terminal and out the front door onto the street where a mariachi band played and fans chanted, "Ra-úl! Ra-úl!" A police car escorted an exuberant parade of cars honking their horns and flashing their lights into Monterrey to another reception in front of the ornate, pillared government palace, which was lit up with huge spotlights. Alcalá and his girlfriend Adriana Maldonado were driven around the palace plaza in a convertible sports car bedecked with flowers and Mexican flags in front of more cheering fans and another mariachi band. One fan had painstakingly copied the top 10 general classification from the 1987 Coors Classic onto a sign with Alcalá's name in capital letters at the top. Another waved a placard reading, "Alcalá para Presidente."

"We have a saying here for such occasions," said Professor Faz. "When Mexicans celebrate, they throw the house out the window."

"Bicycle sales have definitely gone up in Monterrey because of Raúl," said Rolando Arreola over dinner with the Alcalá clan that night. The owner of the Deportes Arreola Hnos. bike shop and long-time friend of Alcalá, Arreola said that a typical bike purchase at his shop now averages $500. It is the first time in six years that his store, which only sells Mexican-made Benotto bikes, has turned a consistent profit.

One of those infected by Alcalá's cycling success is his youngest brother, Rigo. The 16-year-old was grinning ear to ear, as were most of Alcalá's seven siblings, as he watched his brother across the dinner table. "Why are you so happy?" Viggio kidded Rigo. "Because the guy with the big eyebrows is back," Rigo answered.

Rigo also races but had recently broken his old frame and unsuccessfully tried soldering it back together. Raúl rendered him speechless when he unveiled a new frame purchased for Rigo from a Boulder bike shop.

Alcalá's generosity is becoming legendary. The fifth of eight children, Alcalá is buying his mother Ernestina a new house and completely outfitting it, from furniture to forks. Separated from Raúl's father, a car mechanic, she has lived in an apartment downtown for the past year with four of her children (five when Raúl was home). Alcalá said that being able to do this for her is ample motivation for him to work even harder in the future.

"My mother says, 'Ahh, it's too much money!' but it isn't. Not for my mother," Alcalá says proudly.

Tears welled up in Ernestina's eyes as she said, "It means a lot to me because of all the suffering and sacrifice he had to endure to achieve this. 'Ruly' never gives up and that is what is so important in his success. He's always been that way."

Raúl Alcalá was 12 years old when he first discovered bike racing. He was in a neighborhood soccer game when he heard sirens wailing on the next block. He hopped on his bike to see what was happening ... and found a bike race. On impulse, he joined the boys' event and promptly won a trophy. "That trophy really motivated me," Alcalá remembered. "I had been playing soccer, but it is too hard to win a trophy in soccer. It would take a whole year. Besides, soccer is too violent and dangerous. So I raced in citizen bike events for the next two years and then joined a junior cycling team."

His bike was a heavy single-speed relic, so he pretended it was a racing frame. He had never heard of the Tour de France, but there were Mexican stars he would try to emulate. At about this same time, though, corruption and deceit corroded Mexican team management and the sport, so sponsors pulled out and the government took over. Today, no trade teams exist. It is strictly amateur clubs with little money or prizes, and Mexicans race just for fun. Clubs can only supply clothing, and the meager prizes barely buy new equipment.

Alcalá wanted to make the system work for him, so he moved to Mexico City in 1980 when he was 17 to do battle against more demanding competition. The only rider around Monterrey who could challenge him was his arch rival Rosendo Ramos. Alcalá then competed for the Mexican national team in the 1983 and 1984 Coors Classics with little ambition other than to gain international experience. He trained in earnest for the 1984 Olympic road race but blames inexperience for his still not so shabby 11th place.

In 1985, Alcalá moved again, this time to San Diego, California, with another Mexican racer, Marco Antonio Lopez, to live with Arturo Valencia, the director of the Tour of Baja — the biggest bike race in northwest Mexico. Alcalá turned professional to take part in the 1985 CoreStates USPRO Championship at Philadelphia with its $100,000 prize list, assuming he could make a living racing for himself in the United States. He made this bold move even though he had never won a major race.

As is his style, Alcalá regards that period as an important part of his destiny. "Those were the most beautiful experiences of my life, because it taught me how to work with a team and how to lose," he said. "The first thing you have to do in bike racing is learn how to lose, not learn how to win."

It was during the Tour of Baja in April 1986 when his ambitions began to come to fruition. The 7-Eleven team participated in the Mexican race when, because of the U.S. crisis with Libya, the team withdrew from the Tour of Spain at the last minute. In Baja, the

American team's coach, Mike Neel, became intrigued by the aggressive Mexican who defended the overall lead of his Benotto teammate Martin Esparza by chasing down attack after attack launched by the 7-Eleven squad. He sensed that Alcalá — who still managed to finish third in the Baja race — could lend strong support in the Americans' first long and grueling Tour de France later that summer, and he began lobbying the team sponsor to get him on board.

"In the beginning, most of the riders were skeptical about me," Alcalá recalled. "Doug Shapiro and Bob Roll were immediately my friends, but the others gave me a cold reception. It took them time to warm up.

"I didn't speak any English, but Mike Neel spoke some Spanish, so that helped. He is a good coach, he understands the personality of each rider and deals with us in different ways. He cares and probably suffers as much as the riders do in a race!" said Alcalá, laughing.

Alcalá took part in his first Tour de France only six weeks after his 7-Eleven debut, and he fought hard to earn the respect of his teammates and prove to himself that he belonged there. Unlike some of the team's stars, Alcalá *finished* the race. In 1987, he was the highest placing rider on 7-Eleven (ninth overall) and earned the white jersey recognizing the best rider under 24. His impressive performance throughout the Tour attracted serious offers from European teams including PDM, Carrera, Fagor, BH, Panasonic and Reynolds. In fact, too much attention.

Viggio came to the rescue. "When I arrived at the Tour, Raúl asked me to talk to them because they were flashing all this money in front of him and disrupting his racing. He needed to calm down and think about his future, not just see the dollars. They were offering him Mercedes and nice apartments. The other teams were very disappointed when I finally told them that Raúl had decided to remain with 7-Eleven," Viggio said.

Alcalá is grateful for what 7-Eleven has done for him. He used to fantasize about possibly being signed to a Spanish team, but he never dreamed he would be picked up by a major American team. At the same time, Alcalá does not feel that his jump from being a Mexican amateur to an international professional was too difficult, because this team was maturing along with him, allowing him room to grow. He emphasizes that the quality of the team support and equipment was good for his morale, even though he sometimes felt like a stranger in a strange land.

Adriana Maldonado is not a typical Mexican woman. At 26 years old and single, many bluntly ask her what's wrong, why isn't she married — everyone else has been married six years at her age. Instead, Alcalá's striking girlfriend, who is three years his senior, owns two dress boutiques, has her own apartment and car, and races bikes. They've been dating since November 1986, when they met as spectators at a triathlon, but the Mexican media already has them engaged. Alcalá's oldest brother, Rodolfo, joked that only he should decide such familial matters and that "Raúl cannot get married until he wins the Tour de France."

It was Adriana's Chrysler Le Baron that Raúl was driving Friday night when he was late for a television interview at Monterrey's Channel 28. The station was visible on the hillside but Raúl couldn't find the road to it, just dead-end streets. When he finally came across a street leading down the hill from the TV station, Raúl turned the car up it and floored the gas pedal, driving the wrong way up a one-way street on a hill. With a curve. In the dark. Cars going 40 mph downhill passed on either side as Raúl yelled "Aiiyee!" in mock horror. Adriana looked out the window with serene resignation. The car roared relatively safely into the parking lot, Alcalá dashed into the station and he was hastily led onto the news program's set as they cut for a commercial. Sixty seconds later, Raúl was on the air, slightly out of breath but nonetheless composed.

When Alcalá stepped off-camera, station crew members lined up for autographs. After scribbling his name for 10 minutes, he then announced that he wanted to visit his 83-year-old grandmother, because she had been on his mind lately and he worried about her health.

A boisterous woman with snow white hair and failing eyesight, Josefa Gonzalez avidly asked Raúl about his travels before he kissed her goodbye and hopped back in the car, this time to attend another party in his honor at a popular sports bar. Many old friends and former race rivals cheered his arrival as a video of the CBS Sports coverage of the Tour de France played on a big screen. It was a time to kick back with a Bohemia and reminisce.

The next day was again packed with appearances, interviews and appointments. Alcalá first visited his two brothers, Rodolfo and Ezequiel, at their car repair shop: Servicio Automotriz Alcalá. Girlie calendars and posters of Raúl decorated the office walls, and a pit bull, Nero the Perro, guarded the garage entrance. Alcalá acknowledged that he would probably be working there, too, if his racing career hadn't succeeded.

As he leaned against a dismembered Chrysler, whose engine parts were scattered about the concrete floor, Alcalá somehow suddenly looked more Mexican. He was simply dressed in Levis and a cotton button-down collared shirt, so perhaps it was because he was finally relaxing for the first time in months. His eyes looked sleepy and heavy lidded, like his brothers'. His movements were slower, as if there were no reason to hurry. Alcalá was home.

Still, business and fans were waiting. He left the garage and drove to a tuxedo rental shop where owner Reynaldo Castillo fitted him for a custom-made tux in honor of his success. Then Alcalá drove to a midday meal at his mother's with all siblings, spouses and nieces in attendance.

Alcalá's mother was becoming exasperated with her jangling telephone, which had been ringing off the hook all day with calls from reporters wanting interviews. She complained to one journalist, "I'm sick of all these phone calls!" The reporter responded, "So who told you to have a famous son?"

Alcalá couldn't stay long because he had been invited to a pro soccer game where he was to kick off the match between the hometown Tigres and Mexico City's Atlante. He was late arriving at the stadium: the teams were already on the field warming up as Alcalá introduced himself to the security guards and explained why he was supposed to be on the field. "Ah, Raúl Alcalá! 7-Eleven!" exclaimed the two guards. Instead of letting him in, they wanted to chat about the Tour de France. And while Alcalá tried to instill the urgency of the situation upon them, the game started without him.

Even though Alcalá claims he hasn't changed with success, he has still come a long way from the eight-year-old who sold ice cream from a street cart — and lost money, because he ate more product than he sold. One wonders what Alcalá thinks today as he looks at the children selling gum, candy and windshield wiper blades to motorists pausing for traffic lights.

And the future? His cycling goals include winning the Tour de France. If the opportunity presents itself in 1988, he will attempt it, but he thinks that his own maturity and preparation is better timed for the year after. His greatest accomplishment is not, unsurprisingly, cycling related. "My greatest accomplishment is buying that house for my mother. That is my most, most, most biggest accomplishment," he said happily.

"My biggest *wish* is to have a beautiful, happy family with four kids."

"Three," Adriana whispered quietly.

The last veneer of Alcalá's Americanism peeled away Saturday night when eight of his friends took him to Restaurante Palenque, which features a colorful, even patriotic, dinner show. Traditions from different regions in Mexico are honored by costumed dancers, mariachi bands, singers and a mock cock fight on the central stage, which is surrounded by dinner tables on raised levels. Raúl knew every folk song and lustily sang along while downing tequilia, beer and steak fajitas.

"I am so happy!" he kept announcing as he toasted his friends. When the show's host discovered Alcalá was in the audience, he invited him down to the stage, where the famous cyclist was warmly greeted with whistles and applause.

"Raúl treats his friends no differently now than before his success," his friend David Martinez remarked after dinner, as restaurant patrons lined up for autographs. "I think the English word for him is humble. And what we love about Raúl is that he got where he is by himself. No one helped him. Raúl earned it.

"And we are so proud of him."

*Clockwise from top:*
**U.S. HERO I** Sara Ballantyne took the Grundig World Cup in 1990 and '91. In the first of her five 1990 World Cup race wins, she forded a stream at Aviemore, Scotland.
**U.S. HERO II** After one of his more than 300 road wins, Davis Phinney was hoisted into the night sky in Reno, Nevada, at the '85 Coors Classic.
**U.S. HERO III** Steve Hegg was the reigning Olympic champion when he placed fifth in the amateur pursuit at the '85 track world's.

V. Ekimov          F. Maertens

F. Casagrande

*Clockwise from top center:*
**HOT WOMEN** Any help was welcomed by Italian ace Maria Canins in her break-away battle with French mae-stro Jeannie Longo at the 1985 world's in Italy. Longo won. **HOT PURSUIT** American Peggy Maas is congratulated by fellow rider Betsy Davis after Maas reached the semi-finals of the pursuit at the '85 track world's. **NOOOOO!** New Zealander Craig Griffin — now a track coach with USA Cycling — slipped up at the '88 Tour of Texas.
**IRON CURTAIN** The 1987 Tour de France started at the Berlin Wall. **MOUNTAIN MAN** Gert-Jan Theunisse made a long solo break to win the Alpe d'Huez stage of the '89 Tour. **NO GOLD** At the '81 track world's, Eric Heiden was unsuccessful in using his speedskating muscles in the pro 5km pursuit: He was 17th of 17 starters. **CIRQUE DE SOLEIL** Besides being a prolific prologue winner, Frenchman Thierry Marie was an accomplished clown.

B. Julich

M. Cipollini

S. Novara

*Clockwise from far top left:*

**TOP SPRINTER**
Japan's Koichi Nakano
won an unprecedented
10 consecutive world
sprint championships
from 1977 to 1986.
**TOP TEAM** Danny Clark
and Tony Doyle scored a
world record 19 six-day
team wins in the late
1980s and early '90s.
**THIRD TEAM** Jane
Marshall (r), Jeanne
Golay and Leslee
Schenk earned a bronze
with Phyllis Hines in the
team time trial at the
'88 world's. **THE PRO-
FESSOR AND THE
PRIEST** Laurent Fignon
in 1990. **SQUIRT** An
unexpected shower for

Roy Knickman.
**BALANCE** Czech riders
Vitezslav Voboril and
Labomir Hargas took
third at the '87 world's;
an event that ceased to
be a championship in
1994. **LONE STAR** A
19-year-old amateur in
1991, Lance Armstrong
raced in the Portland
round of the Mayor's
Cup. **GOING DOWN**
John Lieswyn bumped
into an Athlete not in
Action. **SMILE!** In
1989, at the unofficial
European world's (l to r),
Julia Ingersoll, Sara
Ballantyne and Susan
DeMattei swept the
women's cross-country.

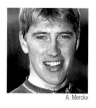

E. Breukink

A. Merckx

A. McCormack

G. Bontempi

*Clockwise from top:*
**HARD LABOR** Nothing like muddy logs to make a course: Lembeek, Belgium, 1986. **BREATHLESS** Despite winning five world titles, Rebecca Twigg was always a bundle of nerves before a final. **NOT THE WAY TO GO** Davis Phinney collided with a team car at the '88 Liège-Bastogne-Liège.

*The 1980s saw a surge in the sales (and use) of mountain bikes in North America, giving rise to huge problems of where the new bikes could be ridden.*

# The battle for terrain: No trails, no races?

**BY TIM JOHNSON**

Six years ago there were about 200,000 mountain bikes being used in this country. By the end of next year, if industry projections hold, 10 million off-road bikes will have been sold in the nation during this decade.

With this seemingly endless stream of bikes rolling out of the shops, there shouldn't be much surprise to the news that not everyone else out on the trails is happily welcoming these off-road riders. It isn't just the sheer number of riders out there, but the attitude and image the sport projects.

Consider these headlines:

"Mt. Tam's Bad Bikers" —*San Francisco Chronicle*, July 14, 1989.

"A New Menace Lurks in the Wilds: Supersonic Cyclists" —*Wall Street Journal*, October 18, 1989.

The *Chronicle* article described riders "stopping halfway up the summit to smoke marijuana ... and discuss 'killer rad bikes'.... Now mountain bikers as a creed are the most feared and hated element on Mount Tam since the Trailside Killer."

The front-page *Journal* article wasn't nearly as harsh on riders and the sport as the headline read, but it did describe an incident in Napa Valley, California, where speeding mountain bikers (on a trail specifically closed to them) spooked a horse. The animal broke its leg and was later destroyed. The cyclists left the scene and were never identified.

Until recently, off-road riders could have read accounts like these, shrugged and said, "So what? Newspapers sensationalize the situation — that's not the way it really is," and then go out for a ride. But it isn't just bad headlines that are being generated. Antagonism has grown between cyclists and other trail users, and those on two wheels have been coming out on the short end of these battles.

Trails across the country are being closed to mountain bikers due to damage and confrontations — real or exaggerated. Decisions are being made fast and furiously — and often without due process. They include the following:

• Pennsylvania shut down 1000 miles of state-managed back-country trails on August 31 — without any public notice that there had been problems, or any hearings to discuss solutions.

• South Carolina is *considering* a ban on mountain bikes within state parks, and yet park rangers are already enforcing such a ban.

• Georgia's Kennesaw Mountain National Battlefield Park, a mecca for Atlanta-based off-roaders, banned mountain bikes from all unpaved roads and trails October 1. The decision restricts riders to 2.5 miles of pavement during the week, and just a mile on weekends.

• Cougar Mountain, just east of Seattle, was closed by the King County Parks Department in April. A local hiking group, which had originally helped establish the park designation in the 1970s and cleared many of the trails, led the fight against bikes.

• California is undergoing a review of use for trails and fire roads within state park boundaries. Unless designated otherwise by the January 1, 1990, deadline, all fire roads will be open to mountain bikes, and all single track (those trails 60 inches or narrower) will be closed to them.

The good news is that cyclists around the country are organizing and working to fight for open trails. The groups, many formed in crises situations, make up an alphabet soup: NORBA, ROMP, NEMBA, IMBA. Even groups generally associated with touring and road riding concerns, such as the League of American Wheelmen and Bikecentennial, have begun to focus on off-road trails access. Whereas the National Off-Road Bicycle Association once led the charge with land-access issues, it has in recent years focused on the racing scene; but it is being supportive of the mountain bikers' cause.

A coalition has slowly grown between some of the smaller, regional organizations and those at the national level, with a unified approach evolving from numerous turf-givings and compromise meetings. At the Atlantic City Interbike show in October Jim Hasenauer, a board member of the International Mountain Bicycling Association, presented an ambitious plan developed by IMBA, Bicycling Industry of America, League of American Wheelmen and Bikecentennial to promote responsible trail use and continued access for mountain-bike riders.

His presentation took place at a meeting planned to update the industry on the groups' efforts — and to solicit financial support from manufacturers and dealers.

"Manufacturers told us to develop a joint plan. The groups had been doing these things individually," Hasenauer said. "At the Anaheim show, we laid out what we wanted to do." And the Atlantic City meeting outlined how the groups hoped to accomplish their goals, dividing up responsibilities for press relations, fund raising, educational efforts, advocacy and trail development.

"By spring, we should be able to move on a coordinated effort for a national program," he said.

To raise funds for IMBA and help educate riders who may be unaware of trail etiquette, Specialized Bicycle Components is selling water bottles with IMBA's "rules of the trail" imprinted on the sides and passing part of its profits along to IMBA. Fuji is also contributing to IMBA's work: a portion of the money it receives for catalogues and posters is earmarked for trail-access activities. West Coast Cycle presented IMBA with a check for $1600 at the Anaheim Interbike Show. The money was sales proceeds from a T-shirt designed to promote responsible riding.

Pro teams are pitching in as well. At this summer's Winter Park Mountain Bike Festival, riders from the KHS and Gary Fisher racing teams worked to promote the U.S. Forest Service's Tread Lightly program. Originally designed to educate motorized off-road users of federal "wild lands," the program has been expanded to help mountain bikers learn about the impact they can have on the terrain.

"Tread Lightly doesn't just focus on mountain bikes," said KHS team manager Tim Mehl. "It is to help inform all people — hikers, horseback riders, mountain bikers — about appropriate use and responsibilities in the forest." Information is passed along via trail signs, flyers, posters and fender stickers. In addition to trail etiquette, the program helps explain the rationale behind the regulations governing federal lands (such as wilderness status, wildlife protection, and erosion control).

More riders means a higher visibility for the sport out on the trails, but the increase in numbers alone hasn't brought on the closures. Irresponsible riding — as highlighted in the *Wall Street Journal* article — has also contributed to the problem. Adding to that is the public's perception of irresponsible riding as they watch an off-road racer jet by on a training ride.

What's a racer to do? Well, it is possible to ride hard off-road, but it does take a little planning. As Linda DuPriest, Specialized publications editor and *de facto* land access coordinator, said, "I got into mountain biking because of racing. I love to descend fast on single track — but you just can't do that all the time. When you ride in a way that pisses someone off, they're going to go back and tell someone at the ranger station about you."

# 89

*Following his Tour victory over Laurent Fignon in 1989, five teams fought a six-week battle for Greg LeMond's signature. The battle reached a crescendo the day he won the world's a second time.*

# The first $2 million cyclist

**BY JOHN WILCOCKSON**

The silent engine of the big, silver Mercedes-Benz was still hot as it stood on the wet sidewalk. Its American occupants had gone through the plate glass doors of the plush, but unpretentious, Park Hotel in Grenoble, France. Outside, the mercury glow of streetlights just penetrated the soft drizzle. Evening had come early.

For seven hours of that damp day in late August, the driver of the Mercedes was piloting a very different kind of machine: a bright lemon yellow, 14-speed, carbon-fiber racing bicycle that bore a Team LeMond logo on the front and the inscription *Maillot Jaune* on the side. Cheered on by 150,000 fans, he'd pedaled it 21 times around a grueling, hilly road circuit before sprinting to his second world professional cycling crown.

In contrast to the crowd-trampling frenzy he left behind an hour's drive away in Chambéry, only two "outsiders" awaited Greg LeMond in the hotel lobby in Grenoble. Both French and in their 40s, Roger Legeay and Roger Zannier of the Z team were ready to talk business.

"I have to go to my room and shower," the new world champion said to his guests before disappearing into the wood-paneled elevator. "I'll see you in 20 minutes."

Legeay and Zannier sank back into two of the lobby's brown leather armchairs and continued their low-voiced discussion as they jotted down figures on graph-paper notepads.

The two French executives seemed content with the way things were going. For several weeks, they'd been trying to get LeMond's signature on a contract to join Z in 1990.

This Sunday evening, August 27, was important because the 7-Eleven team directors had given LeMond until midnight to accept their already lucrative salary offer of about $1.4 million a year.

The 28-year-old Tour de France champion was being cagey about the negotiations. Earlier in the day a French journalist asked him, "Can you confirm that the French teams Fagor and Z are joining forces to sign you?" LeMond replied, "I don't know anything about that."

Nothing was definite yet. Other teams were still in play. Besides 7-Eleven, Fagor and Z, the Toshiba and Coors Light teams were also trying to put deals together. The Toshiba team director Yves Hézard and its financial director Camille Le Tierce breakfasted that morning at the Hotel Bristol, Aix-les-Bains, where LeMond stayed the previous night with the rest of the U.S. world's team.

Now, after showering and changing into jeans and a black T-shirt, LeMond was ready to continue his talks with Legeay and Zannier. Also present were his father Bob LeMond and personal advisor Fred Mengoni, the owner of the Mercedes. The five men were ensconced in an upstairs room for the next two hours.

Meanwhile, the rest of the LeMond clan had taken over the hotel's intimately elegant hotel restaurant, La Taverne de Ripaille. Four generations of the family were present, from great grandfather Art LeMond to baby Scott. LeMond's other son, five-year-old Geoffrey, was playing among the restaurant's velvet cushions and brass rails, a world championship gold medal swinging from his neck.

When his dad finally came back downstairs, Scott was crying and Geoffrey was ready for bed. But the world champion still hadn't eaten dinner. "The restaurant's run out of pasta, I'll see if I can get you a sandwich," said Kathy LeMond.

Her husband flopped into one of the lobby chairs. "I'm completely dead," sighed the American bike racer. It had been a long day. But he soon became animated, talking about the travails of team negotiations.

"Roger Legeay first spoke to me way back (in early July), long before 7-Eleven approached me," revealed LeMond. "But I dismissed it. I didn't think they (Z) had the money."

We recalled a conversation during the Tour de France at Villard de Lans, the day that Laurent Fignon increased his lead over LeMond to 50 seconds. Trying to avoid the crowds milling around the entrance to his night's accommodations, he went out the back door and sat on a boulder overlooking a valley. The sun was setting behind the mountains.

While we spoke, a 7-Eleven team car drove into the parking lot. LeMond waved. "Hi, Mr. Ochowicz," he called to the American team manager. He then whispered, "I can't make it too obvious," indicating that 7-Eleven would be his new team. That was July 20.

Negotiations continued strongly with 7-Eleven into August, although there were some sticking points. The American team has a deal with Eddy Merckx to supply bicycles through 1990, which would prevent it using Team LeMond machines until 1991. The two parties also had to settle the conflict between the team's suppliers and LeMond's endorsements for Giro helmets, Brancale shoes, Time pedals and Oakley sunglasses.

At the World Cup race in Montréal on August 6, Z's Legeay and Toshiba's Hézard confirmed their interest in signing LeMond, while Coor's Light's Len Pettyjohn was asking for more time to conclude a co-sponsorship deal with a major European firm. But 7-Eleven was still the front runner.

It seemed that a deal would be concluded by August 15, but then Z "came back with the Fagor deal, and the offer was too good to refuse," said LeMond, taking up the story in Grenoble. "7-Eleven couldn't go any higher, and gave me a deadline of tonight."

And what was Z offering? "More than I ever expected," he continued. When pressed, he said under his breath, "It's about 30 percent to 40 percent more (than the 7-Eleven offer)." And for how many years? He held up three fingers.

Besides the money, another interesting aspect of the new offer was the decision by Cycles Peugeot to end its commitment as bike supplier to the Z team. LeMond pointed out, "It means that I can ride my own [Team LeMond] bikes."

By the time the world championships came around, it was also agreed that LeMond could retain all his endorsement contracts. "That's important," he explained, "because they (Time, Giro, Brancale and Oakley) all stuck with me when things were bad."

When LeMond left Grenoble next morning to catch a 9 a.m. flight from Lyon (he was racing that afternoon in west France), he confirmed that the Z-Fagor arrangement had been agreed. "Everything should be on paper within 10 days," he told the French media.

However, Toshiba hadn't given up hope of tempting back LeMond to its team (he raced for Toshiba and its predecessor La Vie Claire from 1985-87). The CEO of the group that owns those companies in France and oversees the team, Bernard Tapie, is a boundlessly ambitious businessman. Since the team's glory days in 1986 (with the LeMond-Hinault one-two at the Tour de France), his money and initiative had made his Olympique Marseille soccer club the best in France. Perhaps he would now return to cycling.

Tapie invited to his yacht, the CEO of Fagor, a Spanish appliance manufacturer. As a result, Fagor canceled its commitment to Z in the belief that Tapie (and Toshiba) had a better chance of wooing LeMond than Zannier (of Z). That proved a big mistake.

Zannier now had to guarantee the total amount of the new contract for LeMond — until he could agree to terms with one of two potential co-sponsors. To clinch the deal, Zannier had to deposit a letter of credit with the Crédit Lyonnais bank in New York. It arrived September 11, and plans were confirmed for the press conference in Paris two days later. The three-year contract with Z is worth about $5.7 million, with the third year making LeMond the first $2 million-a-year cyclist.

As the 1980s closed, VeloNews *gave a warning of a new drug that could prove to be a potentially huge doping problem for cycling in the 1990s....*

# Killer-drug EPO: Scourge of the '90s?

**BY THE EDITORS**

As rewards in cycling become higher and higher — $1 million salaries and $100,000-a-day prize lists will soon become common-place — so does the temptation to use drugs. In the past decade, anabolic steroids and blood doping were the easy, danger-fraught way to improved performance. In the 1990s, as athletes search for ever more sophisticated shortcuts to success, a more sinister drug has entered the picture: erythropoietin, or EPO.

This new threat to our sport was mentioned in this space two months ago in connection with its possible abuse by three Dutch cyclists who have died from heart failure in the past 18 months. And there is widespread speculation that the members of at least one major professional team have been experimenting with the drug.

It's thought that EPO can improve oxygen transportation in endurance athletes (particularly road cyclists) even more effectively than blood doping. Yet the new "wonder drug" needs none of the complicated subterfuge required by blood doping — which includes storage and transfusions of the athlete's blood. EPO is easy to take, and virtually impossible to detect because it quickly disappears from the body, yet its benefits remain.

Erythropoietin is a synthetic drug developed about five years ago for patients suffering from kidney failure to help correct their anemia. In its naturally occurring form, it is a hormone produced by the kidneys to stimulate the production of oxygen-carrying, red blood cells in bone marrow. If synthetic EPO is injected into a fit athlete, his or her hemoglobin (red blood cell) level is artificially raised.

Proof of its performance-improving effects was recently provided by a series of tests conducted on eight Swedish athletes by Professor Bjorn Ekblom, the man who first revealed the potential benefits of blood-doping in 1981. His latest tests showed that the athletes injected with EPO increased their oxygen absorption by up to 10 percent!

Such injections can be made by the athlete at any time with little fear of detection. However, there are dangers. Dr. Scot Bradley, head of the U.S. Cycling Federation sports medicine advisory committee and a participant in the U.S. Olympic Committee drug control program, says that without strict medical supervision, too large a dose of EPO could result in life-threatening side effects. "EPO stirs premature, red-blood-cell production that can lead to blood clotting. Clotting can induce stroke and heart failure (believed to have caused the deaths of the unfortunate Dutch riders).

"Worse, by tampering with the body's red-blood-cell production, EPO may both shut down this production and greatly increase the risk of leukemia."

Research has been undertaken at the sophisticated Olympic drug facility in Los Angeles, and USCF liaison Bradley told *VeloNews* that the facility is close to finding a method that will detect EPO in an athlete's urine or blood sample. He was so confident of a successful completion to the research that testing for the drug may be possible at the Tour de Trump in May.

On the negative side of this breakthrough is the fact that EPO is not included on the lists of substances banned by the UCI, the world governing body for cycling, which has already issued its proscribed list for 1990. So, even if the drug were detected, the culprits could not be punished: at least, not this year.

It is understood that the use of EPO may be more widespread than presently thought. The magazine *Track & Field News* has reported that certain U.S. athletes used the drug at the 1988 Olympic Games and praised its effectiveness. And while the black market price of erythropoietin was once as high as $15,000 a dose, Bradley reports that the drug recently went into commercial production and now sells for hundreds, not thousands of dollars.

Bradley said EPO is potentially more dangerous than steroids because it affects the body's basic metabolic functions. "We don't yet know all the consequences (of the drug), and if it gets into common use among athletes, I predict we will see some really sad stories."

## 90

*A trip following the 1990 Giro d'Italia proved to be an emotional journey for a copy editor from* VeloNews, *on her first visit to a European bike race.*

# 'Dov'é il Giro?'

## BY RIVVY BERKMAN

You should know from the start that I am neither a racer nor an aficionado. I am a copy editor for *VeloNews,* but my interest is purely a literary one. And while I do enjoy riding a bike, my search is always for that elusive route which has all downhills and no ups. Then what was I doing following the 1990 Giro d'Italia?

Simple. I live with a bicycle journalist, and, after accompanying him on several U.S. races, I was lured by the mystique of a major European tour. ("It's so different in Europe," I had heard him and other writers and racers say, ad infinitum.)

"Why not keep notes while you are there," suggested another editor at the magazine. "You'll probably notice things people intent on the race might not." Indeed.

So I went with J. to the Giro and this is what I saw....

### May 26: Arriving in Bra

My favorite "bicycle" postcards have always been artistic shots from Italy: narrow alleyways, ochre-colored plaster facades with fuchsia flowers spilling out of window boxes — and, in front of a turquoise-painted door, one perfect bicycle. I remembered those cards the morning we arrived in Northern Italy, the Piedmont region, for the second half of the Giro. Driving through the old part of Bra, there they were: the ochre buildings, the window boxes of flowers, the narrow streets and alleys — but the bicycles were not just resting; they were being pedaled through the streets, and by all kinds of people. I think what struck me most was seeing so many older people — proper matrons, their gray hair in buns, bearded men in spectacles and berets — cycling not for pleasure, but just to get around.

That's when it first struck me that Italy (like many European countries) is the perfect setting for a bicycle race. It is a place where bikes are naturally interwoven into the people's lives — and so, too, is the race. When I told our concierge that we were here to follow the Giro, his eyes grew warmer and he told me he was rooting for Bugno. It feels good, for once, not to feel like I am part of some eccentric fringe world. When I was in New York City on the day the Tour de Trump came to town this year, few people I met there had even heard of the race, let alone known that it was happening that day. Well, the Giro is happening here, all right, and most everyone knows it.

### May 27: Time trial at Cuneo

It's Sunday, so the beautiful boutiques are all closed. Their windows are decked out with some of the most fanciful clothing I've ever seen; and, in the arcade of stores alongside the finish line, miniature and real bicycles, or copies of *La Gazzetta dello Sport* (the newspaper that promotes the race) are artfully woven into their window displays.

The Italian crowd, lining up to watch the race, is older and more dressed-up than what I've seen at American races. People in their 30s, 40s, 50s and 60s are smartly costumed, with Italian flair: The women are in elegant pant suits, the girls wear white stockings, and many of the men are in sport jackets or trench coats on this overcast day. Similarly, the race announcer's voice has a more serious and formal tone, which, added to the fact that he's speaking in *Italian*, makes it all seem somehow more significant, cosmopolitan and historic.

I've never seen so many people at a bike race! Throngs line the streets and the grandstands. Many of the baroque, three-storied buildings on the boulevard have balconies; and, on most of these, families stand watching.

As I walk away from the finish line, block after block after block is filled with waiting fans — along with Roman columns, arches, piazzas. It all evokes the Olympic races of old, and I am struck by how the grand architecture seems to befit this noblest of sports....

I am about eight blocks away now, but I still hear the announcer's voice, booming from loudspeakers on every corner, and rising to a crescendo as certain riders come through. And I am still surrounded by children, grandparents and couples, who stand waiting and watching under archways or umbrellas, as a light rain has now begun to fall.

Stopping in an ice-cream bar — *"Dov'é la toilette?"* — I glimpse on their huge television set, helicopter shots of Grinzane Cavour, the medieval castle where the race started, and close-ups of each racer poised on the platform from which he will launch.

Returning to the streets and back toward the finish, I see old men bicycling to the race. With their dark, buttoned cardigans and neat trousers, they look like the background people I've seen in so many foreign films ... I feel like I'm in an Italian movie! Suddenly, one of the racers zooms by us, followed by cars and shouts of "Bravo!" and I'm amazed, as always, that even at the finish, after 68 kilometers, they race faster than I can begin to comprehend!

As the stage nears its end, the crowds grow so thick I can hardly walk. It seems like the whole town is here. I see members of the Italian army with their feathered hats, *polizie* decked out with silver buttons, gloves and epaulets — even a few black-gowned nuns. It's truly an event, and the Italians are all so friendly that it feels like a big party we're all at together.

Flashing my press card (well, it actually says "seguido" — literally, follower), I am allowed up on the press stand and discover that I'm the only woman there. The European sports press is such a men's world, that sitting here now, I feel like a spy. I'm perched behind a Venezuelan radio sportscaster, who is speaking into his tape recorder in such rapid, excited Spanish — stopping only every three minutes or so for a breath — that I fear he'll have a stroke. Apparently, a Venezuelan rider is doing quite well.

At the end of the stage, when Italy's Gianni Bugno comes in second (and keeps the leader's pink jersey), the crowds rush forward. Fathers hold children on their shoulders, and as far as I can see the streets are filled, sidewalk to sidewalk, with people roaring Bugno's name.

Back in the press room — *la sala stampa* — we are given press packets filled with beautiful travel guides to the region, and rum-filled chocolates that just might be the best I ever ate. The room itself, in a municipal building, looks regal: marble floors, the Italian flag and crest of Alba, and heavily carved, long, oak tables. The horde of journalists sitting all around — each with his own typewriter or laptop computer — looks like a group of English barristers in these serious environs.

### May 28: Stage finish at Lodi

Just one day later, and the press room is in a high school gym — how quickly the mighty fall.... But the cans of Sprite (a race sponsor) have bicycles printed on their labels, and, what I thought was a bowl of vanilla ice cream, turns out to be a huge wheel of cheese, from yet another sponsor, Grana Padano. So that's what that gigantic, round, yellow balloon I saw at the finish line was supposed to be.

### May 29: On our way to Baselga di Piné

A critical part of covering a tour is getting there — or *not* getting there. Leaving Lake Garda and heading for the mountains, we are stopped by a line of parked cars in front of us, heading toward the only tunnel. After waiting for some time, J. walks to the tunnel and sees a sign stating it is closed for repairs for the next two hours. Surveying his map, J. decides we'll go up, around and down the mountain, figuring that would be only about an hour out of our way.

Twenty minutes later, the street becomes a dirt road; 30 minutes later, there's some dirt, but mostly rocks and we are climbing around and around, at 10 mph, what seems to be an endless path. *"Ferma!"* warn some motorcyclists at the turn. "At your risk," they say in broken English, showing with their hands that the road, already narrow, will become much narrower still. J. is determined though; he's worried about missing the end of the race and not being able to fax back the story he'd written this morning.

Soon, I am trembling and finally, praying, as we inch along a rocky path, only two meters wide, and thousands of meters above craggy peaks and valleys I can see all too clearly from my side of the car, since there are no barriers between us, and a drop too deep to consider.

I consider begging, bribing J. to stop, or walking back down — it's too narrow to turn around — but fear that if we don't die from a dizzy fall, we could from starving or freezing in these alpine heights. The scenes of cliffs, clouds, pine trees below and Dolomite mountains above are some of the most beautiful I've ever seen — and, I'm thinking, probably the last.

Turn after turn, approaching the top of the mountain (we've been told that the other side is mostly paved — a piece of cake), we stop some other motorcyclists coming down and ask if we're almost at the peak. About two kilometers, more, they say, and then shake their heads and fingers warningly, telling us that the end is too steep for an auto.

J. curses out the foreign map which didn't show that this road was unpaved (not to mention life-threatening), but finally sees reason. He decides that our lives are, after all, worth saving, and at a blessed corner where it's possible to edge backward up a hill, he turns … and we slowly, carefully, inch our way back down the mountain.

We return to the tunnel, which is now open — since our little detour took two hours — and after five hours of driving, we plod onto the race, arriving about an hour after it's ended. The press room is still busy with those who stay and work after the crowds and fans have gone. J. catches up on details, gets his Xeroxed copies of results … and it's back to business as usual.

**May 31: Klagenfurt, Austria**

I wake this morning with horrid stomach cramps — the result, no doubt, of last night's cheese dumplings in butter sauce, served at 10 p.m. when we finally got to our hotel. The thought of missing the race for a day in the room, close to the *toilette*, seems incredibly appealing. However, I follow J. instead, proud of my martyrdom. Bike racing always sounds pure in concept, but I realize now what it means to have days when your stomach hurts, or it's cold and raining and you have to continue traveling nonetheless — not to mention racing! I'm awestruck at the stalwart stoicism of bike racers. I mean, it's all I can do to drag myself out to see them; and to picture someone like Bob Roll in the throes of dysentery, still pedaling up and down mountain roads … well!

On the way to the start, we pass the most beautiful lake I've ever seen: aquamarine, surrounded by stands of pine trees, flower-bedecked chalets, and the foothills of the Alps themselves. How lovely and exciting, I think, for them to race through such varied and spectacular beauty. But then I wondered if the cyclists, speeding up to 60 mph, concentrating with all their might and focusing all their strength, have the capacity to even notice where they are. I mean, you never get a post-race quote from say, Steven Rooks, declaring, "The pace was intense. I attacked with Roche and LeMond and suddenly I glimpsed this incredible, aquamarine lake, surrounded by stands of pine trees, flower-bedecked chalets...."

On a shady street in the center of this Austrian mountain town, the stage begins. The crowd here, lined up three-fold, is, like their town, quieter, plainer and more old-fashioned than in Italy. The woman standing opposite me wears a black skirt and a high-collared, long-sleeved white blouse, and has a typically prim but friendly look. People clap politely as the race caravan passes — beaded by the flag-wielding, red-faced race organizer Vincenzo Torriani — but give some slightly more spirited calls as their plump-but-stately local dignitary is driven by, smiling and waving.

The stage ends in another, even quieter part of town. Here, the street is lined for about a half-mile with more well-behaved Austrians. Mothers hold bonneted babies out of high windows in old stone houses. J. and I, with our official cards, are allowed, as always, to stand with the press behind the *"Arrivo"* banner in the center of the street, between the policed crowds. Awaiting a great view of the winning riders, I move about with a practiced nonchalance, but actually feel the same excitement I experienced when I had front row seats to see Richard Burton in "Hamlet."

The speakers are broadcasting a constant race narrative in German. Suddenly, we hear, "Allan Peiper! Und Pascal Poisson ... neunzehn Sekunden..." and I grow visibly excited: first of all, because having understood all these words, I am under the illusion that I now miraculously understand German. I am also thrilled because I *know* Allan Peiper — someone I *know* is winning! Well, I never actually met Allan, but I do edit his articles for *VeloNews*.

J. and Roop (another Aussie) are also excited and continuously write down the data the announcer calls out. "Allan Peiper ... vierzehn Sekunden" "Allan Peiper ... neun Sekunden."

Uh, oh ... the chase group is gaining, and even I, the novice, can sense it doesn't look good, that a group has more momentum than two lone leaders. They are only one kilometer away, the announcer says, and almost immediately after, we can hear the motorcycles leading in and we see Allan Peiper, arms up (just like in the photos) and winning! I yell, "Allan, yeah, Allan!" with all the others, and feel an editor's maternal pride and delight. My boy Allan has won.

### June 1: San Candido

I am in a tiny, Tyrolean village, surrounded by forests and astounding views of the Dolomite Mountains. A few dozen locals and some *polizie* stand with me on a roadside at the edge of town, waiting for the race to pass. Now, like the other villagers, I keep looking at my watch. They were supposed to pass our town at 4 p.m. It's 4:05, so where's everybody? Cars from the entourage come by in spurts, but no grand parade, no real Giro....

Now, motorcyclists pass and the cars grow closer together. More villagers gather, wearing overalls, and some are even in traditional alpine knickers and hat. 4:08. Humph. I've been standing here since 3:45, all to wait for a glimpse that will last only a few minutes. Oh well, I can smell the pines, the sun shines brightly, tiny swallows dart into the creek and … they're coming! I can hear the helicopters buzzing overhead, a true sign of their arrival. Sure enough, a small group of cyclists whiz by to our applause; another group follows; and then, about 50 cars pass, each loaded with bicycles and wheels and looking slightly comical, kind of "overdressed."

On this narrow street, the riders pass close enough to touch. It's over so quickly, it's almost ephemeral, illusory, yet I'm so close that in some way it feels more real than most sports do.

### June 2: Dolomites

We're driving up the Dolomites, around curvy, narrow, mountain drops on either side. Here we see a boy and his father, bicycles parked, awaiting the race. There, perched high, is a man with his camera. Now some groups are seen sitting along the grass by the road; old men are laughing together, festive with the event. We pass through towns so small we zoom by them in a minute, where crowds of more than 100 are lined up behind the *polizie* who give directions to the traffic.

Higher and higher we go, the mist making it seem even more as if we've entered heaven. In fact, the tops of the mountains before us are now shrouded in clouds. And still, there are people waiting, watching, biking, hiking, getting ready for the Giro. Our car wears an official sign that allows us through and causes some children, on seeing it, to smile and wave as we pass. I feel as if we're part of a parade — but it's two-way, and I'm watching all of them as well.

On the top of the first climb, far, far away from anywhere, there are only white, rocky peaks and craters around us, as if we're on the moon. And here, even here on the moon, we find dozens of people — picnickers whose tables are laden with bread and wine, bike club members in uniform, old folks sitting on deck chairs.

I feel queasy from the constant curves, steep views, and up-and-down altitude changes, and again, I find it incomprehensible that some men are about to race these roads, twice as fast as we're driving … and on bikes!

As we drive up the last climb to get to the finish before the racers do, the roads become lined with hundreds, thousands of spectators. Tents and camping vans, wine and barbecues are everywhere. Some people hold homemade banners, most of which honor Bugno. And surrounding them all are looming Dolomites, rising like gigantic stalagmites from the earth.

On the very top, we can hardly move because of the crowds, but we are close enough that I can see the riders arriving and notice that many look half-dead, the way they *should* look after such an ordeal.

### June 3: Aprica

Driving, endless driving, that's the dark, flip side of following a tour. We are now on the road from Bolzano to Aprica, and the sun is hot and glaring. J. said it would be but a couple of hours driving today at most. I'm beginning to feel I've seen enough mountains, churches and picturesque villages to last a lifetime.

Traffic jams on mountain tops ... who'd have thought? "It's because of the race," J. mutters. We finally reach a sign that says 15km to Aprica. More than 40 minutes later, when we finally reach Aprica, I proclaim what I've been suspecting for the last four days of driving: "The Italian road signs lie. They say 15km when it's really 30km." J. laughs. "That's what some of the racers say, too," he says, and now I know it's true.

By the time we arrive at the finish line, I feel they should be cheering us as well, the unsung heroes of the Giro, all the *seguidos,* the followers who must also traipse from town to town.

I'm at once dismayed and relieved to see that American nationalism in sports crowds is not an anomaly. The Italians are here to honor Bugno and to encourage their other native sons. When Leonardo Sierra, after seven hours of difficult mountain climbs, becomes the first Venezuelan ever to win a stage of a major tour, the applause is controlled. But when Bugno brings in a chase pack, a few minutes later, the crowd goes berserk.

### June 4: Lake Como

Nearing the end and nearing Milan. You can tell a big city is imminent: the traffic is faster and louder, and neon lights mar the natural beauty. I guess it seems right for the race to end in Milan. But I feel a sadness as we leave the small towns and villages. In many ways, they seemed the right and perfect setting for a tour: ancient sites, human-sized and human-paced, where people still close everything for two-hour lunches, and have the time and interest to watch this most human of sporting events as it passes right by them, close enough to hear the whirring sounds of the wheels, close enough to touch.

### June 6: Milan

As always, the press room is strikingly different from all the others and seems reflective of the city or town we're in. Here, we enter a night club, whose foyer is so dark you can't see your feet. In the main room — painted black, and hazy with tobacco smoke — the reporters sit around the drum-filled stage, at small tables lit by flood spotlights. They all look like Humphrey Bogart.

After planning to meet J. near the finish, I take to the streets, which remind me of a 17th century version of Manhattan. (The last stage — a circuit race — is taking place in Italy's answer to Central Park.) Trying to find my way back, I ask a *signora, "Dov'é il Giro, bicicletta toura?"* She doesn't know what I am talking about. It's so different here than in the towns before....

Through some strange meanderings and a dollop of charm (ahem), I end up where, previously I'd been told, only official photographers are allowed. I can't find J. or where the journalists are. So, here I am, right at the finish line, a lone *seguida,* standing with the *paparazzi,* some city officials and even a few black-robed Fathers. Suddenly, the cyclists, in a bunch of about 100, fly by us so fast it's amazing — I almost lost a foot, and the *polizie* yell me back.

I see what looks like a press stand and make my way there. Standing on a chair on the stage, I still have a good view to watch the cyclists and look for J. No J., but the Venezuelan announcer is here before me and talking into his tape as fast and excitedly as ever. *"Finito!"* he finally shouts, and it's true, the Giro has ended.

It all feels a little anticlimactic. Bugno won, of course. But I guess I expected the crowds to scream more. A few minutes later, however, the screaming begins, as Bugno mounts the podium to the sound of his name shouted by thousands filling the park. As everyone else rushes forward, I try to leave the course and look for J. — our plane leaves in an hour. Weaving through the hysterical, stampeding crowds, I turn a corner — and there he is! We smile with surprise, and get ready to say *arrivederci* to Italy.

So I went with J. to the Giro ... and that is what I saw.

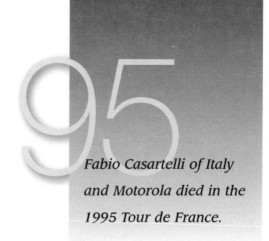

*Fabio Casartelli of Italy and Motorola died in the 1995 Tour de France.*

# A death in the family

**BY JOHN WILCOCKSON**

For Stephen Swart, the awful reality of his teammate Fabio Casartelli's death didn't fully hit him until the next morning. "When I signed in today," he said before the start of the 16th stage, July 19, his voice quivering with emotion, "they'd blanked out Fabio's name. That's when it really sunk in."

Swart was sitting alone in the covered Victorian marketplace in Tarbes, which minutes earlier was bustling with the noise of the Tour Village. This is the place where the race followers gather each morning to exchange greetings, grab some food, read the papers, and discuss the race. That day, Casartelli's fatal accident was the only topic of conversation. And now, just a few minutes before joining the rest of his Motorola team on the start line for a minute of silence, Swart solemnly talked about the previous 24 hours.

"We were told (about Fabio dying) when we were climbing the Aspin, but we had to get to the finish. We didn't have a chance to talk to each other about it then, so it didn't really sink in what had happened ... until now."

His teammate Alvaro Mejia didn't know that Casartelli had died until he crossed the stage's mountaintop finish line above Cauterets. After hearing the news, Mejia had to ride the five kilometers back down to an awaiting team car. There, without saying a word, he sat down, shaking with emotion, buried his head in a towel and sobbed.

Casartelli was one of the newer members of the European cycling peloton. But like everyone who had survived the first 14 stages of this Tour de France, he was a skilled professional.

On paper, the 15th stage was the toughest of the race, with more than 17,000 feet of climbing in its 206km. The day started quietly, with a thick mist hanging over the Pyrénées. Riding slowly, the 129 riders heard the rushing waters of the Lez River ... and the uplifting sound of church bells being rung in the hamlet of Illartein. They saw the valley's tiny fields of wheat, barley and corn ... and the cathedral-like, snowy peaks emerging through swirling, morning fog. They felt the thick humidity of the woodlands ... and felt the first heat of a summer's day.

These were the last sensations of Fabio Casartelli in his final hour on earth, as he climbed with his colleagues out of the valley of St. Lary ... raced as one past the moss-covered stone houses of Portet d'Aspet ... and made the last few turns of the climb, rising steeply past sloping green meadows.

The Col de Portet d'Aspet is an easy climb from the east, but the descent on the west side is the steepest in the Tour: 15 percent for most of its continuously twisting five kilometers. Although there were no attacks, the pace was still fast, because of the steep grade. The riders were descending single file, and had almost reached the bottom when there was a pileup on a left-hand turn. It's not known what caused the crash, but it's possible that a tire blew ... or a rider mis-read the turn and overlapped wheels with another.

There are no safety barriers on this narrow back road, just square concrete blocks marking the edge, and a low stone wall on the outside of the curves. Dante Rezze, who fell into the ravine, said, "I wanted to throw myself on the ground, but I was on the wrong side, and I couldn't avoid going straight on."

Casartelli didn't go over the wall. He either hit it, or more likely collided with one of the concrete blocks, given the severity of his injuries and the damage to the front part of his bike. One of the riders following, François Simon, told *Le Parisien* that he saw Casartelli fall: "His front wheel was stopped, and he went head first over the bike."

Casartelli was knocked unconscious, and lay on the road, a meter away from one of the concrete blocks. The first person to examine him was the race medical officer, Dr. Gérard Porte, who said that Casartelli was losing "an enormous amount of blood" from severe lesions on the right side of his head, between the cheekbone and the skull.

The medical report described a serious cranio-facial traumatism, with a deep coma and a severe hemorrhage, as well as multiple fractures of the skull. With emergency equipment, the assistant race doctor was able to revive Casartelli after three successive heart failures on the helicopter flight to the Tarbes hospital ... but he had lost so much blood that the surgeons had no chance of saving the cyclist's life.

The 24-year-old Italian was not yet a star. Although he won the gold medal at the amateurs-only 1992 Olympic road race in Barcelona, that was no more than his qualification into the paid ranks. But after signing for the Ariostea team in 1993, his pro career began well. He won a stage of the pro-am Settimana Bergamasca, finished 107th in the Giro d'Italia, and then took two second places in stages of the Tour of Switzerland. Unfortunately, Ariostea pulled its sponsorship, and Casartelli ended up riding for the low-budget ZG-Selle Italia team in 1994.

Although then only 23, Casartelli was called up to ride the Tour de France. He retired on the seventh stage, from Rennes to Futuroscope, because of a knee injury that eventually required reconstructive surgery. His injury brought the Italian into contact with Dr. Massimo Testa, who lives in Casartelli's hometown, Como, and is the team doctor of Motorola. With Testa's recommendation, along with that of new signing Andrea Peron, Casartelli was added to the Motorola team when 1994 ended.

Through the spring, mainly riding stage races in Spain — he was third on a stage of the Tour of Murcia — Casartelli gradually regained the strength in his knee. So much so that he was penciled in as a potential member of Motorola's Tour de France team — a selection that was confirmed when he raced strongly at the Tour of Switzerland.

The 24-year-old Italian was looking good in this, his second Tour. He'd been in an early attack the day that Lance Armstrong finished second in Revel, and was lying 87th out of 129 riders after the first of three stages in the Pyrénées....

Casartelli was from a close-knit family, and his parents Sergio and Rosa had fully supported their son's cycling career. He and his wife Anna Lisa had a baby son, Marco, just four months ago. It was only after speaking with Anna Lisa Casartelli that the Motorola team continued in the race.

For the riders who have children, like Swart, it was particularly hard to continue. But as the New Zealander said, "We have to face up to it one day. So it is probably better to do it right away."

The day after Casartelli died was also a difficult one for the other riders. Armstrong described his feelings during the 16th stage, the one that the six Motorola riders were allowed to finish in line abreast, 300 meters ahead of the peloton: "We were out there eight hours. There were 120 guys there, and about 115 of them didn't say a word for eight hours. It was the hardest day of my career ... bar none. Even though they were going easy, it was hard and it was hot, and physically it was damn hard. Mentally, I was just so far away ... I don't ever want to have a day like that again. That was the hardest day of the Tour de France."

On that same day, though, Armstrong was supported by a different impression of the peloton than he'd ever had before, one of solidarity and compassion. "I can't say enough for the guys of the peloton," he added. "It's not easy to concede a stage of the Tour de France. That's a stage somebody could've won ... could have made their year ... or their career. And for everybody to sit up and say we're not going to contest it, this is not a day to race, this is a day to mourn.... That says a lot. Certainly my attitude towards the sport, towards the peloton, completely changed that day. I was impressed by their class."

He didn't say it, but Armstrong now knows that the men he races with are all part of one big community. One family. And he also now knows how they react when a member of their family is lost.

*Two months after Lance Armstrong was diagnosed with testicular cancer, VeloNews paid a visit to his Texas home in December 1996.*

# 'As long as I have a chance'

**BY JOHN REZELL**

The telephone rang just about every five minutes, with an irritating fake urgency echoing throughout Lance Armstrong's spacious Mediterranean-flavored villa on the shores of Lake Austin. Life bustled within the elegant walls, and there was no time for constant interruptions. Besides, everyone inside recently had forged a clearer picture of what truly qualifies as urgent. So the phone rang on and on, slowly fading from consciousness.

Aside from his chalky, pale complexion and the horseshoe-shaped scar atop his shining chrome-like dome, few signs show that Armstrong has spent the past two months battling for his life. His handshake remained firm, his spirits bubbled and his voice boomed with confident strength — although his always intense blue eyes appeared to probe deeper than ever. "I feel great," Armstrong said, as he settled into the chair at his desk for a chat.

Despite all the comforting distractions of everyday life, though, the battle at hand never strayed far from Armstrong's thoughts. It was the first week of December, and in four days the champion would face his final scheduled round of chemotherapy at University Hospital in Indianapolis. The first two of the four rounds were like child's play, so much so that Armstrong found time to sneak out of the hospital for dinner a time or two. But the reality of the fight hit hard in the third round, his reaction to the chemotherapy violent enough to prompt doctors to sedate him. Although all the tests proved that Armstrong was winning his fight and was recovering rapidly, there was no telling what the final week of chemotherapy would be like.

"I've never felt the cancer," Armstrong said, his face quickly drawn to a whiter shade of pale, while his eyes dropped to concentrate on a paper clip dancing between his fingers and the desktop. "But I've felt the chemo'. And it's hard. It's *real* hard."

In the blink of an eye, it became apparent what Armstrong and others with cancer mean when they say cancer is something that will be with them forever. It changes a person at the core, no matter how well the physical impact can be hidden.

An eight-foot-tall cardboard get-well card smothered with signatures of well-wishers leaned against the wall in the foyer. Meanwhile, back at his agent's office in downtown Austin, four boxes stacked four-feet high sat near secretary Stacy Pounds's desk. They contained most of the letters sent to Armstrong — all but those from Armstrong's cancer-inflicted brethren. Armstrong kept those at home, never far from his reach.

"There are dark days," Armstrong said, "dark moments that aren't easy. But I read those letters and I walk out of this room motivated to continue the fight."

On this day, a stack of some 30 e-mail messages arrived. The outpouring of support has been moving and enlightening. What immediately captured attention was the common theme throughout the messages of those who have been touched by Armstrong's career. It's a theme Armstrong never understood before.

"Ninety-nine percent of those start off with, 'You inspired me... " Armstrong said. "I mean, I knew people knew about me, some say they've seen me race, or seen me on TV, or read about me, or a friend has told them about me ... but I've never realized that I inspired people. That's not something I think about when I'm racing. But now I know I have the ability to inspire people, and even if I never race my bike again, I just want to keep on inspiring people. I know I can do that, and that's a big reason to live. There are a lot of reasons to live."

And throughout the day, Armstrong recited the reasons to live, all aspects of life that had passed by him as unnoticed as the wonderful French countryside during a frantic stage of the Tour ... until that day in October when doctors told him he had testicular cancer.

"Yesterday was a good day," Armstrong said, despite the fact that rain drenched central Texas under cold cloudy skies the day before this interview.

"There *are* no bad days," he explained. "Some days are better than others, but there aren't any bad days."

After Armstrong's final scheduled chemotherapy, doctors planned to tell him the next step. It could be more chemotherapy, or radiation treatment, or surgery. Or, as Armstrong hoped, a clean bill of health. With pleasure, he noted that there is a scale from 1 to 100 which doctors use to rate a patient's chemotherapy. "Most people score around 30-40," Armstrong said, "my doctor said I'm as close to 100 as he has ever seen."

The doctors in Indianapolis rave that they have never had a cancer patient begin a fight in such fine physical condition. Armstrong hesitated to give that aspect too much credit. "I was doing some incredible things late in the year," Armstrong said, "and I had the cancer in my lungs at that time. It's something you just aren't aware of. That's the scary part of it."

Many argue that mental attitude is a major key to fighting cancer. Armstrong agreed: "I always raced 90-percent physical, 10-percent mental. This is closer to 50-50. And that extra 40 percent is a lot of work. It's very hard."

Still, every step of the way, in the face of challenging revelations, Armstrong's positive attitude has shone through. Even in the most trying moment.

"At first the chemo' was easy, but the news was getting worse," Armstrong said. "Now, the chemo' is getting harder, but the news is getting better."

Aside from the initial shocking news that he had testicular cancer, the worst day came when the doctors told Armstrong he had two lesions on the brain that required surgery.

"I sat there in the office with my mother and my girlfriend," Armstrong said. "When they came in and told me they had bad news, that it was in my brain, I started bawling ... but you know, every step along the way, even when the news was bad, there was still a positive side to it. That day they said the two spots were small and easy to get to. So, I said, 'Let's get them.' Every time they give me news, they tell me what the chances are. And you know what? I don't care what they are, as long as I have a chance. I can't imagine what it's like for those patients who have to hear the doctor say there's no chance. I can't imagine it. I don't care if I have a 50-percent chance of recovery, or 40 percent or 10 percent or 5 percent. Just give me a chance to live, that's all I want. Just give me a chance...."

Once again, Armstrong's mind wandered off to a place that so many thousands of cancer patients know.

"I feel changed, yeah, certainly," he said. "The letters from cancer patients, a lot of them say that we're the lucky ones and everyone else isn't. We get to see how precious life is. I don't know if I buy that, but I understand it. You know, the sun setting on Lake Austin. That's a reason to live. Getting up each morning. That's a reason to live. Starting a family someday. That's a reason to live."

So each day, no matter how up or down Armstrong feels, he climbs aboard his bicycle. Just a few months ago, he did so totally for one reason: It was his job. He admitted freely then that he wouldn't ride if he didn't have to. That has changed. He loves getting on his bicycle. He loves riding, even if it's the hardest part of his battle.

Then slowly, the impact of his battle crept to the forefront again. Armstrong stared out the window of his office, to the sunset lighting up the forest-green hills and the wind gently ruffling the leaves of the palm trees lining his driveway, which leads to the garage. Inside the garage, a shiny black Porsche and a sparkling Harley-Davidson motorcycle sat as testament to his success as a bicycle racer, just as the luxurious home did. Armstrong cringed and bit his lip.

"You know," he said, "the house, the car, the money, the fame ... I'd give it all away in a second to be cancer-free. I really would. I'd be homeless if I had to. It all really doesn't mean anything unless you have your health. That's everything."

PERSONALITIES

*The life of a Polish immigrant was tough in the United States of 1977.*

# The double life of coach Eddie B

## BY DAVE CHAUNER

He's doing just what you might expect a typical Polish immigrant to be doing. During the winter, he punches the time clock at a drab, turn-of-the-century iron foundry in the heart of New Jersey's industrial district. When spring breaks, he joins a Polish road crew that works its way south to Mississippi painting outdoor storage tanks. His clean but cramped apartment is on the 12th floor of a shabby high-rise overlooking clogged highways, parking lots, and Union College's mud-brown football field. And, like the 25,000 other Poles concentrated in this particular northern New Jersey community, he speaks very little English and hangs tight with small groups of his countrymen — all of whom share the somewhat discomforting feeling of constantly trying not to look back.

For Eddie Borysewicz, 37, one of the world's most knowledgeable cycling coaches, trying not to look back is perhaps surpassed in difficulty only by trying to learn English.

It's understandable. Borysewicz (roughly pronounced Boris-veech) spent nearly 15 years working his way up through one of the most demanding sports coaching systems in the world. When he left Poland in the summer of 1976, he was at the absolute top of that system, teaching sports physiology and doing physical therapy at Warsaw's Academy of Physical Education. He was one of between 10 and 15 "special" coaches in Polish cycling, and he talks with fondness about famous friends and pupils he has worked with — the best of whom collected world championship medals. By Polish standards he had made it: a comfortable apartment, his own car, color TV, privileged travel, national status and a stimulating job.

So why did he leave? That was the first question I put to him after we'd settled down with an interpreter at the small Polish-American travel agency where most new arrivals generally congregate as they begin the long, agonizing process of assimilation into American society.

The answer didn't just come tumbling out. In fact, I quickly got the feeling that it might have been the wrong question to ask. Officially, I was told by the interpreter — between furtive glances and much chatter back and forth in Polish — that Eddie is on a visit to the United States and Canada and may decide to stay rather than face a worsening family situation at home. But ultimately the decision to remain in the U.S. will hinge first on Borysewicz's ability to learn English (a task he is finding somewhat easier now that he is taking a crash course at a nearby college), and secondly on finding a job as a physical therapist.

So how will American cyclists be able to benefit from the vast information this new arrival brings from behind the Iron Curtain? His "discovery" by Mike Fraysse of the North Jersey Bicycle Club led to a highly successful stint this summer at the Olympic Training Center in Squaw Valley and subsequent clamor from our national-class riders for the U.S. Cycling Federation to "take care of this guy" by further involving him in U.S. coaching programs. The federation has responded quickly, and offered him a full-time position as national coaching director.

What an asset he should be. Borysewicz's racing career began in 1958 as a promising club rider in the small town of Lodz, traditionally the Polish breeding ground of cycling talent. As a junior, he was twice national champion of Poland in the individual and team pursuit events and, after turning senior, became a member of the 100km team time trial squad that took the national title on two occasions. As a member of the Polish national road team for six straight seasons, he competed in up to 12 major stage races every year. And those were the brutal beginnings of the Iron Curtain classics that today travel on much better roads and stop only in showcase accommodations. When Borysewicz rode races like the Tours of Poland, Czechoslovakia, Yugoslavia and Austria, and the Peace Race, it was incessant cobblestone roads and cold water hotels. In 1962, he received Poland's "Champion of Sports" award, roughly the equivalent to America's athlete of the year and an honor that has been bestowed on no more than 15 Polish athletes — in all sports — since World War II.

By 1968, he was at the height of his career and expecting to make the trip to the Mexico City Olympics. But during a routine medical check-up, doctors diagnosed some spots on his lungs as tuberculosis and he was socked into a hospital for six months. He still claims that no one really knew what was wrong and that he wasn't sick at all.

But it was enough of a blow to end his racing career and encourage him to take — and pass — the rigid entrance exams for admission to the renowned Academy of Physical Education in Warsaw. Within two years he became the first Polish racing cyclist to graduate from college with what in the U.S. would be a master's degree in physical education.

Even while still racing, Borysewicz enjoyed working and training with younger riders, making it natural for him to gravitate into formal coaching following retirement from competition. But in Poland, nobody becomes a coach just because he's available, happens to campaign the loudest, or pays a few zilotigs for a card and a hat. There are currently 10 to 15 first-category coaches in Poland. Borysewicz has been one of them for nearly 10 years.

Although, initially, Borysewicz was asked for three years to become a general coach, he preferred instead to instruct at the academy as a "special" coach with status and duties similar to those of an American college professor. Like civil servant jobs in the U.S., each rung up the ladder becomes a higher pay bracket, and Eddie's position netted him 8000 zilotigs per month (roughly double the average worker's wage) plus all the fringe benefits associated with esteemed stature in a national sport.

In spite of the fact that Borysewicz rarely took teams to international events, he came in contact with and influenced some of Eastern Europe's best cyclists. He has worked closely with Ryszard Szurkowski (three times a world champion). His own closest protégé, Mieczsław Nowicki, won silver and bronze medals at the 1976 Olympics, was a world champion in 1975 (100km TTT) and just recently took a bronze medal in the Venezuela world's.

Because cycling is one of Poland's biggest national sports, a lot of government money is funneled into local clubs. Youngsters who show promise get a chance to compete for use of one of their club's "racing" bikes, usually a clincher-tired, steel-cranked, Polish 10-speed.

Before getting too serious about training and competition, a cyclist will be given a series of physiological and psychological tests. If he scores high enough, he will be given a few hours a day off from his government job to train with his club.

These tests are administered every three months to those who have been given time off or, one step further, been given phony jobs so training can be full-time. Any rider who fails to pass at any time may be asked to hang up his wheels. The cream soon rises to the top and, for sure, only the fittest survive.

Under such a rigid, no-nonsense program in the world's most demanding sport, why are there any racers in Poland at all? The answer is the most classic paradox found within the Communist system — sport is business and comrades in sport, for the most part, are as committed to capitalism as Henry Ford.

Borysewicz puts it quite bluntly: "Work in factory — one month, 4000 zilotigs. Win big race — 100,000 zilotigs. No money, no sport."

The exuberance and enthusiasm Borysewicz has seen in the American cyclists he has met is something that he says is not found nearly as much in Polish athletes. For Americans, it's not such a life-or-death struggle to become a top racer, and Borysewicz isn't yet sure how big a role that struggle plays in turning out champions. Not until Americans reach a higher degree of technical knowledge and support will we really be able to tell.

Eddie B will be a key in giving us some answers.

*Shortly after winning three medals — including the road race gold — at the 1979 world junior championships in Argentina, Greg LeMond spoke to* VeloNews.

# America's world junior road champion

**BY ED PAVELKA**

G reg LeMond is the best 18-year-old road rider in the world. That's a very good place to start. And LeMond knows it is just the beginning.... When talking with LeMond you hear quiet enthusiasm, an honest opinion, a lightness that lets you know it's not all so very serious.

So much good news was made by LeMond and the rest of the U.S. team in Argentina that we really thought we were dreaming when told of the silver medal in the individual pursuit. By who? You're kidding! Yes, it was LeMond, who had previously ridden only one pursuit in his life. Then came a bronze medal for LeMond, Jeff Bradley, Mark Frise and Andy Hampsten in the team time trial; followed by a gold for LeMond in the road race: the first-ever world road title for an American junior.

**VeloNews** You had two days between the team time trial and road race. When you got up that day, did you feel fully recovered from your rides in the other two events?

**Greg LeMond** Yeah, I felt pretty good for the road race... and I wasn't near as nervous as I was the year before.

**VeloNews** What was the course like?

**Greg LeMond** Flat, dead flat. Not one hill in it. There were wide turns, and I thought it would be hard to ever break away. Early breakaways would get away for a kilometer or so and then be caught. There were eight laps of 14km, and with four laps to go there was an eight-man breakaway followed by a five-man group. Jeff Bradley and I were in the second break and we bridged the gap to the eight guys. Then the other three caught up so there was a

13-man breakaway. And we stayed away for about half a lap. That was the first dangerous break, but the field caught us.

Then there were some more little attacks. On lap six, the crucial breakaway went, going off in little groups at first. Then there was a total of 14 riders away. They got about 35 or 40 seconds. At the end of lap seven, going into the last lap, a Dutch rider and I broke away for a kilometer or so. We got caught and when I got back into the pack I attacked immediately, right after we got caught.

**VeloNews** You were really going for it at this point?

**Greg LeMond** Yeah. I kinda figured I had to start doing something. So I attacked, and this time Kenny DeMaerteleire and I got away. We picked up 20 or 25 seconds quickly — the others had just got done chasing me and the Dutch rider and they kind of rested. At that time, the whole pack caught the break group and everyone was together with Kenny and me off the front.

**VeloNews** Were you prepared to go it alone if you could?

**Greg LeMond** Yeah, but I figured somebody would come. We worked together pretty good for about a kilometer or so, but then Kenny said he was dying and he started not pulling through so good. I was doing something like 70 or 80 percent of the work for the whole last lap. He kept saying, "Come on Greg, you can do it, you can win."

**VeloNews** He's talking to you in English?

**Greg LeMond** Yeah. See, I know him fairly well from my racing in Belgium. All the Belgians speak English, a little English. He made an offer to me — for $500 I can win.

**VeloNews** Huh?

**Greg LeMond** (*Chuckle*) If I give him $500, because he was sitting on, he would let me win. I didn't say anything, I just kept going. A couple of times I did slow down to where I made him pull through, and he did pull through after I started yelling for a few seconds. But I was pulling maybe for two minutes at a time. And this whole time we were only 20 or so seconds ahead. I could see them back there and it was just an all-out effort. I was in my biggest gear the whole way.

**VeloNews** What was that?

**Greg LeMond** A 53x13, a couple of times into the 12.

**VeloNews** We understand that all five Russians went right to the front of the chase.

**Greg LeMond** Yeah. Jeff was sitting on the Russians, but with about six kilometers to go I remember looking back and seeing five red jerseys at the front, stringing out the whole pack and just doing a team time trial. The last five kilometers were on the autodrome and you could almost see the whole lap. I could look back and see the Russians pulling, and I think they took seven seconds out of the 20 we had when we entered. Kenny pulled just once or twice that whole last lap.

**VeloNews** So it was totally up to you to save it or lose it.

**Greg LeMond** Yeah, Kenny was just sitting on and probably saving it for the sprint. I would kind of drop him after he'd get done pulling, so I guess he was pretty tired. Still, I think he could have pulled a little more than he did. But that's the world championship and you can't do anything about it. I knew it was do or die. If they caught us I knew I couldn't sprint because I was just too tired, so either I would get second or first or else get nothing. I just put my head down the last two or three kilometers and just went all out. Then with 1000 meters to go I think the whole pack, the Russians, just gave up.

**VeloNews** So you could forget about the Russians and the others, but what about Kenny?

**Greg LeMond** Coming into the sprint, he still wouldn't come through. I didn't want to slow down entirely because I knew the pack could still catch us, so I kept in the 53x13 and I went to the side. I was watching him. I started slowing down just to rest and with about 300 meters to go he jumped. I got right on him — it was fairly easy to get on him. He was shifting sides of the road and when he got to the other side he started going straight toward the finish. I was coming around him and I think my front wheel was up to his handlebars — I was definitely coming around him with speed and I guess he saw me coming. He pushed me over into these automobile tires. It was a hook. I hit a tire and went over it and there was about an eight-foot section where I could ride my bike up to the crowd of reporters and everyone, about a hundred people at the finish, but they wouldn't move. I started to draw even with Kenny and I had to switch over — this is the last 100 meters — and some guy moved a tire and I shot through the space! I was sprinting up the side and Kenny came back over, and this time he touched me — his hip or something touched my arm. I rode right into the tires and in the last meters I rode over every automobile tire until the finish. I had to put on my brake — the crowd was just right there in front of me and I had to swerve to miss them.

**VeloNews** These tires were just lying flat on the road?

**Greg LeMond** Yeah.

**VeloNews** How the heck do you ride a bike over automobile tires?

**Greg LeMond** (*Laughing*) I don't know! I thought for sure I was going to crash. It took eight spokes out of my wheel. By the finish my wheel was just totally wrecked. I was amazed I didn't crash. The tires did have a little give to them, but I hit every one — about six of them in the last 100 meters.

**VeloNews** So that put Kenny well ahead at the finish?

**Greg LeMond** Only by a bike length … a bike and a half. Each time he put me into the tires I lost about a bike length, and each time I picked it back up even with him. I was coming around him the first time clear, just definitely coming around him, but I was a couple of lengths behind after I got into the tires.

**VeloNews** As far as getting to the line, then, Kenny was the winner. Was there an immediate protest filed?

# Paraskevin: Queen of the sprint

## BY GEOFF DRAKE

At the 1984 world cycling championships in Barcelona, an official tried to hand Connie Paraskevin a silver medal in the match sprint. Now if that medal had been hers, she would have taken it. Gracefully. But it wasn't. A protest had been made by the U.S. coaching staff, and a re-run was scheduled for the following day. And when the final race was run off, it was all Paraskevin. For the third consecutive year, her world's medal was gold.

Now 23, Paraskevin won her first national track championship in 1973 in the midget girls class. She went on to win two national titles as an intermediate (1975-76), and two more as a junior (1977-78). In 1981, she was national criterium champion, and in 1982 and '83 she won the women's sprint title.

In the following interview, Paraskevin talks about her world's wins from her new home in Los Angeles, where she has been training at the Olympic velodrome.

**VeloNews** What thoughts do you have on your world's win last year?

**Connie Paraskevin** It was a close call. I don't know one word to describe it. I was really lucky to be able to come through with it. But I haven't won any of my championships easily. I mean, if you look in the record books, it says *boom, boom, boom* — three years in a row. But I didn't dominate any one of them. So last year was another case where I seemed to go through all the semis and the qualifying rounds pretty easily, but in the finals it was pretty tough. And the Soviet rider (Erika Salumae) was very aggressive.

Anyway, none of my rides have been easy and (last year's world's) was just another one that was too close. You know, I was riding a warm-down while the protest was going through, and the commissaires — who aren't in with what's going on with the judges stand

— one of them starts grabbing me and saying, "Ah, Paraskevin! Ceremony! You must come!" And I'm saying, "No, no! It's not over — there's a protest — we're having another ride!" And then he said it again, and this time I just shook his hand away from me and kept riding. Then he did it again! So by now I'm freaking out, right? And so then finally somebody came over and told him, "Cool it man, there is no ceremony." It was pretty hairy.

**VeloNews** You've been competing in the world's off and on since 1977. How has the competition changed in those years?

**Connie Paraskevin** Well, let's see. The first couple years when I rode I was pretty young and I was more just into speed — I didn't really know a lot about tactics. So I tried to rely on my speed — hit the 200-meter line and go. But I think in the last few years women's races have been getting more tactical. And they are getting faster.

And there are better riders, better bike handlers. You can find women that can do pretty much anything on the bike, like balancing — which I'm not saying is good — as opposed to just straight leadout sprints.

**VeloNews** Roger Young is your coach now. Can you describe that arrangement and how it's working out?

**Connie Paraskevin** It's great. Roger's been my coach since '81 when I started riding again. Before that I had decided I'd take a few years off from cycling to concentrate on speedskating for the 1980 Olympics. I got back into cycling and it was like — I'm going to try it out for this year, and if I like it, I'm going to go all the way or just quit completely. And I decided I did want to go for it. So I started working with Roger. He's helped me not only in my conditioning — in my speed — but in my thinking. You know, trying to analyze my rides, what happened, and what can happen.

One big asset that Roger has over other coaches is that he works with the riders. He's on the track doing the workout with us. And in match sprinting, I think that's really important because if somebody's sitting in the infield and watching a practice or a race going on, you can't see the subtle pedal movements. But with him on the bike, when I try to make a move on him he can see those subtle pedal movements, he can feel them and he can know if it's done right, right there at that very second.

**VeloNews** Connie, what is it about you mentally and physically that makes you good at sprinting, and what things do you have to work hardest on?

**Connie Paraskevin** I have to work hard on everything. Everything is hard for me. But I don't know what makes *me* good. I think what makes anybody good is just the desire, or the determination, to do something. I don't really believe in a natural athlete. I think people have certain natural abilities, but you still have to work on it.

But I love to do it, and I think that's all it is. I'm a pretty strong-minded person — if I set my mind on something, I just go until I get it.

*A professional racer for 17 years, Dutchman Joop Zoetemelk won the world road title in his 16th season, in 1985, at Giavera del Montello, Italy. At age 38, he was the oldest rider in history to win the world's.*

# Zoetemelk: the unlikely world champion

BY PAT ENNIS

If there were ever a champion who almost wasn't, it is the new world pro road champion, Joop Zoetemelk. Born December 3, 1946, he began cyclo-cross racing at age 17. He became the Dutch national champion in that specialty, but his dream was to become a champion on the road.

As an amateur, he participated in the 1968 Olympics in Mexico City, on the Dutch team time trial squad, and the following year he won the Tour de l'Avenir. He turned professional in 1970.

Zoetemelk was nicknamed "the rat" and "*biberon*" (feeding bottle) for his opportunistic, wheel-sucking tendencies. A contemporary of both Eddy Merckx and Bernard Hinault, he placed second in the Tour de France six times (twice behind Merckx, once behind Lucien Van Impe, and three times behind Hinault). Of his second place to Merckx, he said in answer to his critics, "To stay on that wheel for any length of time was an accomplishment in itself."

In 1974, during the first stage of the Midi-Libre stage race in France, Zoetemelk collided with a car that strayed onto the course during a sprint finish and suffered a fractured skull. Fortunate enough to recover from a coma and a death-threatening case of meningitis (which left him without his sense of taste), he decided to retire from bike racing and manage the hotel he bought with his wife. But he returned to the sport that he loved the following year. In 1980, at age 33, he won the Tour de France.

"I'm a stage racer," Zoetemelk explained after winning the pro road championship on September 1. "It is more logical for me to win the Tour than the world's."

In fact, he almost didn't enter either race this year. Had it not been for the urging of Jan Raas, ex-racer and new director of the Kwantum team, Zoetemelk would have retired earlier this season. But because Zoetemelk had won the Italian stage race, Tirreno-Adriatico, in the spring, Raas convinced him to ride the Tour for the 15th time. After placing a very respectable 12th, the Dutchman spoke again of retirement, but Raas convinced him to continue racing through the end of the season.

"I was working for Johan Van der Velde," Zoetemelk said of his championship ride. "I had noticed some rivalries in the field earlier, but when I escaped [just over a kilometer from the finish], I didn't know what would happen. I was astonished that no one chased. It almost didn't seem true.

"I can hardly believe I won. The full impact won't hit me until I return home ... to my family, and the celebrations."

And how much longer will he continue to race? "One more year," Zoetemelk replied. "But I won't compete in the Tour next year. It is no longer a race for me, at my age."

Now 38, Zoetemelk is the oldest pro rider ever to win the world's. Stan Ockers (Belgium) won it in 1955 at age 35, and Fausto Coppi (Italy) was 34 when he won the world championship in 1953.

*French road racer Jeannie Longo was at the height of her fame when she was interviewed in 1987, having won three consecutive world road titles, a Tour de France Féminin, and three Coors Classics.*

# Longo: Woman of the decade

BY **MARILEE ATTLEY**

I
n 1987, Jeannie Longo won the Tour de France Féminin, PostGirot Tour of Norway, Coors Classic and world road championship (for the third straight year). She currently holds world hour records at both sea level and altitude, as well as 10km and 20km. Her native France has awarded her the Legion of Honor medal, and she was named Athlete of the Year in 1986 by *Vélo* magazine. She may be the dominant female cyclist of the decade.

Yet Longo, 29, has also been known to chastise teammates in public and push other riders in the pack. After she first lost the yellow jersey in the 1987 Tour Féminin, she reportedly took a swing at the Dutchwoman who had stolen her lead.

Longo makes no claim to being a diplomat, and she says the hostilities stop when the racing ends. But neither is she a one-dimensional super-athlete. For example, she's an accomplished pianist who studied the classics from age seven to 17. She has a college degree in math and computer science, and is currently pursuing advanced studies in sports economics and law at the University of Grenoble, France.

She has been married for two years to Patrice Ciprelli, a former French amateur racer who has become her personal coach. Not only do they plan her training program together, but Ciprelli and Longo go over each route before a race, planning when and where she should attack. "I owe many of my wins to him," she said.

Longo began cycling in 1979, initially as training for downhill skiing, and found success early on the bike. Soon she began pursuing it in her methodical way. "I do my sport like the best. All the training I do, the rest, everything I do is around cycling," she said.

This year, her main goal was the Tour Féminin, because it was the one major victory that had eluded her (besides the Olympic road race). She knew that to beat two-time winner Maria Canins of Italy, she had to improve her climbing. "All winter, two times a week, I would climb mountains," Longo said. "My husband would wait for me at the top and drive me down in the car because sometimes it would be snowing. Then in May and June I climbed every day in the mountain passes around my home in Grenoble...."

So intent was Longo on winning the Tour that she was willing to jeopardize her chances at defending her world pursuit title. "I didn't do any speed work at all before the Tour," she said. It showed. In the Tour she didn't win a single sprint finish, but she came through where it counted — in the mountains. On one of the toughest ascents, she left Canins behind and powered on to a two-minute lead. She held that margin to the finish.

A month later she claimed her third straight Coors Classic, finishing six minutes ahead of runner-up Inga Thompson. Then, in the world road championship, Longo attacked in the final miles and no one could go with her. The same move enabled her to win two stages at the Coors Classic. Sometimes it seemed to be the only tactic she had — or needed. "But I don't use the same strategy in every race," she said. "My strategy depends on my shape and the course profile."

While the course profiles vary, Longo's shape seems only to improve. "I thought last year I was at my peak," she said, "but this year I am better. I can train with more maturity. I know what I need to do."

Among the things she wants to do are improve her altitude hour record and win the Olympic road race.

How much longer does she intend to race? "I think about the Olympics in 1988, but I don't know about '89. In my city, Grenoble, they are building a track. I work for my city, so I'll be involved somehow, as a rider or ...."

She feels that sponsorship opportunities are improving for women. "I think the future of cycling is not amateur and professional," Longo said. "But we need money in this sport. Sponsors give girls motivation because, if you must work to earn money and then after work train, you are tired and cannot race at your best."

Racing at her best is something Longo knows plenty about. That's how she managed to become the only racer, male or female, ever to win three consecutive Coors Classics.

Still, she doesn't consider the Coors to be in the same league as the Tour Féminin. "They are very different," she said. "The Tour is a huge organization. There are millions of people along the roads. The competition is more international. There are no foreign teams at the Coors. That's a pity."

But whatever the race, Longo must carry the burden of being the most-watched rider in the peloton. "The pressure of being on top is always hard," she said. "But I am used to it."

*The first man to win five Tours de France, Jacques Anquetil died of cancer in 1987.*

# Anquetil: One of the greats

**BY GEOFF DRAKE**

Jacques Anquetil, the great French pro and five-time Tour de France winner, died of stomach cancer November 18 in Rouen, France. He was 53.

At his funeral in nearby Quincampoix, his birthplace, a Tour de France yellow jersey was laid on his coffin. Many famous cyclists attended, including Raymond Poulidor, Ercole Baldini, Felice Gimondi, Luis Ocaña, Bernard Thévenet, Eddy Merckx and Bernard Hinault.

The French cycling monthly, *Vélo,* published a special issue dedicated to Anquetil. Included in the magazine were statements from French president François Mitterand, former Tour directors Jacques Goddet and Félix Lévitan, and riders Jeannie Longo and Bernard Hinault.

What kind of rider was Anquetil? Some say he had one of the most beautiful pedaling styles in the history of bike racing. His toes were always pointed down and his heels high. One rider confessed that he would sometimes get on Anquetil's wheel just for the pleasure of watching him pedal.

In their book, "Road Racing Technique and Training," to be published by *VeloNews* in the spring, Bernard Hinault and Claude Genzling describe Anquetil's style this way: "His pedal action didn't look like anyone else's and it aroused the admiration of spectators and peers.... Anquetil perfected his style in training, with a concentration that made him resent the presence of other riders around him.

"This partly explains his extraordinary domination in time trials. His style was certainly inborn. But he cleaned it up and perfected it, searching for his own best way to put the greatest possible tangential force on the crank during the full rotation of the crank arm."

One of the most famous moments in Anquetil's career came in 1965 when he won the Dauphiné Libéré stage race and the following day won Bordeaux-Paris, a 347-mile classic race, half of which is done behind a motor. In his book, "Continental Cycle Racing," Noel Henderson describes Anquetil's feat this way: "Anquetil had been engaged to ride in the Dauphiné Libéré, ending in the afternoon of May 29, and in Bordeaux-Paris, starting at 2 a.m. on May 30.... Some suggested that Anquetil would treat the Dauphiné as a training ride for Bordeaux-Paris, others that he would withdraw from the latter race. Those who knew him best suggested that he would try to win both — but only try.

"Anquetil, always joining the correct break, took the lead in the Dauphiné by winning stage four at Oyonnax. Two days later, over four passes, he dropped everyone, but Poulidor, and won again. Another two days and he was winning the time trial at over 27 mph. When the race ended in Avignon, Anquetil led Poulidor by one-and-three-quarter minutes....

"The final stage ended in Avignon at 3 p.m., having begun at 9 a.m. Then followed two hours of receptions and interviews. When all was over, Anquetil flew to Bordeaux in a specially chartered plane, had three hours rest, and got up for his pre-race meal.

"During the night (the race started at midnight), he was unable to eat anything because of a severe cramp in the stomach, and continued against advice."

But in the Chevreuse Valley, after 300 miles, "Anquetil was away, pursuiting his way to Paris, to win by less than one minute."

Anquetil started racing in 1951, and the next year he was French amateur road champion and took a bronze medal in the team race at the Olympic Games. The following year, he turned pro at age 19 and won the Grand Prix des Nations time trial for the first of nine times in nine starts over a 14-year period.

He excelled in time trials and often won road races by breaking away. In 1967, he improved the world hour record. Anquetil again improved the record in 1967, covering 47.493km, but that mark was disallowed when Anquetil refused to take a drug test.

Later in life, Anquetil was involved in cycling as a coach, cycling journalist and race director of the Paris-Nice stage race.

*After blazing onto the mountain-bike scene in his teenage years, John Tomac, then 21, took a change of pace in 1989, when he was interviewed by VeloNews correspondent Owen Mulholland.*

# A man who knows where he's going

## BY OWEN MULHOLLAND

Contrary to popular impression, mountain-bike whiz kid John Tomac is a warm and talkative sort. To appreciate that, you have to work past two problems: to get the guy to stand still for a while, and to get him alone. Since most people encounter Tomac at bike races, these problems can be insurmountable. Even away from races he can be difficult to pin down.

The first time I phoned him for an interview, his sister told me he'd "just left for the track." The next time I called it was well after dark and she was a bit worried because he'd left on a "two-hour mountain-bike ride seven hours ago!" When we finally got together the following week, Tomac was still grinning about that ride.

"Me and some friends got lost exploring some new trails in the San Gabriel mountains," he explained. "I left them to take a shortcut back to the truck, but I took a wrong turn onto a five-mile climb. It was pitch black, I ran out of food ... wow, it was great!"

With Tomac, what you see is mostly what you get. He loves, loves, loves riding bikes. He always has — well, almost always, since age four; and as far as he or anyone can tell, he always will. But right now this talented 21-year-old cyclist confronts the difficulty of which type of bike to ride.

No one doubts that he can go on being a dominant force off-road. Pursuing the narrow line between ridiculous false modesty and equally ridiculous self-aggrandizement, Tomac is perfectly clear about where he stands in the off-road scene. "At the beginning of 1987, I was worried about a few guys, and after a while, just one [Ned Overend, of course].

I can win a lot of mountain-bike races, but they won't mean as much as the road. Once you get to the front it's just a grind the whole way," he said.

"My friend Thurlow Rogers is always bugging me to do road, to do a 'real' sport. He's right regarding the competition right now, but mountain biking is just as legitimate as the road. Racing over rough terrain can be tougher than anything else. Three hours flat out is all anyone can take, I don't care who it is. But I've pretty well done that, and I thrive on new challenges."

The downside risk of changing camps, and it's a small one, is that Tomac's financial future is pretty secure with mountain bikes. "The way things are going, after four or five years I might never have to work again," he revealed. Before the 1988 season, he said, "If all my deals go through, I might get close to six digits this year."

That's as close to money talk Tomac likes to get. Cash is not what really makes his life happen but he knows its value. Shortly after arriving in Los Angeles from his native Michigan, he enrolled in a technical school specializing in electronics. He graduated at the end of the summer of 1986 and told the school's placement office to hold off for two weeks. Then he told his old BMX sponsor, Mongoose, to consider a contract for 1987 if he did well at the Ross Fat-Tire Four-Day race and the national championships. Tomac won the Ross event in New England and was leading the nationals when his bike broke. Mongoose needed no more convincing, and the school's job placement was put on permanent hold.

Last season would have been a bit awkward if his principal sponsor, Mongoose, were the inflexible sort. With a "signature" John Tomac mountain bike heading its line (a fairly "rad" bike with a 72-degree head angle), Mongoose might have expected Tomac to stick to the dirt. Fortunately, they understood his potential well enough to know that an Olympic year was not the time to thwart whatever road aspirations he might have had.

For that, Tomac is very grateful. He rode with the Sunkyong-SKC road team and put himself in contention for the Olympic team by brilliantly winning the national criterium championship at White Plains, New York. This was ironic in view of his earlier statement: "I like road races better than criteriums. I just don't dig going in circles."

He was also put off by some of the attitudes he encountered. "A lot of cycling people aren't nice to others, especially newcomers," he observed. "There are cliques in skinny tires. There's always an elite group that thinks they're better than anyone else. They didn't pay any attention to me until I beat them all. Then all of a sudden I'm their friend."

You might think Tomac would be attracted to this nastier side of cycling. One of his ads claims he's "Bad to the Bone," another that he's into "Bar Hopping." Throw in the dark shades and the buzz cut which established his image, and the casual reader could be excused for wondering how cycling started to attract punks.

"My hair thing goes back to my Christian elementary school. After eighth grade, I went to a public school where all I found were clean-cut, preppy athletes or the stoners. I was in between, so I got into something new, sort of New Wave."

His buzz cut was such a turn-on for the kids in Tomac's neighborhood that they lined up in his garage for the "me-too" treatment. And they'll probably follow now that he has longer locks.

But who could blame the kids for their adulation? They sensed that this was one guy who knew where he was going: that if he'd been a little out of step with society from time to time it was because he had to be in step with himself.

The attraction of doing well at a sport as complex as cycling is an obvious amp in one's life. By age seven, Tomac was hooked. It was hard to convince his parents at first, but he made such a stink they finally capitulated. Ever since, "it's been the only thing I've ever done, only thing I wanted to do every day," he explained.

Less obvious is another inner pillar of Tomac's strength, Christian faith. It goes back to his elementary school days. "A lot of people get out of those schools," Tomac observed, "and either blow it off or turn into a full rebel. That didn't happen to me. Everything sunk in the way it was supposed to. I never show it that much. I don't push religion on anyone, but that's the core of my personality."

I was certainly appreciative of his mature confidence on our bike ride, his first, in Marin County, California — the birthplace of mountain biking. He just cruised through a four-hour downpour enjoying the camaraderie and scenic wonder of the redwood forests with nary a thought for pecking order.

Two days later he went to Michigan for a month with his family. Michigan and recharge are somewhat synonymous for him. It's also his favorite fishing area at other times of the year. Come January, he planned to be back at his sister's in the San Fernando Valley of Los Angeles.

Tomac knows his experience is limited, but he finds cause for optimism in not having made the same mistake twice. He is particularly proud of his criterium title last year, and his eighth-place performance at the 1987 National Amateur Road Championship, which capped a meteoric rise from complete novice just a few months before.

Last year, Tomac failed at the Olympic road trials, despite winning one of the three heats for the national championship road race. "I wasn't too disappointed, as I hadn't given the trials my full effort," he said. But his promise has secured him a place on the USCF national road squad.

Whenever possible, Wayne Stetina, the multi-Olympian and national road champion, has served as Tomac's mentor and riding partner. Obviously, Stetina is not one of those elite clique riders. Stetina, Rogers, Tomac's sister and brother-in-law, and just a few others make up Tomac's social set.

"I spend so much time bike racing and preparing for it. I want to do it good, so I just don't get involved with other stuff," he commented.

*In June 1992, Miguel Indurain's first Tour de France win was behind him ... and he had just taken his first Giro d'Italia. Racer Allan Peiper wrote this appraisal of the Spanish ace.*

# On Miguel's wheel

.....................................

**BY ALLAN PEIPER**

I've ridden with Bernard Hinault, Francesco Moser, Sean Kelly, Laurent Fignon and Greg LeMond, but in my 10 years of professional cycling, no rider has impressed me the way Miguel Indurain has. This isn't based solely on cycling ability. In my first Milan-San Remo, in 1983, I spent 100km riding behind then world champion Giuseppe Saronni — I was so under the spell of that rainbow jersey! There were moments in this Giro when I nearly felt the same, on days we'd be lined out on the side of the road, and I would be behind Miguel. I think I must have counted every spoke in his back wheel at least 100 times!

Those wheels: Campagnolo hubs shining with a brilliance; flat spokes, radial on the front and left side at the back, crossed on the right; and Mavic aero' ceramic rims, with smaller-than-average racing tires. Then, there was his ceramic Pinarello frame: click-shift levers on the down tube, none of this brake-lever shifting for Miguel. The other top riders changed bikes for the mountains ... not Miguel, he already had his weapons out.

He's always so cool, never seems to be nervous. I said to one of my teammates that if Indurain weren't careful, Claudio Chiappucci would be gone without him one day. Sure enough, on stage 15, from Riva del Garda, a break went on the opening climb with Chiappucci, Roberto Conti and Franco Chioccioli — but no Miguel. The peloton was blown to pieces.

From previous experience, I knew a stage like this could be fatal, if you were dropped on the first climb. I gave it everything and was in the second group at the top. Four Banesto men rode the gap — after their screaming, panic-stricken director came up to tell them to chase. Forty kilometers later, the eight escapees were back in the bunch. Miguel sat upright, no hands, and clapped, saying, "Come on, boys, attack."

Never ruffled, he always looks cool. He never perspires, his hat is always just right, and he never has marks on his shorts from wiping his hands. Once, on a long descent with Miguel on my wheel, I thought, "I better be careful. Miguel is behind me.... I'd hate for him to crash because of me."

Miguel has respect in the peloton because he is so *normal*. He isn't a loudmouth, and he has respect for all his fellow riders. Maybe his appeal is that he's so relaxed. Journalists say he is a dream, so polite and genuinely friendly. He even seems shy! One evening, we were in the same hotel as Banesto, and Miguel came to the table late. Before he sat down, he put his hand on his brother Prudencio's shoulder, and I saw the light squeeze of his fingers. It moved me to see such brotherly love. But then, that's Miguel.

What's most impressive, however, is how strong this man is. In the time trials, he had no competition; and in the mountains, he just rode the gaps as they attacked. In the longest mountain stage, there was an early break of 25 riders ... 220km later, at the foot of the final climb, there were still two riders in front. In the vastly diminished front group, attacks were coming fast and furious. My fellow Australian Neil Stephens (ONCE) asked Miguel if he wanted him to make some tempo to stop the attacks (Indurain's director had asked Neil if he would be prepared to give a hand, if Miguel got into trouble). Miguel coolly replied, "No, there is 20km uphill, they will come back."

After the 16th stage to Sondrio, photographer Graham Watson said that Indurain never has to go hard, but when he *does*, it's incredible. Indurain had gone with Chiappucci and Mario Cipollini, as they attacked on a wet descent. At the bottom, the gap was 40 seconds. Thirty of us were in the group behind. Motorola (for Andy Hampsten) and GB-MG (Chioccioli) chased for 20km through the valley to the last climb, and didn't make any impression on the lead trio ... such was Indurain's riding. Sean Yates (Motorola) said he was "screwing his legs off" trying to get on the wheel, after a stint on the front chasing — and there were seven or eight chasing.

Believe me, it's not who will win the Tour de France, it's who can race Indurain.... I'll again be trying for a stage win, and I'm getting a new pair of wheels ... just like Miguel's.

*Successful at racing both road and mountain bikes, Canadian Alison Sydor was interviewed in 1993 — prior to her winning three consecutive world cross-country titles and the Grundig World Cup.*

# A cyclist for all seasons

BY MARTI STEPHEN

Alison Sydor is a combination of tenacity, athletic prowess, smarts, confidence, humility (yes, humility), and maybe even that old battleground quality, valor. And while Sydor is clearly more than the sum of her parts, her qualities — and how she feels about them — reveal an athlete ideally suited to her profession.

"I'm a disciple of the philosophy that if you just keep going and trying your best, one day it will happen," the Canadian cyclist told *VeloNews*. "And that's exactly what happened to me about four years ago. I had some success, but limited success, internationally as a road racer, but just kept plugging away. And all of a sudden the break came, and after that there's just a snowball effect. All you need is sometimes that one result to act as a catalyst to pull everything together."

The result that launched Sydor's high-profile road-racing career took place in the 1991 Tour de l'Aude, in which she captured the leader's jersey and held it for six days. Soon after that, Sydor won the World Cup mountain-bike race in Chateau d'Oex, Switzerland, launching a second career in mountain biking. And later that year, she won a bronze medal at the world's road race.

It was the sign of a gifted athlete coming of age, and it really couldn't have been too big a surprise. After all, Sydor had practically been *earmarked* for an athletic career. "I grew up sort of downhill skiing," she said, in her clipped Canadian accent, "and at the time, I guess, they approached my parents to take me for ... uh, I must have shown some sort of promise ... to take me for the national team. But my parents made the decision not to get me involved. They wanted me to have a more balanced growing-up, and to do a lot of different activities rather than focus at such a young age on one activity.... And who knows where it would have led, but I think they made the right decision."

Sydor's "balanced growing-up" involved "anything that was going" — including hockey, basketball, volleyball, and track and field. And everything she tried she excelled at — so much so, that Alison's parents steered her sister in different athletic directions, to keep the two from colliding.

With medical school in mind, Sydor's balanced youth also included getting a degree in biochemistry. But once she tried bike racing during her college years, Sydor found something that deserved her total attention. "I have to admit," she said, "I have a big passion for cycling."

Can that passion encompass two disciplines, though? Until now, the dilemma of whether to focus on road racing or mountain biking has never bothered Sydor much. She would dip out of her road racing career to triumph in mountain biking — a Cactus Cup here, a World Cup race there, a silver medal in the world's. Just this year she is both the reigning Canadian road champion and the No. 2-ranked woman in off-road racing. But as the stakes get higher in mountain biking, she may be forced to choose. "I'm starting to think that maybe I will have to make a decision soon," Sydor conceded, "if I want to be at the top of *either* sport."

Yet she readily acknowledged that it will not be an easy decision. "I'm a big fan of road racing," Sydor noted, "but at the same time, I think I'm ultimately better at off-road racing." What she appreciates about road racing are "the mental aspects and the fact that even on days you are not feeling great, sometimes it comes to you during the race — or you make a good tactical choice and you have a chance of winning." Sydor finds this a contrast to off-road racing: "In the men's races, I see the pacing having more of an effect, because the races are longer. But for the women, after the first lap, things don't change very much."

The quality that makes Sydor think she's ultimately better suited to mountain biking is her all-around ability — not a pure climber, but a good one; not a pure sprinter, but possessing a good sprint. And to make the most of her talents, she rides a course until she's almost bored with it. And after every race, Sydor sits down and reviews how she rode and how it could have been better. In these post-race refinements, she's discovered that she still has "a long way to go as far as getting more speed out of the descending."

Proud of her home country, she can also be rightfully proud of herself. For Sydor is an athlete destined and determined to do her best — no matter what the circumstances — and to be pleased with any results, as long as they reflect her best effort. In other words, she's an athlete's athlete. There can't be any higher accolade.

*In 1993, Juli Furtado won the World Cup for the first time. She was interviewed by VeloNews correspondent Paul Skilbeck.*

# Furtado: the enigmatic superstar

**BY PAUL SKILBECK**

The surprising thing about Juli Furtado's winning the 1993 Grundig World Cup is not that she whitewashed the opposition, but that it took three years of trying before she succeeded ... for she is as talented as cyclists come. Yet if her face is very familiar by now — after a long, industrious sporting career, whose ups and downs have made her wily and wise — few of her mountain-bike colleagues would claim to know what makes this enigmatic rider tick.

Furtado herself is more concerned with knowing what makes the *world* tick. She likes to keep well informed, and leisure for the Durango, Colorado, resident is occupying a table in the Durango Coffee Company, drinking endless espressos and scouring the paper to satisfy her interest in current affairs.

"I love reading the paper and magazines," said the University of Colorado business school marketing graduate. She also loves "big, thick books; I used to go through one of them in a weekend. I like gossipy stuff — well, not exactly gossipy, but definitely not political theory. I like pretty smutty books (big smile), Robert Ludlum, mysteries.... I don't like serious books. When I do read, I feel like I should be *doing* something."

Which explains why Ned Overend once described her as "kinda driven," and why even Furtado once pointed out that "carefree" was not a word she would use to describe herself. Indeed, she generally has the appearance of someone on a mission — this year in particular.

But after her World Cup victory, sitting on the grass immediately after the final in Berlin, Germany, Furtado wore a very different expression. The combination of satisfaction, relief and pleasure on her face showed that the title was the culmination of three years' hard work. It looked then as if she had finally arrived at her destination, and had just let go of the drive that had propelled her so forcefully throughout the season. And with the World Cup crown so long in coming, no one could fault her for now letting go.

In light of this, Furtado's mediocre showing at the world championships two weeks later was hardly surprising. In an interview with *VeloNews*, recorded three days before the cross-country championship at Métabief, France, she displayed an almost ambivalent attitude to the task ahead of her.

She explained, "I've been more motivated for the world's in other years, and when I got here and looked at the conditions.... My motivation's fine, I always go into any race wanting to win, but I accept that my main goal was the World Cup, so any result I get here is icing on the cake."

Since Furtado had already been a world champion, the World Cup was going to be her one to win. "It's partly because I hadn't won it," she explained. "I mean the world's is a great title, all people regard it as the most important ... but the World Cup has many different courses and is all season long, so I think it shows who rode better throughout the season."

Success in the World Cup also attracts a far more enduring publicity than world championship honors do. Yet despite its value to sponsors, the scrutiny of the public eye is something Furtado accepts more than revels in. And it is with mild incredulity that she responds to the suggestion that being in the limelight might be a motivating factor.

"To win stuff? I don't think so. No, it's more.... I don't know why I want to win."

And next season? "I don't think I can ever repeat what I did this year. I don't know how I did it. I shocked myself...."

This self-deprecating quality is puzzling in an athlete as abundantly talented as Furtado. It sometimes sounds almost as if she wants to talk herself *out* of something. "I'm a great descender in race situations, but I can't do it on any other day of the week," she says of her downhill prowess. Then, when reminded of her recent downhill racing record — a rainbow jersey and third place at the NORBA final — she starts looking coy and cites courses that were "perfect" for her and something about being an "instinctive downhiller" as the reasons for her success.

As for her reputation for psychological toughness, Furtado not surprisingly discounts a lot of what is said. "Having a mentally strong head comes from having a physically strong body, and (this year) I had no bad days on race day — which is a lot of luck."

Hard as she is on herself, Furtado is equally uncompromising when talking about her rivals. When one competitor suggested that she had made a conscious decision to let Juli go in a race, Furtado's response was caustic: "It's always easy to say in hindsight when you're sitting there and not breathing hard, but when I went, if she could've gone, she would've gone. That's all there is to it."

# Fignon goes out with a fizzle

BY SAMUEL ABT

*Few racers made as much impact on the 1980s as Laurent Fignon, the dynamic Frenchman whose roller-coaster career ended in 1993.*

That meteor, that lightning bolt called Laurent Fignon has blazed out. Riding in a minor French race late in August, Fignon coasted to the side of the road halfway through and got off his bicycle for the last time as a professional. The authority for that is Fignon himself, and he can be believed.

Blazed out or burned out, how to decide? What can be said is that after a dozen years of majestic heights (two victories in the Tour de France, one in the Giro d'Italia, two in Milan-San Remo, one in the French national championship) and profound depths (a heel injury that cost him peak seasons, last-stage losses of both the Tour and the Giro, two positive drug findings), Fignon, at age 33, has retired as a racer.

He went out his own way, announcing beforehand that since he had no interest in competing in the world championships, the unsung Grand Prix Ouest-France would be his farewell. He would have already slipped into retirement, he said, but he owed it to the fans to be there.

The statement was pure Fignon: An arrogance that was almost touching in its naïveté. Or, if you wish, a naïveté that was almost dumbfounding in its arrogance. By the time he retired, nobody came to see just him. The rider ranked 201st in the world considered himself a fan attraction? A two-page photograph in *Vélo* magazine, the bible of bicycle racing in France, inadvertently said it all. There in the foreground was Fignon — the familiar ponytail, granny glasses and strained look — and there in the background were five fans ... all looking down the road away from Fignon.

Time has moved quickly since 1982, when Fignon emerged from an obscure amateur career and startlingly won the Critérium International in one of his first races as a professional with the juggernaut Renault team. Bernard Hinault was the Renault leader then (Greg LeMond was a young hope), but by July 1983 Fignon was sweeping the Tour de France and the country was glorying in his triumph.

The ex-champion is not speaking publicly these days, and so his latest thoughts date back to the interview he gave to *L'Équipe*, the daily French sports newspaper, the day he retired. From the beginning of the interview he was vintage Fignon, remote and brusque.

Had it meant something to him to start his last race? *L'Équipe* asked. "Something?" Fignon repeated. "No, why should I have felt something?"

Not a heavy heart or sweaty palms?

"No. There was no reason for me to feel sad. I'm rather happy to retire. I decided on this many months ago.... Since I signed with Gatorade (before the 1992 season), I knew I was joining my last team. Only the dead are sad and, as far as I'm concerned, don't talk about a burial.... So don't be sad for me."

Cold, defensive and ungrateful: Let us now praise famous men. Fignon won the Tour de France twice, in 1983 as an unknown, and in 1984, when everybody went gunning for him. A month after he lost the Giro — in the final day's time trial, when Francesco Moser used his new aerodynamic bicycle to overtake him — Fignon overpowered the field in the 1984 Tour de France, winning five stages. The victory was a demonstration of sheer dominance.

But then, just 24 years old, Fignon was struck down. An operation for tendinitis in his left heel sidelined him for most of 1985, and not for years afterward did he fully recover. Then, in 1988, he won Milan-San Remo, and the next year he repeated this triumph, before going on to win the Giro, and be first in the Tour ... until the final day, when LeMond beat him by 58 seconds in the time trial and by eight seconds overall.

Everybody remembers the photographs of a spent Fignon slumped and weeping on the Champs-Élysées, after he crossed the finish line to find himself a runner-up. Few remember that he placed third on that stage, the fastest time trial in the long history of the Tour.

Now, at the end of his career, what seems clear is that Fignon was really always fighting with himself.

Like Hinault, Fignon had an excess of character. Born in Paris, and a longtime resident of the capital, he was the archetypal Parisian, indifferent to everybody but himself. Fignon snatched victories from teammates (Thierry Marie, at the 1989 Tour of the Netherlands; Gérard Rué, the 1988 Tour of the European Community); helped rivals win by chasing down his own teammates (Thierry Claveyrolat, at the 1989 world championship); and treated them like hired hands — "They're paid to ride for me, not be my friends." He was respected in the pack, and at his peak, he was feared, not admired. He was Parisian to his fingertips and not many riders will miss him. But he was also a champion and an electric presence, and the sport, especially in France, needs more like him.

# Davis on Davis

*With more than 300 victories in an 18-year racing career from the late 1970s to the early 1990s, Davis Phinney was America's winningest rider.*

### BY JOHN WILCOCKSON

The phone call came just before Thanksgiving: "I've ended my career as a pro cyclist. In fact, I haven't taken my bike out of its bag since finishing The Norwest Cup in September." The caller was Davis Phinney, who had spent the last three years starring for Coors Light, after six years as the big-time pro sprinter for 7-Eleven, and nine years before that as an amateur. As with his 1993 teammates Alexi Grewal and Roy Knickman, who have also retired from racing, Phinney was a leader of the class of '84 — the formidable U.S. national team that blazed through the Los Angeles Olympics, and still includes current pros like Ron Kiefel and Andy Hampsten.

Phinney was already an American star when he joined the paid ranks in 1985, having won more than 200 races as an amateur — most of them criteriums, including the 1983 USPRO Criterium Championship at Baltimore, ahead of such European racers as Laurent Fignon, Stephen Roche and Allan Peiper. The Olympics brought Phinney a bronze medal in the 100km team time trial, and fifth place in the road race — in an event that he still feels could have brought *him* the gold and not teammate Grewal....

This and many other tales of Phinney's career came tumbling out in the interview he gave to *VeloNews* just before Christmas. The 34-year-old Boulder, Colorado, native was at ease in the living room of his rambling, open-plan home, which looks out at the snow-covered rock formations of the Flatirons in the Rocky Mountains' Front Range. As he talked, his wife Connie Carpenter — the 1984 Olympic gold medalist in the women's road race — was baking a pizza, and three-year-old son Taylor was anxious to get his dad's attention.

We take up the story when Phinney and the rest of the amateur 7-Eleven team decided that they wanted to race as pros in Europe....

**VeloNews** After the 1984 Olympics, the 7-Eleven team collectively decided to turn pro?

**Davis Phinney** It was at the Olympics that we were talking of being pros — and we decided that in '85 we should do this as a team. We'd been successful because we'd been involved with this organization (7-Eleven), with these riders, with this personnel, with (the coach) Jim Ochowicz....

Oh man, it was an experience! It took a long time to get the organization up to speed, and that's part of bringing on Mike Neel. We asked him to be our director for the Tour of Baja (in Mexico in May). Just before, when we rode the Tour of Texas on returning from the spring trip to Europe, Ron and I remembered how well Andy had ridden in the William Tell. And we told him, "You've gotta turn pro, this is cool, this is the way to go." So he got on the Raleigh team for Baja ... and after that, Andy turned pro, and went over to Italy with us to ride the Giro.

Then, two days before the Tour of Italy, Bob Roll calls, and Ron Hayman's gotten sick, and Mike says, "Gee, Bob, d'you think you wanna ride the Tour of Italy?" So Bob says. "Oh ... kay." And he flies over and does the whole thing ... and really impressively.

That's what was fun. You couldn't do that kind of stuff today. No way. But that's when the Giro was just like a Francesco Moser country-club stroll. You'd ride all day at glacial speed ... until with 60km, 80km to go, the helicopters would come in, and — bam! — you'd be doing 60 kph flat out.

So a lot of people got brought along in that race — Andy obviously, and Mike Neel, and Bob Roll ... and the rest of us. Andy and Ron both won a stage. And we were tied in with Boyer — Jock replaced Hayman as the one who was, like, in the men's club; and we were all knocking at the door. Boyer was my "pilot" that first year. I would just follow that guy the last 80km of every race. He would get me to the front with one kilometer to go, no matter what. He was really classy....

**VeloNews** How were you developing as a rider? Were you getting close to winning any stages in the Giro?

**Davis Phinney** I was third twice, and I was in the top 10 probably eight or nine times. That first year, I was really keen. I had a lot of confidence. And the first stage of the '85 Giro really stands out for me....

It was a really long stage, and we rode a pretty pedestrian pace, and then built up to a crescendo. Of course, you have the jet helicopters up above — so you can't hear a thing. You're just flying along the road, riding totally by visual and by instinct. I was just following Jock ... and there were all these fantastic sprinters on Italian teams, like Freuler, Rosola, Mantovani and Bontempi. These big giant guys were just banging into me, and I'm not giving up any space, just holding my position. Then we come to a kilometer to go, and I can see the finish down there, and I'm in about sixth place, saying "This is *great*!" Then Bontempi takes off, and I go with him. He's leading with about 400 meters to go, and he starts to fade. I pass him with about 200 meters to go, and I'm leading my first stage in the Tour of Italy with 100 meters to go.... And then Rosola starts coming by, and ... I don't remember who won, but I got fourth.

I'd had some success already — like a second place to Vanderaerden in the last stage of Tirreno-Adriatico — but (it was a shock for) Andy. He had no expectation for this team. After the Giro stage, Mike was going "good job, good job." So Andy asks, "What happened?" "Well, I got fourth," I said. And he said, "No *way*, no *way*..." He got so excited, and said right away, "We can win a stage here."

It was really fun. It was like we were part of this magical thing, and that totally went into the next year in the Tour de France, when Alex (Stieda) did his amazing ride (to take the yellow jersey on the first day); and the first time I go to the front, I follow (Robert) Dill-Bundi into this break, and I (unknowingly) win the stage. That's been well-chronicled, and you were at the finish line, and you captured my famous words, "I don't believe it! I really don't believe it...."

My very best memories of those times are not myself throwing my arms up winning a stage, it's the expression on the faces of the people you first run into. I remember when I won the stage into Bordeaux in the '87 Tour. It was our second year in the Tour de France, it was into the second week of the race, we hadn't gotten any big result, and Och' was getting kind of uptight.... And after coming across the line, there's Och' with this biggest smile on his face, his arms are raised, and he's so ecstatic. So I reflect on that — the people who really supported me — those times when you are able to make *them* happy. And giving Jim the keys to the BMW after (I won) the '88 Coors Classic, and seeing him almost collapse (in shock). I love stuff like that....

**VeloNews** You were able to win events like the Coors Classic, and stages at the Tour de France. So why did you never win a one-day classic?

**Davis Phinney** I don't think I was strong enough, and I didn't put the focus into it. What always happened to me in Europe was: I'd prepare well in the spring, and be really firing in February, getting good results ... but it always took too much out of me. And so by the time I got into the spring classics (in April), I was already flat. It's just hard to win a race in Europe ... phenomenally hard. In fact, I have so few victories from Europe. It's like, "You won over 300 races, how many did you win in Europe?" "Well, I won five...." "Huh?"

**VeloNews** You said that it was always your desire to do something that people didn't expect you could do. Are there any particular stories that reinforce that statement?

**Davis Phinney** My most favorite story is from the 1990 Tour de France.... I wasn't even supposed to be there. I told Och' that I'm not gonna come, we're having a baby in mid-July, count me out.... But Taylor, a little boy, comes early, and three days before the Tour Och' calls: "Do you want to come?" And I'm over there the day before the race.

Noël Dejonckheere, the team director, says, "Okay, Davis, we need you for 10 days because it's good to have a sprinter, good for morale. But you are finished after 10 days, because you have no preparation." So I thought, "Right, pal, I'm getting to Paris."

It was a wonderful year to be with the team, because Bauer gets the yellow jersey, we have a good team time trial, and hold the jersey for 10 days. And I'm getting in there at the finishes ... but then we get to the mountains. I start suffering through it, and start coming off (the back) really quickly on all the climbs. Then my real Waterloo comes on the stage from just outside of Chamonix to L'Alpe d'Huez....

We went over one climb directly, and that was okay. And then we went up this little bump before the Col de la Madeleine, and I was getting dropped. So right away I'm just gritting my teeth and suffering ... and pretty soon I look back and there's just three guys left. And it's *right* at the bottom. And I see these signs: "28km to the top of the Madeleine."

I rode up the mountain with one other guy. I get to the top, there's about 100km to go, and I'm 20 minutes down. I'm now by myself, as the other guy's quit ... there's no way I'm gonna make it within the 40-minute time limit.

So I kind of relaxed. I'd given it my best shot ... and I knew there was a feed at the bottom of the hill, where I could just climb off my bike. I went down the hill thinking, "This is nice. I'm out in the middle of France, by myself ... and it's over."

Then, I'm down in the town, going past all the parked team cars, and I don't see a 7-Eleven car. And I don't believe it: "They won't even wait for me to quit." Then, right before you turn left to go up the Col du Glandon, a 7-Eleven musette just swings out ... and I grab it. And I keep going, thinking, "That was really dumb."

But I started to feel better, and I picked up my pace on this new climb ... and I started to get the idea: "This is *my* Tour de France. It's just me against the time." I was just gonna go as hard as I could go to L'Alpe d'Huez. It just became the most important thing I could do at that time. I was a half-hour behind and people were leaving the mountain, and then they would spot me, and start cheering me on....

I get over the Glandon, and catch a guy on the descent. We were picked up by a moto gendarme, but the other guy flatted ... and once again I'm on my own. So I just rode hard to the bottom of L'Alpe d'Huez. I had no idea where I stood (on time), but I rode flat out up that hill — and that hill is such a wonderful experience because of the whole fervor. Even though it's 40 minutes after the leaders, the people are just going nuts for you ... slapping me on the back, the whole nine yards. I was giving it absolutely everything I had....

And I can still remember taking that last left turn and sprinting up to the line. Only two people had waited for me — Jim Ochowicz and Sean Petty (of 7-Eleven). I just about fell over at the line. Och' grabs me and throws a jacket around me, and whispers in my ear: "You made it pal. Two minutes." I was so happy; it was like I had won. Then, at the hotel, Noël was talking to some reporters; he looked up and said, "You finished, huh? You come in the car....." And I said, "I made it, Noël. And I'm making it to Paris." And I did.

# Story of an Olympic champion

BY JOHN WILCOCKSON

No name in cycling arouses more mixed emotions than that of Alexi Grewal. And his racing career — which has just ended — will be remembered as much for his outlandish "bad boy" outbursts as for his outstanding performances. The eldest son of an Indian Sikh father and German mother, Grewal apparently inherited characteristics from both, resulting in the volatile, talented, enigmatic personality who has been such an inextricable part of American cycling for the past 15 years. However, as this interview made evident, it was these very characteristics that enabled Grewal to become the first-ever American to win a gold medal in the men's Olympic road race.

**VeloNews** When did the Olympics become a target?

**Alexi Grewal** One year prior, 1983. That was a pivotal year, because I first got coaching. I learned a system where I could compete, and control my fitness ... from a guy ... I'll call him Arnold. I can't say his real name ... he'd kill me!

He lived in Aspen, and once said to me, "If you ever need any help, and need a place to stay, call me." So when I came home from the Milk Race (in Britain) in '83, I didn't have a place to stay, and I called him from the airport. He said, "Okay," and I moved in with him. I learned more from him about being an athlete than anyone else, about the lifestyle, how you sleep.... The training I was most successful with at *any* point in my career was the training that (I did with him). He said, "This is how it used to be when I was training with Coppi." I said, "Okay, I'll do it."

So in '83, I lived in a trailer on his property. He took care of me hand and foot, from

May to the end of the season. And that's when I won the Morgul-Bismarck stage at the Coors (Classic), won a stage at the William Tell (in Switzerland), and won a stage in the Tour de l'Avenir (in France). That was also the year I was second in the nationals.... That was when I decided (to aim for the Olympics) ... because the nationals were in San Diego, in similar conditions and on a similar course, similar everything. So I said I'll have to try to win the Olympics, because I was on a really bad day in San Diego. The heat wore the other guys down. I still felt bad, but I was okay. I was away with Kiefel, and he dropped me with about three kilometers to go.

**VeloNews** This Arnold character, is he Italian?

**Alexi Grewal** He's Swiss. According to him — which I really believe — he was this super-talented, strong rider who'd break away at the beginning (of a race).... There's pictures of him with snow on his shoulders.... He really had a good feel for fundamentals, with a great heart. In '84, I lived with my father, but after we went through all the different things just prior to the Games (*including Grewal's positive drugs test for a Chinese herb in the Coors Classic that was then overruled*), I was in Boulder the evening before I had to fly out to L.A. I called Arnold and said, "I have this flight tomorrow, will you come out and take care of me at the Games?"

He hadn't heard from me ... but he packed his stuff and flew down to Boulder in his little private plane. We picked him up and stayed the night at Len Pettyjohn's house, and then flew down to L.A. together. He pretty much waited on me the whole time I was there. A lot of people helped me, but without his help in that one week before (the Olympic road race), I never would have made it. I'd felt terrible, stressed out....

**VeloNews** How did Arnold help you?

**Alexi Grewal** He bought all the food, cooked every meal for me, and gave me an hour-and-a-half rub *twice* each day. We didn't talk about a whole lot of things ... but when I went out to train the fourth day prior to the race, the air was really bad. I couldn't even breathe. I was thinking, "I'm not even gonna start the race." That was the only time I got real negative, and I remember asking him, "What d'you think?" He replied, "I think you've got the right stuff," that sort of thing. He wouldn't say more than one or two sentences ... we'd sit staring at each other ... and then I'd turn the TV back on.

On the one day I did a long training ride of four-and-a-half hours on the course, three days before the event, he rode over there with the cooler, strapped to the back of this single-speed Schwinn. He sat there the whole time ... made friends with someone living on the corner, and would throw cold water on me and feed me bottles.

**VeloNews** Did he do the same in the Olympic road race?

**Alexi Grewal** I couldn't get him a credential, so he went up to about the same area where he'd fed me in training — about two-thirds of the way up the long, gradual hill at the bottom of the course. He stood there the whole time with the cooler. When I went by the first lap, he waved, "Here I am." The place was packed, and it was about six-to-seven deep where he was; but the people made a little space for him to work in. And this hand would stick out of the crowd with a bottle, and I'd just grab it. Later in the race, I'd ask for a particular piece of fruit, and there would be a peach, or whatever, the next lap.

**VeloNews** In the race itself, what made you break away alone so far from the finish?

**Alexi Grewal** Looking back on it, it was just *right*. I'd made a little move at the top of the hill; and when I made these little moves, (Steve) Bauer would come up to me, and he then would motor by. And the other guys would chase. This time, when I made my move, Bauer came up and pulled quite *hard*, for quite a ways. I wasn't in trouble on his wheel, but I wasn't gonna pull. The other guys caught us — Dag-Otto (Lauritzen) pretty much brought 'em back up. Thurlow (Rogers) and Davis (Phinney) were the last guys to get there, I think. But they got there fairly quickly. And then Bauer went again. I got right on his wheel, and we came to this little riser before these small rollers. And everyone had their tongues hanging out, and I thought this was the opportunity to get a little space. I knew we were coming to the last lap — so why wait for the steep hill?

I'd pretty much ridden that hill at one speed all day. And I couldn't really go any faster than that. I don't think I thought of it logically, but all of a sudden there was this big opportunity … there was a lull … not that many guys … and I was on a wheel. We'd gone over a rise, some guys had pulled and we were a little stretched out. And I had speed on the guy in front of me. I was coming up on the guy already, so (I thought) I would pull out, carry that speed past him, and jump from there. I don't remember anyone being real close on me, so I thought, "This is perfect, I'll make this big attack right now."

I was gonna go with a lot of speed, and go flying by. But right when I pulled out to do that, the TV motor pulled in, because of a coned-off lane. And I couldn't go between the motor and the other rider without it being tricky. So I had to brake a little bit, and I waited for the motor to go, then coasted past (the rider). I wasn't even thinking about attacking until I coasted past him … 10 meters … 15 meters clear … coasting. And then there's a downhill, I'm already up to more speed than they are, and there's another riser. It was a perfect time.

I had 15 meters for free, and so I then just started pedaling … checking consistently to see if they were coming after me. I started pedaling, and looking underneath my arm a little bit. If they'd come after me right away, I'd have stopped immediately. But by the time I got to the bottom of that little hill, I slowly wound the gear up until I was going at full speed. So I was in the 12, going at full speed down this hill, and when I looked back they hadn't even begun pedaling. Then I decided, "I'm going now." I already had like 10 seconds. And I just started going hard. It wasn't premeditated, it was just a great opportunity.

I don't want to call it luck, because I don't believe in luck. If I hadn't done that, the last time we'd have gotten to the hill, they would have all dropped us. It would have been those two Norwegians and Bauer, and we would have been chasing them. And they would have killed us, because they were *all* stronger than us. I think Bauer was the strongest, but those other two guys weren't a lot less powerful at the end of the race. And the last time up the hill, I didn't go too fast!

**VeloNews** That's where Bauer caught you, right?

**Alexi Grewal** Right. I had a lot of trouble getting over that hill. If all six of us had gone into it together on the last lap, three would have come out in front, and three behind.

Later, when Bauer caught me, he was 10 times stronger than I was. I was doing everything I could to stay on his wheel, faking that I was halfway decent. He could've dropped me on either one of the two long uphills. All he would've had to do was jump once, get me out of breath, then jump again. He almost rode me off his wheel on the long, gradual one … when someone hit me with this huge bucket of cold water, right at the right time. I just gasped, got a deep breath again, and got back on his wheel.

**VeloNews** What did Bauer do wrong in the sprint?

**Alexi Grewal** That's another interesting story, because his coach — who I talked to a year or two later — told me, "I was watching the race on TV, and thinking I've gotta run down and tell Bauer to go from 500 yards." So he was trying to run down to the last corner, and he had plenty of time, but a policeman stopped him.

If Bauer *had* gone from a long way out, he would've blown me out of the water. As it was, I got past him, held it, and was probably losing a little bit toward the very end. So he waited too long. He waited until it was the perfect distance for me. It was what I was best at. I was light, it was uphill, and I'd trained to accelerate from a slow to a fast speed. That's the sprint that I've always been good at. And so he handed it to me. I was thinking, "This is awesome. Keep going."

If he'd gone at 500 yards, and enticed me out into the wind, he would have shed me immediately.

**VeloNews** Did the crowd have any affect on you?

**Alexi Grewal** The crowd had an affect on *every*one. Of all the races I've ridden, I've never ridden one in which the crowd was so loud. On the steep hill, it was so loud, it was like you were inside a culvert … you felt good when you got out of it. The roar was like *too* much.

I remember riding with Len to the start. We had to ride two miles to the course, then around half the lap. And we were riding up the hill … Len was carrying my wheels and water bottles. He could barely get up the hill, he had all this stuff — he was sweating. People would see us coming, and they would just start this roar as we started up the hill. And I just turned to Len and said, "There's no way I can lose." I was pretty convinced I could win the race before it started. Actually, I was *totally* convinced that I could win that particular race. And I think the crowd had a lot to do with it.

*Eddy Merckx, who retired in 1978, was arguably the greatest road cyclist of the 20th century. He turned 50 in 1995....*

# The Cannibal turns 50

BY OWEN MULHOLLAND

Eddy Merckx and I have two things in common: a love of cycling and the same age — he turned 50 on June 17. I first learned of Merckx in 1964 when he burst onto the international stage at age 18 with a blow-'em-away victory at the world amateur road championship. And as subsequent years rolled by, I was left to contemplate what I might have done if I'd been born in a different body in a different place.

I was not alone. All my generation had similar thoughts. From the most distant observers, such as myself, to his professional rivals — such as 1976 Tour de France winner Lucien Van Impe, who once observed, "It was unbelievable; he was always a gear above us." Or perhaps 1965 Tour winner Felice Gimondi, who paid him this compliment: "They say when Colombians ... or Americans race in Europe, Eddy Merckx will be surpassed. But I don't believe it. He will always be the greatest." Yes, the majority of observers agree that he was the most significant person ever to put a leg over a bike ... and here's why.

Stats: With Mr. Merckx they never end, but here are a few. He won five Tours de France, five Tours of Italy and a Vuelta a España. He won all the classics (except the flattest one) ... and most numerous times. He took four world road championships, virtually every important (and not-so-important) race on the calendar. He also broke the world hour record, won numerous six-day races ... and that's just the start of the list. Several times, he set the record for most victories in a season, and he virtually owned the Super Prestige Pernod trophy (similar to the current World Cup) for nearly a decade.

Well, you get the idea. And yet, impressive as they are, dry stats are tedious. It was the way those stats were created that really puts Merckx in his own category.

For all riders but Merckx, conservation of energy is a primary consideration. But Eddy seemed to have his private energy source. I first laid eyes on him in his first Tour de France, 1969. On the first stage, an admittedly dangerous break of four was a minute up the road. Standard strategy would have been for Merckx to marshal his troops at the front of the peloton to chase down the break. But what did I see? Here was the Belgian himself at the head of a 160-rider line, merrily towing everyone along. I rushed into a bar and watched him on TV as he played choo-choo for the next 20 minutes. Later, he set up the sprint for one of his teammates, Julien Stevens. And later yet that afternoon, he powered his team to victory in the team time trial and took the yellow jersey. Day after day, Merckx gave new meaning to the French expression, *la course en tête* (racing at the front). Foolish? Wasteful? Undeniably. But beautiful? A thousand times yes. And when that Tour encountered its first mountains, Merckx showed no signs of slowing down. He was genuinely astonished when he won the Tour's first uphill stage by over four minutes. Later in the same Tour, in the Pyrénées, he doubled his eight-minute overall lead in *one* stage, having soloed the last 140km.

The word "panache" has come to be associated with Bernard Hinault, but it would have fit Eddy Merckx even more so. Normally, he rode at the front at such a frightful pace that other riders would eventually drop off … and leave him to cruise in for the victory. I have a picture of Merckx leading an echelon in the Tour of Flanders. He looks serious, but all the others look like they're in a full sprint. Of course they couldn't keep that up forever, and one by one they cracked and dropped back.

Occasionally, the bike gods would handicap Merckx, like the day in the 1971 Tour when he lost nine minutes to Luis Ocaña. An impossible handicap, one might have thought, but Eddy vowed to make every remaining day a classic. The very next stage, he broke clear with a teammate and a handful of others in the first kilometer of the 240km stage to Marseille. Their break took back two of the lost minutes — and set a record for the fastest stage in Tour history!

Eddy's last win in a single-day classic was a record seventh success at Milan-San Remo. I have a French book showing him flying down the tortuous Poggio with a caption that captured his spirit, "*l'attitude suicidaire.*"

Because he was not only a winner, but an electrifying rider to watch, the fans loved him and flocked to see their insatiable hero, for he was always ready to do his best, always committed to winning. Go back and read of his exploits. All great riders had some, but his were endless.

For myself, I am grateful to have lived in the same era as Eddy and been lucky enough to witness firsthand the greatest phenomenon our sport has ever seen.

## 95

# Twigg back on track

**BY DEBORAH CROOKS**

Although it's been 18 years since Rebecca Twigg entered her first bike race, and despite her four-year "retirement" — from 1988 through 1991 — she's still one of America's brightest cycling stars. After all, Twigg can count four world titles (and a silver) in the 3000-meter pursuit and a couple of Olympic medals — a silver in the road race at Los Angeles and a bronze in the pursuit at Barcelona — as well as innumerable national road and track medals to her credit.

After a national time trial championship in 1994, Twigg had been notably absent at the races this season. But after taking most of the spring off to go to school — she already has an AA in computer science and a B.A. in biology — she decided to race in Idaho to train for the upcoming track world's.

**VeloNews** Where have you been this season?

**Rebecca Twigg** I've been in school at UCS in Colorado Springs. I've been taking classes to try to get into graduate school in computer science. It worked out well. Then I can race without worrying about what I'm doing afterwards.

**VeloNews** Have you been training much?

**Rebecca Twigg** After finals, I started training every day. But it doesn't matter what time of year it is, the first race is hard. One of my biggest goals (in the races) is to train to get in shape. As the season goes on, I'll get into road racing a little more, but my heart is still in pursuiting. My focuses now are just on the nationals, world's and Olympics.

**VeloNews** Do you still work with Eddie B?

**Rebecca Twigg** I'm riding on his team [Montgomery-Bell] and I still talk to him and get coaching advice. I have so much experience, and a lot of it comes from him. I can almost coach myself, but there are still times when I need it.

**VeloNews** When you look back, do you have mostly fond memories, or has it been hard?

**Rebecca Twigg** Well, you know, it *is* hard. It's a hard sport and it's tough. I've had pressure on me…. I've really gained a lot of self-confidence from cycling. But I've also *earned* that.

**VeloNews** You've done things that people only dream about — the world championships, records, the Olympics…. Has it all been worth it?

**Rebecca Twigg** Oh, absolutely. Sure, there have been struggles and hard times; but being able to travel and see other countries, that's been exciting. And getting the recognition's been great.

**VeloNews** You've had such an accomplished life and you're only 32! You started college at 14, and began bike racing the same summer. Do you think this has taken a toll on your personal life?

**Rebecca Twigg** Probably, a little bit, yes. You make sacrifices. Certainly, at times I've felt socially awkward, because I haven't had time to brush up on those skills. I guess I'm starting to learn them now. At least I hope!

**VeloNews** Didn't you marry young, too?

**Rebecca Twigg** Yeah. I was married at 21 or 22 to Mark Whitehead. It was too young. We were opposites. We just weren't compatible, really. You have to have the same values and beliefs…. Now, I really realize how important it is, and what a commitment it is. It's very scary, because I don't want to make another mistake.

I'm definitely more spiritually aware now. I've been exploring a lot more religions and realizing that there are more similarities than differences. The more I've explored, the more I realize there is a truth to spirituality.

**VeloNews** Is this new to you?

**Rebecca Twigg** We were raised Unitarian and we did arts and crafts. So, no, I wasn't exposed to any religion before. It's been really eye-opening. It makes me feel more secure … comforted. I feel more healthy now, more well-rounded.

**VeloNews** Did you ever suffer from depression?

**Rebecca Twigg** Oh boy … I don't really want to go into *everything*. Not really depression, but I had different weaknesses. Right now, I have a really positive attitude. I have a place. If I do feel like I'm slipping, then I'll meditate or pray more and find more guidance, to go on the path that's going to help myself and everybody else the most — to be the most useful.

**VeloNews** Useful?

**Rebecca Twigg** Doing the most good overall — for the benefit of myself and anyone else.

**VeloNews** Even when you came back to cycling the second time, in 1992?

**Rebecca Twigg** Yes. Part of it has got to be *for you*. Sure, it's great to want to do it for the good of everyone, but it's got to be good for you, too — or it's going to be really hard to talk yourself into doing these things. They're painful. Cycling's hard.

# Ballantyne on balance

BY MARTI STEPHEN

On a peg near a claw-footed bathtub in the log house that Sara Ballantyne and her husband Chris Haaland built near Breckenridge, Colorado, hangs a white terry-cloth bathrobe with chain-grease marks on it. The bathrobe belongs to Ballantyne, who may have retired after 10 years of mountain-bike racing, but who still hasn't slowed down.

In fact, without a race and training schedule to chain her to the bike, Ballantyne appears to have speeded up. On this December day, she had just finished snowshoeing in the pine-covered hills out her back door and was packing to go to Bolivia. The trip was scheduled for the morning after she picked up her lifetime achievement award at the Korbel Night of Champions featuring the *VeloNews* Awards in Los Angeles. Before any settling happens, Ballantyne will co-lead a January bike trip in Mexico's Copper Canyon, and spend the rest of the month at her parents' new house in Baja California, Mexico. She'll join Rock Shox founder Paul Turner in Whistler, British Columbia, at the end of February. In March, she'll join her husband in Argentina to do some climbing. And at the end of April, she's going heli-skiing in Canada "with the girls."

Ten years of mountain biking has been a long career, and the final year was the hardest by far, says Ballantyne. "So now I'm rewarding myself with continual vacations," she quips. "I've gotta figure out when I'm gonna have kids."

Ballantyne confesses that her natural job choice is coaching, a career that the 1990 Grundig World Cup winner realizes is filled with challenges. "I've been led by the hand before," she notes. "It's going to be a challenge [to lead someone else]...."

Ballantyne is ready to move on, though. "I knew at the start of the season it'd be my last season," she says. "It's a great sport.... But it's just gotten to a level where ... you have to be able to live a pretty anal lifestyle."

For a woman whose kitchen sink has a view of Breckenridge's Peak No. 8 and Peak No. 9 — mountains that she and her husband routinely hike up and ski down in the winter — a singular devotion to the bike was numbing. "I felt like I was giving up a lot on a powder day to go ride a bike," she explains. "But it definitely paid off [Ballantyne's efforts earned her third place in the Jeep National Cross-country Series], and I'm glad I did it. I think life is meant to be a series of challenges...."

Ballantyne's challenges have ranged from being the first American woman pro mountain biker to race in Europe — and win the Grundig World Cup — to bringing equal prize money to women's racing. Her career has spanned developments from the grass-roots start-up races of Northern California; to the first official world championships in Durango, Colorado; to her own bronze medal at the 1994 world's in Vail, Colorado.

At those first world's in 1990, she was the hands-down favorite to win the rainbow jersey, but her pioneering European travels had left her tired. In fact, in order to defend her title in the World Cup that year, she had to fly back to France to race in the finals just one week before the world's. By the time she got to the world's, she was exhausted. "I remember being on the starting line, and I remember my body shutting down," she recalls. But she bears no grudges over the circumstances, and says that she felt "very happy" for Juli Furtado who triumphed that day.

In talking to Ballantyne, whose face is supple from frequent smiles, it's clear that she has no regrets over the decade she devoted to one sport. And despite her many athletic accomplishments, the achievement of which she is the most proud has more to do with activism. She and several other well-known women in the off-road peloton got together and lobbied for women's prize money to be equal with the men's for the top three places. They got what they wanted; however, Ballantyne laments that the process stopped there. "It's never going to be equal," Ballantyne says about the size of women's and men's fields, "but I don't think that should penalize the women who are doing this for a living. They train as hard as the men." Ballantyne also served as riders' representative to the National Off-Road Bicycle Association.

As Ballantyne steps out of the sport, it is rolling into a future of even more international competition and Olympic hoopla. When people look back at the early years of mountain biking and her participation in it, what would she like them to see? "I would like to be seen or remembered as an approachable person," she says, "someone helping the sport to progress."

Of course, there's another way that she'll be remembered by her peers. "That girl, she brings the term 'fun hog' to a new level," says Olympic bronze medalist Susan DeMattei. That's right, Sara Ballantyne may have retired, but she's not slowing down.

## 96

*America's most successful mountain biker, Ned Overend, reached the end of his pro career at age 41.*

# A talk with the master

### BY MARTI STEPHEN

For years, one of the chief pleasures of covering the mountain-bike circuit has been the opportunity to talk with Ned Overend. At once gracious and straightforward, Overend has a masterful perspective on bike racing. And when the race is on, no one is tougher. Small wonder he has been a champion several times over. He was the sport's first official world champion in 1990, and he has won six national championship series.

Having raced mountain bikes for 14 years, Overend is dialing back his efforts in 1997. As he puts it, "I'm not calling it a retirement ... I have a mutual agreement with Specialized to switch emphasis." The emphasis will move to more research and development.

"What I'm looking forward to is some camping trips," he says, "summer camping trips. Pack everyone into the car and go to the Grand Canyon...." You can be certain that Pam, his wife of 16 years, daughter Alison, 10, and son Rhyler, 6, are looking forward to the same thing. But for the fans who won't be going camping with Overend, here's some extracts from a long talk with a true professional.

**VeloNews** Of all the many satisfactions of your career, which one seems to be the highlight?

**Ned Overend** It seems I remember the more recent races more vividly. I'd have to say the Italy and Switzerland World Cup wins in 1994 ... those were big wins for me. The NORBA points series wins ... those were important, too.

**VeloNews** What about the world's?

**Ned Overend** That was a huge deal, but because of all the pressure, it was "Thank God it's over." But still, you can call yourself world champion all your life. I'd have to say the world's was the most satisfying.

**VeloNews** Are there any laurels that you missed that you really wanted?

**Ned Overend** Not winning the World Cup overall. I got second in '94.

**VeloNews** In your mind, what is the true spirit of mountain biking?

**Ned Overend** It's a feeling that you get on certain trails, of when you're reacting like you and your machine are just one thing. It's the feel of physical exertion and speed and technique all wrapped into one.

**VeloNews** What are the secrets to winning?

**Ned Overend** Be confident that you're capable of winning. Line up with the imagery that you can finish in first place. But then during the race, you've got to assess how you're going to mete out your energy. Of course, it's backed up by your training program. I'm constantly reading about training, and then using what works for me.

**VeloNews** What's the secret to staying motivated?

**Ned Overend** What's helped me have been distractions in life. I have a family ... it's given me a focus other than training. I do other things, too. I'm interested in weaving and other Native American arts, politics — at least reading and arguing about them. I think, too, that physically I'm not an overtrainer. I train 11 to 14 hours a week on average, more in spring. And I don't dick around when I'm out training, that's for sure. I also cross-train in the winter — mountain running, Nordic skiing — and so I approach the season fresh.

**VeloNews** Why do you think you won six national championships?

**Ned Overend** I think it relates to part of that off-season motivation. I bet some of those guys who I beat in the finals would have been kicking my butt in March. It leaves me fresher in August and September, which is when I've clinched those national championships. I'm usually spent after a race. What I'm saying is, you may be talented, but you may not be prepared to suffer....

**VeloNews** What is the most important thing about mountain biking as a competitive sport?

**Ned Overend** Besides the physiological benefits, it's the sense of accomplishment from doing something hard. The mental toughness required for the discipline leads to real personal growth.... It's shaped my character.

**VeloNews** What was the most exciting race you've ever been in?

**Ned Overend** In '89 at the (unofficial) world's in Mammoth, I flatted in the first 10 minutes. They set off the experts at the same time, and all 175 guys passed me. Then, throughout the race I had to pass them. I think Charlie Litsky was the announcer, and I was so far back he was just ignoring me. Then spectators started to catch on that I was catching up. On the last lap, I moved into first. Whenever you come from behind, the crowd appreciates it.

**VeloNews** What is the best way to handle disappointment?

**Ned Overend** Learn from it and focus on the next race.

**VeloNews** And success?

**Ned Overend** (Laughs) Appreciate it, because it fades quickly. You shouldn't look at it like you're going to have too much of it. It doesn't come easily.